CW00672144

Amongst Ourselves

A Self-Help Guide to Living with Dissociative Identity Disorder

Tracy Alderman, Ph.D., and

Karen Marshall, L.C.S.W.

NEW HARBINGER PUBLICATIONS

Publisher's Note

This publication is designed to provide accurate and authoritative information in regard to the subject matter covered. It is sold with the understanding that the publisher is not engaged in rendering psychological, financial, legal, or other professional services. If expert assistance or counseling is needed, the services of a competent professional should be sought.

Distributed in the U.S.A. by Publishers Group West; in Canada by Raincoast Books; in Great Britain by Airlift Book Company, Ltd.; in South Africa by Real Books, Ltd.; in Australia by Boobook; and in New Zealand by Tandem Press.

Copyright © 1998 by Tracy Alderman, Ph.D. and Karen Marshall, L.C.S.W.
New Harbinger Publications, Inc.
5674 Shattuck Avenue
Oakland, CA 94609

Cover design by Poulson/Gluck Design.
Cover illustration by Karen Marshall.
Edited by Angela Watrous.
Text design by Michele Waters.

Library of Congress Catalog Card Number: 98-66702
ISBN 1-57224-122-5 Paperback

All Rights Reserved

Printed in the United States of America on recycled paper

New Harbinger Publications' Website address: www.newharbinger.com

First printing

To Sophie, Opie, Garbo, and Fishie

Contents

Acknowledgments

Thank you to New Harbinger Publications for being willing to address issues that are controversial. Special thanks to Angela Watrous, an exceptional editor with a great sense of humor, with whom it was our pleasure and honor to work. Kristen Beck, you are an amazing woman who plays a mean Scrabble game.

Karen

It has been an extremely hard struggle for me to come to terms with myself. I have spent many years trying to understand myself and how to heal from my past. I have been very lucky to find people who can really accept me as me. I know that I have challenged them in many different ways, because I have made them relook at life and what they assumed life was about. Those of us living with DID are extremely isolated, and many of us live in a closet of silence and fear. I know that life with DID isn't easy, but I do know that healing is possible and that there are people who will accept you for who you are.

To Tracy, my partner, thank you for being my shero. I know that we are not always easy to live with, especially when everyone gets into their own mess. I love you for being you! Thank you for being my lover, my partner, my friend, my supporter, and my play-mate.

To Pam Badger, my therapist: you know that you really did save my life. I began to think that the only thing that was constant was horror and shame. You taught me the tools to heal and the skills to grow. You are a wonderful guide and have given me the path through the thorns and taught me to see the flowers growing amongst those thorns. Thank you for your skills, your support, your willingness to work with this issue, and your continuing fight against people attempting to discredit people with DID, who are simply try-ing to heal.

I also want to thank my friends, who have become my family and continue to support me even as I do something crazy and come out of the closet once again—this time as a person living with DID. I thank Joanne Odenthal, Eugenie Newton, Mitch Block, Jerry Lowell, Marci Seigel, and Becca and Amy (my stepdaughters), for letting me be me and teaching me about healthy families.

I have been very lucky to find people who have supported me and helped me learn about myself. I found that I had to find a way to accept my body and live in it, instead of feeling like it was an object that I and the rest of the alters had to carry around. We knew that bad things were done to the body, and that in order to reclaim our life, we had to find a way to come to terms with ourself. We did this through bodywork. I did a lot of research to find someone who understood DID and was lucky to find several people. Thank you to Carole Osborne Sheets, our massage therapist, who taught us that we had a body, and that we might as well live in it since we had it. By the way, Rosalee still feels bad for scaring you when she drove home that day; that is why she is 121 years old—so she can drive! To Diana Panara, thank you for all you do to help us heal, so we can reclaim our body. You are very patient with all of our questions and com-ments and answer all the little ones' questions with humor and kind-ness.

To my belly-button family—Sue, Bob, Pat, Bill, and Kathy—I thank you for supporting me. I know that I keep you on your toes, but you've continually been there for me, and I appreciate that more than you know.

To people who also have DID, I have to say the worst is over. I admire the way each of us has learned to survive and to make sense of things that are unimaginable. For each person who feels crazy and alone (well, as alone as you can be when you have all these little ones and big ones inside talking to you about life), you have support. I also acknowledge the courage that you each have to make a decision to live instead of giving up. It really does get better—not perfect, but better.

Tracy

Among the many people who have been helpful and supportive throughout the process of writing this book, several deserve special thanks. First, I thank my family for their continued support and interest. Alyson Shaff helped to create the title for this book for which I (and probably everyone else who picks up the book) am particularly grateful—the title was pretty boring before. Finally, I would like to thank my partner and love of my life, Karen et al., for being so honest, insightful, fun, open, loving, and just generally wonderful. Each day with you is the best gift I could ever imagine.

Introduction

There are many voices found within this book. We have collaborated in writing the informational text (found in normal print). What we write is based on our years of clinical practice, research, reading, and personal experience with issues of Dissociative Identity Disorder (DID). Our voices are combined and merged within this writing.

Additionally, Karen lends a unique and immensely important perspective to this book, in that she is able to speak as both a therapist and as an individual who has DID. As you read this text, you will have the opportunity to learn what living with DID is actually like, not only through Karen's voice, but also through the voices of her alters who she will refer to as "the little ones." The sections that are written by Karen and the little ones are presented in italics. Unless otherwise indicated, the writers of these sections are Karen's alters—Rosalee and all of the little ones. When Rosalee and the little ones are speaking, they will be referred to as Rosalee, et al. Rosalee is the more vocal one inside and writes better than the others.

> *Since we want to make this as easy to follow as possible, we will write for all of us inside. Often when we write or draw, we sign the work we do as Rosalee et al. We are the Queen of the Pen! We are the one that are most aware of what happens in the inside world of Karen. We are also known as*

*the wise ones, and sometimes certain people call us a bit of a
smart aleck.*

It is hard to try and explain to people without DID that those
who do have DID are more than one. For this reason, you will sometimes hear people with DID refer to themselves as "we." When there
is a section that is written by Rosalee et al., the section will always
say "we." It is the only term that accurately describes Karen's inside
world, which is filled with a variety of alters. When Karen herself is
speaking, the section will be from the "I" perspective; this is because
the information that is being presented is about being the outside, or
"big," one.

The others who have helped write this book, through the voice
of Rosalee, are Number 1 (two years old), Number 3 (three years old),
Timmie (Rosalee's twin), Nada (the "robot"), Baby Leaf, Round Baby,
Flower Heads, and the rest. Each one of Karen's little ones keeps her
life fun, full, and entertaining. She feels lucky to have developed DID,
because DID allowed her to cope and survive traumatic events. Without DID, Karen might not be alive and kicking.

Karen

I came to write this book with my partner, Tracy, after years of struggling to find out how to live a healthy life as someone who also has
DID. There is information that is available about how to diagnose
someone with DID. There is information that discusses possible
causes of DID and defines the goal of treatment as integration (integrating the host and the alters into one person, rather than coping
with the alters as just another part of daily life). However, there is vir-
tually nothing written about how to live with DID and how to cope
with life on a daily basis.

When I first realized that I had DID, I began to read everything I
could find to try and understand how to heal. None of the books discussed the process of healing in a way that was helpful. I learned
about the cause, the symptoms, and the theoretical discussions on
what happens after a person has completed therapy. After I found a
therapist who was able to help guide me through the healing process,
I realized that the information I was looking for was not available in
print. What I found through my work with Pam Badger, my therapist, was the missing information. The pieces that were missing in the
available materials were the ones that described in detail how to
cope, how to function, and how to heal.

We believe that in order for a person with DID to begin to heal, safety has to be created internally, and there has to be a communication system set up prior to exploring the trauma. This provides a way for the person with DID to cope and learn new ways of handling the traumatic memories and processing the past. The alters have ways to feel safe when they talk about the bad things in the past—without being alone, as they were when the original trauma occurred. The alters also have the host (or big one) inside and people on the outside, who help those who don't know learn the difference between the past and present. This helps these alters understand that their feelings are based on past experiences, and that they do not have to perform destructive behaviors to keep the big one quiet, nor must they create a state of chaos so that the big one gets lost and is unable to focus on the past. This book will present some of these methods and begin to teach those with DID how to live their lives more fully and more joyfully.

Many therapists use the treatment model of reexploring trauma, without first establishing the necessary safety and communication. As the flashbacks occur and an alter comes out to talk about the experience, the therapist will have the little one describe in detail what occurred. At the end of the session, the alter goes back inside, and the adult may sometimes return to the therapist in a state of trauma. As this process goes on, the little ones talk more and more about the bad things that happened, and can get more and more distressed. Without having first set up communication among alters and a sense of safety, the alters may end up living in isolation and a state of fear.

The lack of communications among alters can result in retraumatizing the client. Every time the alters come out to talk about the past and the traumas they went through, there is not an adequate system developed to provide support to or educate the alters. When the little ones come out to talk about the things that happened to bring them into existence, they may experience the moment as being at the same time as when they were created. This may lead the big one to engage in behaviors that are dysfunctional or harmful, because the little ones are trying to keep the adult from talking about the past or doing anything that may seemingly put them at risk. At times like this, the adult may begin to use extreme measures just to cope and get through the day, such as using substances or alcohol, retreating and isolating from others, sleeping, or simply allowing an alter to emerge who can get through the day. The possible result of this approach of therapy, in which the retelling of the original trauma is explored without first establishing safety and communication in the system, is that the client may not heal, but instead be retraumatized over and over again.

A therapist myself, I spoke with many other clinicians who told me they did not believe in DID. I eventually disclosed my diagnosis to them and told them about my negative experiences with the common treatment. I encourage my colleagues to ask questions, get supervision, or refer DID clients to someone who better knows the area.

There is a group of people who feel they are the experts in recovered memories, which they maintain are false memories, who make life awful for those of us who are trying to heal from our past. It amazes me that the same group who questions recovered memories says that therapists plant this information in their clients. Unfortunately, many people find it easier to believe that therapists create this disorder than to acknowledge that child abuse hurts children more than they want to admit. I spent many years trying to make up reasons about why I had the flashbacks, memories, continuous nightmares, etc. When I finally decided to quit trying to hide from the truth, I began to heal.

Tracy

Karen and I have known each other for over a decade. In this time, I have watched Karen struggle and grow. Nearly four years ago, she summoned an amazing amount of courage and told me that she has multiple personalities. It was at this time that I first met Rosalee and began to know Karen more completely. I have witnessed Karen become more and more comfortable with who she is and with the fact that she has DID.

In this time I have also become more educated about DID. As a therapist, I have experience working with individuals who have multiple personalities. But, through Karen's openness, honesty, and great courage, I have had the good luck to learn more of what it is really like to have DID and to experience what it is like to live with and share a life with someone who has multiple personalities. I consider myself to be incredibly fortunate to know Karen et al., and to be able to share my life with her. She is truly an amazing woman and I consider each day with her to be a great gift. Although this book is not really about Karen or her life, there is a great deal of her knowledge and experience included.

Living with DID can be whatever you make it. It can be a struggle, a challenge, a burden, or it can be filled with fun and happiness.

Hopefully this book will teach you how to experience your life in such a way that you get to feel whole and accepting of who you are. There are times in everyone's lives when challenges and burdens seem enormous and cast shadows on joy and happiness. It's important that you learn that these feelings are temporary and that these difficulties can serve to bring out the best in you. You are in control of your life and you can choose how you wish to live it. With any luck this book will show you some strategies you can use so that you can live your life feeling whole, complete, proud, and happy.

How to Use This Book

As the subtitle suggests, this book is designed as a self-help guide to living with Dissociative Identity Disorder. This book is intended to be read and used by people living with DID, as well as their friends, family members, and therapists.

The book is divided into three sections. Part I, "Understanding DID," is designed to provide information about the symptoms, causes, and diagnosis criteria of DID. People with DID, their family, friends, and therapists, and anyone else who wants to learn more about DID will likely find this section interesting and educational. Part II, "Living with DID," discusses what it's like to live with DID, how to manage the disorder, what can be appreciated or gained from the disorder, deciding to enter therapy, and what to expect once therapy is in progress. Part III, "For Others," is written for people who are involved with those who have multiple personalities. Therapists, partners, and family members will all gain essential information about ways to deal with and enjoy those around them who have DID.

There are numerous activities within this book. In order to make the most of these activities, you'll need a journal or three-ring binder and a pencil or pen. By recording your experiences with and responses to these exercises you'll be able to learn more about yourself and continue on your path of self-growth. You may wish to use this book in therapy or as an adjunct to therapy. The material presented in the text, as well as the activities, will undoubtedly help you become more aware of yourself and the ways in which DID affects your life.

This is a guide to help people with DID, as well as their family members, partners, and friends; it should also be helpful to professionals in the field. Working through this book will not be an easy journey, but the work will be rewarding and sometimes even fun. It is a journey that people with DID can undergo in order to heal. Loved ones of people with DID, if they choose to be involved in the journey, will also grow and develop a greater understanding of the person with DID. One thing that is important to remember is that *DID is about survival*. Therapists, partners, family members, and friends are not responsible for you; they cannot take away your past nor can they carry your pain. But if you have DID, you are a survivor, and you will make it through one way or another.

We understand the pain of having DID and the pain loved ones experience as the person with DID goes through the healing process. This is a guide to make the journey a little easier, and while it is not the end-all for each person, we hope it will help you.

> *We are glad we are us. The us part is there, and learning to like ourselves was hard. Now we mostly love being ourselves— it is the best fun. We know that people who are singletons have fun too, but we are sure it can't be like being us! You have to know someone like us to understand. Each person that is part of us is a wonder, and we are just glad we have the many wonders we have.*

Understanding Dissociative Identity Disorder

What Is DID?

As you read this first chapter, you will gain a better understanding of what Dissociative Identity Disorder (DID) actually is, as well as many of its symptoms. You will be able to complete activities which will help you determine if you have DID and understand how this might affect your life. You will also learn some basic information about DID and how it develops. By the end of this chapter you should have a better sense of the role DID plays in your life and the lives of others.

Understanding DID

Prior to the fourth edition of the *Diagnostic and Statistical Manual of Mental Disorders* (DSM-IV), the diagnosis of Dissociative Identity Disorder had been referred to as Multiple Personality Disorder. The renaming of this diagnosis has caused quite a bit of confusion among professionals and those who live with DID. Because dissociation describes the process by which DID begins to develop, rather than the actual outcome of this process (the formation of various personalities), this new term may be a bit unclear.

> We know that the diagnosis is DID and that DID is what people say we have. We'd just like to point out that words

sometimes do not describe what we live with. For people like us, DID is just a step on the way to where we live—a place with many of us inside! We just want people who have little ones and bigger ones living inside to know that the title Dissociative Identity Disorder sounds like something other than how we see ourselves—we think it is about us having different personalities.

Regardless of the term, it is clear that, in general, the different personalities develop as a reaction to severe trauma. When the person dissociates, they leave their body to get away from the pain or trauma. When this defense is not strong enough to protect the person, different personalities emerge to handle the experience. These personalities allow the child to survive: when the child is being harmed or experiencing traumatic episodes, the other personalities take the pain and/or watch the bad things. This allows these children to return to their body after the bad things have happened without any awareness of what has occurred. They do this to create different ways to make sense of the harm inflicted upon them; it is their survival mechanism.

Many people who were sexually abused as children report sitting in the corner of the room and watching what is being done to them. Children who develop multiple personalities develop alters, and the alters are the ones that are hurt (instead of the children themselves). The personality that is created believes that it has done something bad that deserves the treatment it is receiving. After the bad experiences have ended, this personality goes inside and allows the child's main personality to return. This process allows the child to get up in the morning, go to school, and not be aware of anything that has happened to them.

There may be many different personalities developed to handle the various experiences. One personality may be the one who gets to keep the anger. This angry one will come out and express this anger, but only when this acting out will not get the child hurt. If children are being abused or harmed, their angry ones cannot come out, because their systems (the children and their alters) know that they will be placing themselves in further danger. The angry ones are able to take all of those feelings and find ways to let them out later so that the children are not placed in further danger. The children may become extremely aggressive toward friends or siblings without any clear reasons. In these situations, their acting-out personalities are trying to relieve some of the bottled up feelings so that the children will not act out toward their perpetrators.

Not everyone who has DID experiences things the same way. You may have only one alter, or you may have many. You may or may not be able to communicate with your alters or know what happened to you in the past. You may think of yourself as having multiple personalities rather than having DID. Just like with any diagnosis, what you have been through, what you are currently experiencing, and even how you may refer to yourself or your diagnosis may be different from others. However, rest assured that if you have DID, you are not alone and what you feel and think are not crazy.

DID Terminology

Following are definitions that we have developed to help you use this book. Other people may define the terms slightly differently.

- **Alter:** One of several or many personalities. Each alter, or personality, has a name, a role, and a way of being that is different from the others. The personality may be the protector, the wise one (in our case, Rosalee), the one who gets mad, or one of countless other possibilities. There is more to the personality than just a particular mood or feeling; the personality has unique expressions, memories, and reactions, and it functions in a particular way in the world.

- **Dissociative Identity Disorder (DID):** DID, formerly known as Multiple Personality Disorder (MPD), exists when an individual has two or more identities or personalities, each with its own way of being. These personalities are persistent and consistent over time and may alternate in having control of the individual's behavior. DID is typically caused from extreme trauma, usually that of severe physical or sexual abuse, which continues over an extended period of time. Many people with DID experience problems with memory, anxiety, depression, time loss, and dissociation (feeling numb or separate from one's own body).

- **Fragment or Splinter Personality:** This term defines those who are not a complete personality, but who are merely a fragment of a personality. A fragment may hold a memory or an emotion, but it may not be fully formed into its own personality. Sometimes fragments have names, but other times they may not. Usually fragments eventually merge with more fully developed alters.

- **Fragmented:** This refers to the experience of not feeling whole or connected to one's self. For example, when an individual with DID is fragmented, they may feel disoriented, confused, numb, or unable to be aware or in control of the appearance of their alters.

  We define this as when you have many personalities coming out at the same time, and you feel like a revolving door. There isn't any one personality out long enough to let you get focused to do anything.

- **Host Personality:** This is the term that refers to the "out front" person. This may or may not be the biological baby that was born into the world. A host may be a personality that came into being at a young age and has grown up with the body. The host may be the biological one that was born into the world and who continues to keep the person functional in the world.

  In our case, the host is Karen, who is usually out and known to others. She has been around since birth (she is the one who was biologically born into the world).

- **Humor:** What you have to have if you live with DID. It is funny what goes on when you have all of the little ones coming out and doing projects—what a mess! Imagine the result of having three or four different ones getting dressed in the morning—a prissy one, a slob, a boy, and a girl!

- **Integration:** Integration refers to the merging of the alters to form one cohesive personality. The process of integration takes many years and sometimes cannot be achieved. Typically, integration is the long-term goal of therapy for people with DID.

- **Patience:** What singletons need when they live with someone with DID. They have to know that the person with DID is not hiding things on purpose or forgetting things to get anyone mad—it is simply part of the disorder.

- **Recovered Memories:** Recovered memories are those events, thoughts, or feelings that you once experienced, later could not access or remember, and of which you have now regained memory. Often, certain alters will keep memories from the others in the system because they feel that the memories will be too disturbing if they are shared with the others. Later, when the system becomes stronger and can tolerate the disturbance caused by these memories, the holder of the memories will release them to the other personalities. At this point, they become recovered memories.

- **Ritual Abuse:** According to the Los Angeles County Commission for Women (1989), ritual abuse is "a brutal form of abuse of children, adolescents, and adults, consisting of physical, sexual, and psychological abuse, involving the use of rituals."

- **Safety:** Safety is when you feel secure and protected. It is necessary to learn what helps you feel good and safe. Find a place in your home that feels safe. Identify a list of friends you know who can support you when you are in crisis and who are willing to learn what makes you feel good.

- **Singleton:** This is a term that another person with DID came up with (we wish we had made it up). It is a person who has only one personality and was born that way and lives that way. For example, Tracy is a singleton, because she only has one personality.

- **System:** This is the word we use to refer to all of the different personalities in a person with DID. This includes the one who lives out front in the world, the ones who only come out sometimes, and the ones who never come out and only live inside.

Do You Have DID?

Determining if you have DID isn't as easy as it sounds. In fact, many clinicians and psychotherapists have such difficulty figuring out whether or not people have DID that it typically takes them several years to provide an accurate diagnosis. Because many of the symptoms of DID overlap with other psychological diagnoses, as well as normal occurrences such as forgetfulness or talking to yourself, there is a great deal of confusion in making the diagnosis of DID. Although this section will provide you with information which may help you determine if you have DID, it is a good idea to consult with a professional in the mental health field so that you can have further confirmation of your findings.

> *Some professionals still do not believe in DID. We never understand what that actually means. If they do not believe in DID, what do they think we are? If you think that you have DID and you go to see a therapist who tells you that he or she doesn't believe in DID, find a new therapist. Think about this for a minute. If you continuously have a headache and you go to a doctor who says you do not have a headache, you would go to a different doctor, right? If you answered "no" to the previous question then we really must talk. You should find someone who listens to you and understands what you are living with each day. You need to find a therapist who listens to your issues and helps you feel better. If you tell the therapist that you are having some problem and the therapist tries to tell you that your experience is not real or tries to tell you things that you know do not fit with what you have been going through, find someone else to work with.*
>
> *Some people say that it seemed that only certain therapists had clients with DID in their practice. These folks were really meaning that somehow the therapist made all their clients DID. This just isn't the case. We spent a long time trying to find a therapist who could really understand these issues so we could get help. Think of it in these terms: If you have a toothache you go to a dentist, not a cardiologist. If you are struggling with a history of child abuse, seek a therapist who is skilled in treating this issue. If you are finding that you have some symptoms that indicate you may be a person with DID, find a therapist who has experience working with this diagnosis.*

The fourth edition of the *Diagnostic and Statistical Manual of Mental Disorders (DSM-IV)*, published by the American Psychiatric Association, contains all of the psychiatric diagnoses and their criteria recognized by the psychotherapeutic community. According to the *DSM-IV*, the following criteria must be met in order for a diagnosis of Dissociative Identity Disorder to be made:

Diagnostic Criteria for 300.14 Dissociative Identity Disorder

A. The presence of two or more distinct identities or personality states (each with its own relatively enduring pattern of perceiving, relating to, and thinking about the environment and self).

B. At least two of these identities or personality states recurrently take control of the person's behavior.

C. Inability to recall important personal information that is too extensive to be explained by ordinary forgetfulness.

D. The disturbance is not due to the direct physiological effects of a substance (e.g., blackouts or chaotic behavior during Alcohol Intoxication) or a general medical condition (e.g., complex partial seizures).

Note: In children, the symptoms are not attributable to imaginary playmates or fantasy play.

In order for the diagnosis of DID to be made, you must meet each of these four criteria. Sometimes understanding the meaning of each criteria can be a bit difficult, so we'll present them again and expand on their definitions.

A. The presence of two or more distinct identities or personality states (each with its own relatively enduring pattern of perceiving, relating to, and thinking about the environment and self).

This criteria demands that you have more than one unique identity or personality. You may refer to these identities as others or alters or even simply by their names. Each of these identities has its own way of understanding and being in the world. For instance, one of your personalities may be very young and may perceive the world the way that a child would. That personality may speak like a child, act like a child, and even describe their own appearance as that which resembles a child of a particular age. Meanwhile, you may have another personality which is an adult and functions as an adult, going to work or school, paying the bills, driving the car, and perceiving the world from an adult perspective. If you meet this criteria, you probably have a number of personalities each with their own memories, physical appearances, perceptions, and general ways of being.

It's important to remember that these identities must be fairly permanent. Most people have different ways of being in different situations, perhaps dressing or acting differently based upon the demands of the situation. For example, the clothes a singleton wears to work are generally different from the clothes they wear during their free time. They may also tend to act more professional and less goofy when they're around their colleagues than when they're around their friends. The ways in which they act and look can change from situation to situation. However, when they're acting differently from what they would consider normal, they're acting based on a different role, not a different identity. If you have multiple personalities, each time a different identity appears, it carries with it a history and a distinct way of relating to the world. This is one of the key differences between roles and identities. Roles refer to the parts people play in different situations, while multiple identities refer to the presentation of different selves.

> B. At least two of these identities or personality states recurrently take control of the person's behavior.

This second criteria mandates that there must be a change in identities to the extent that at least two distinct identities are controlling your actions. In other words, it's not enough to have more than one identity, but that at least two of the identities must alternate the governing of your behavior.

Recently in the field of psychology a great deal of emphasis has been placed on the "inner child." And, while each person has an inner child, which may need nurturing or loving or attention, the mere presence of this piece of themselves isn't enough to rate a diagnosis of DID. In order for this second criteria to be met, this aspect of a person must be an entity and must control their actions and behaviors at least some of the time. If you meet this criteria, it may be that the two or more identities controlling your behaviors are all adults, all children, or some mixture of each. Again, the distinction needs to be made between people with one personality, who have many sides or ways of presenting themselves, and one person who has more than one personality, each of whom guide or direct the behavior of that individual.

> C. Inability to recall important personal information that is too extensive to be explained by ordinary forgetfulness.

This third criteria states that the individual with DID have severe difficulty remembering information which would normally be remembered. One of the functions of DID is to separate from consciousness memories and events which would normally be too painful to tolerate. Because DID is so effective in doing this, the memory of an individual with DID is often debilitated. If you have DID you may have difficulty remembering things like your birthday or age, your address, the name of the town where you grew up, the names of your parents, or even more day-to-day things like what you had for breakfast or whether or not you walked the dog. Much of this forgetfulness is due to the fact that different identities carry different memories. For instance, if a certain personality wasn't around for a certain event, that personality might have no memory of that event. Thus, while the ability to separate and forget certain experiences may have been necessary in order to survive traumatic events, forgetfulness beyond what is considered typical is likely to be a side effect of DID.

> D. The disturbance is not due to the direct physiological effects of a substance (e.g., blackouts or chaotic behavior during Alcohol Intoxication) or a general medical condition (e.g., complex partial seizures).

> Note: In children, the symptoms are not attributable to imaginary playmates or fantasy play.

This final criteria is simply a way of ruling out the presence of other factors which may produce similar results. Use of substances such as alcohol and drugs can often change the ways in which individuals perceive and relate to the world. In fact, you may be able to think of some people you know whose personalities change very drastically when they are using these substances. The key factor to remember is that it is the substances which are causing the change. With DID, no substances are needed to produce changes in identity.

The effects of certain medical conditions also need to be noted before making a diagnosis of DID. Complex partial seizures are one such type of condition whose effects mimic some of the symptoms of DID. Difficulty remembering, entrance into an altered state of consciousness, and the presence of seemingly different identities are possible effects of this medical condition.

It is also important to remember that DID usually develops in childhood. Sometimes it is difficult to determine if a child is involved in fantasy play or if there is something else occurring, such as the presence of an alternate identity. Many kids have imaginary friends and even more kids are involved in fantasy play. When determining if a child has DID, try to remember that the spectrum of imagination and fantasy is much greater than that of adults and that it may be more difficult to ascertain DID in a child than in an adult.

*

ACTIVITY 1.1: DO YOU HAVE DID?

Place a check in front of each of the following *DSM-IV* criteria which you believe you meet. If you meet all four criteria, you may have DID. However, as was mentioned earlier, it is important that you consult with a professional psychotherapist before identifying yourself as having DID.

_____ A. The presence of two or more distinct identities or personality states (each with its own relatively enduring pattern of perceiving, relating to, and thinking about the environment and self).

_____ B. At least two of these identities or personality states recurrently take control of the person's behavior.

_____ C. Inability to recall important personal information that is too extensive to be explained by ordinary forgetfulness.

_____ D. The disturbance is not due to the direct physiological effects of a substance (e.g., blackouts or chaotic behavior during Alcohol Intoxication) or a general medical condition (e.g., complex partial seizures). Note: In children, the symptoms are not attributable to imaginary playmates or fantasy play.

Remember that you need to meet all four of these criteria in order to be considered for the diagnosis of DID. If you do think you may have DID, remember that it is something that you have always lived with, you just were not aware of why you did some of the things you did. It is important to find a therapist who you feel you can work with, regardless of whether you have DID or another psychological issue. Because this diagnosis is so difficult to make and it will impact your life, it's a good idea to find someone to talk with before deciding this is what you have, just like when you read medical books—you can decide you have the most unusual things, but then a professional needs to assist in the evaluation.

*

Symptoms of DID

Regardless of your actual diagnosis, you may find that you have some symptoms commonly associated with DID. There are reasons other than DID why you would have some of these experiences. Also, these symptoms may or may not be problematic to you.

Dissociation

Dissociation is a term used to describe a psychological state in which your level of consciousness is altered and you basically feel zoned out. For some people being dissociated makes them feel like they are separated from their bodies and are watching themselves in a movie. Others describe the sensation of flying or floating above their bodies when they are in this dissociated state. The way in which you experience dissociation will depend on many things, including the situation you are in. Because dissociation is so important within DID (it's even in the name of the diagnosis) this topic will be addressed more completely in the next chapter.

Time Loss

Given that dissociation is used as a way of zoning out and changing your state of consciousness, it makes sense that if you have DID you would have difficulty tracking time. You have probably had the experience of looking at the clock, checking it again in what felt like a few minutes later, and finding that actually several hours had gone by; you may have no recollection of what happened during that time. In reality, one (or more) of your alters may have been quite busy during the missing time. You may find that you've started building a new addition to your house, gone to lunch with a friend, or even finished writing that novel you had been working on. Or, perhaps you are having to face an upset partner because you are once again late. At times, you may find people upset with you because you are late or you missed a meeting. You may have no idea why they are upset with you, as you may not remember you made an appointment. You may find yourself in trouble again, though you didn't do anything on purpose

> *Who can keep track of time anyhow? Time starts moving and then the next thing you know it's much later—oops!*

Once you begin communicating more effectively with your alters, you'll probably be better able to track the missing time and find out what you've been doing during that lost time.

Losing and Forgetting Things

Everyone loses things sometimes. People with DID tend to lose things more frequently and may never be able to find where they were put. You may find yourself making duplicates of important things just so you'll have less chance of losing them. How many sets of keys do you have?

If you have DID you have probably had a great deal of trouble with losing and forgetting things. Because, in essence, you are sharing your body with others (some of whom are likely very young), the responsibilities of remembering and tracking items is often difficult. For instance, while you may be very intent on holding onto your house keys, your three-year-old alter may not care at all and may have had a great time throwing the keys into a pond and watching them scare the fishes.

> We have many sets of keys in various places; that way we can always get into work, home, and the car. If by chance we do lose the many keys or can not locate them when needed, we have also given keys to other people who we can find easily.

The primary reason for losing and forgetting things is that there is not a consistency in who is responsible for remembering. For example, while you may have arranged an important appointment for Tuesday afternoon, one of your alters may have already booked you for a golf game, and when Tuesday afternoon arrives, another alter may decide that you should have lunch with a friend. As you can see, with so many involved in remembering and scheduling so many different things it becomes nearly impossible to keep everything on track. For individuals with DID, losing and forgetting things is completely normal.

> I always knew that I had to make copies of important (or for that matter any) papers. I would usually end up with ten copies of a report or a grant, usually with the pages not in the right order, and all of the copies had pages missing. It was only recently that I realized that I manage to lose copies as easily as the originals, so now I give them to other people to keep.

Mood Swings

Although mood swings are quite common among people with DID, they differ to some extent from what would typically be considered a mood swing. When individuals with DID become upset they are likely to become more fragmented and allow more personalities to present themselves. When these alters do appear, each may carry a different feeling or mood. Thus, it may appear that the individual is having rapid mood swings, but really the moods of each alter are remaining somewhat consistent—it's simply the alters that are changing. This is not to say that each alter will always have the same mood. Just like everyone else in the world, the mood of an alter will change based upon the present circumstances. However, mood swings, or what appear to be mood swings, are very common with DID.

> *The feeling is very strange, and as you get to know yourself better you will begin to understand what is happening. You can recognize when each alter is coming out and they are changing quickly, and you feel so different with each alter who is out. One second the one who cries is out, the next the little mean one, and then the little mad one. Talk about feeling strange! All of the changing also makes you really tired.*

Depression

The presence of depression or depressive symptoms is common among individuals with DID. Feelings of hopelessness, helplessness, worthlessness, pessimism, and sadness are all common. Many people with DID have suicidal thoughts or attempts because they feel so depressed and hopeless. Some of the suicidal feelings can be traced back to programming or severe threats from the abuser. Most people with DID have been told that if they tell anyone about the abuse, or even mention a single abusive incident, they will die or be killed. If you were told this, know that these people lied to you. You do not have to keep quiet, and you can get even with these people by telling your story and getting healthy.

Although the feelings and thoughts of suicide may be severe, they will pass. For most people with DID, suicidal symptoms are fleeting. Part of the reason for this is that the survival instinct of the other personalities is excellent. Dissociative abilities and alters were developed in order to ensure survival during extremely traumatic experiences. These same survival techniques can be used to combat suicidal thoughts and depression. Thus, even though you may feel depressed and hopeless, you will get better. It takes time and a commitment to do the work to heal.

Several years ago, Tracy worked with a woman in her thirties who had DID. During their first session together she informed Tracy that she wanted therapy so that she could feel better and have enough energy to kill herself. Needless to say, she was pretty depressed. Several months into therapy she did try to commit suicide by taking an overdose of sleeping pills. Fortunately, one of her alters, a teenager who was bulimic, decided that she wanted to live and came out just in time to make herself vomit and purge her body of the narcotics.

The will to live is strong and people who have multiple personalities are definitely survivors.

Anxiety

Dissociative Identity Disorder is borne out of trauma. Many individuals who survive severe trauma will later experience marked anxiety, which may or may not relate to triggers from the original trauma. Individuals with DID are highly likely to have a great deal of anxiety.

There are many types of anxiety that people experience. You probably know some individuals who are often stressed or frequently nervous about something occurring in their lives. For example, many people in Southern California experience great anxiety when driving on the freeways when it is raining (there are countless numbers of accidents whenever it rains). People who have been through traumatic events may experience a particular type of anxiety called Post-Traumatic Stress Disorder (PTSD). PTSD is a particular type of anxiety that is related to having survived extremely abusive and traumatic experiences, such as situations which involve the threat of death or serious injury, or situations in which people actually witness someone being harmed or are physically harmed themselves.

Given that the overwhelming majority of people with DID have undergone some type of severe trauma, it's not surprising that people with DID often have many of the symptoms of PTSD, such as flashbacks, nightmares, body memories, and problems with anxiety and panic. The experienced anxiety and other symptoms may be triggered by things which mimic components of the original trauma. It is not unusual for people with DID to react strongly to loud noises. For example, if loud noises accompanied the original trauma, hearing loud, unexpected noises now may make you highly anxious. Other times, however, you may simply feel scared or anxious and not know what is triggering your feelings.

If you have PTSD, you may reexperience the original trauma in many ways. Sometimes, you may find yourself unable to stop thinking about what happened to you. Other times, you may actually feel as if you are reliving what happened to you (this is usually called a flashback). Nightmares are also common for people with PTSD and DID. Sometimes these nightmares may be flashbacks of actual events you went through before and sometimes they may be symbolic of these events. Also, you may have nightmares that stem from things totally unrelated to the abuse or trauma you endured. In any case, these nightmares are likely terrifying and may cause significant disturbances in your sleep. Insomnia, primarily that which results in difficulty remaining asleep, rather than falling asleep, is frequently experienced.

> *For the longest time we would be awake all night. We have Big Eyes, who sat up and kept watch on the world. At night we have a different crew that likes to play. Oppie likes to draw and write instead of sleeping. Chatty likes to get up at three in the morning and eat chocolate and talk and talk. It is great for us, 'cause when Chatty wakes up she gets candy (usually M&Ms) and milk, and she talks to anyone around—the cat, the dog, Tracy.*

> *Over time, we learned that it was safe in the house and that no one would hurt us while we slept. At first, the little ones were afraid of big people, both inside and outside. We knew big ones had hurt us, so we didn't allow them near us. We would hide from them. Sometimes we would hide under things so we would be safe.*

You may also find yourself avoiding situations which remind you of the original trauma. For instance, you may not like to go to scary or violent movies because they remind you too much of your past and create feelings of great tension and anxiety. They may even trigger flashbacks or greater levels of dissociation.

If you have been through a traumatic experience, particularly one which involves abuse by others, you are probably quite hypervigilant. This means that you are overly wary of your surroundings and those around you. You may spend a great deal of energy trying to be aware of what is occurring around you. You are probably very good at reading cues from other people, and you may work hard to keep the areas surrounding you feeling as safe as possible.

Hearing Voices

Many people with DID report hearing the sound of voices coming from inside their head. If you have DID, you probably had no idea that hearing voices is unusual. During interviews with mental healthcare professionals this question always comes up. There are actually different types of voices that people can hear. Some people hear voices that seem to be from a god or demon telling them to do something. People with DID will have conversations with alters, which may include screaming when a little one is scared or just a lot of talking. These voices or sounds stemming from inside the head are actually the chatter of the alters. The alters may be communicating with each other or with the one who is out at the time. Until you know that you have DID, you may feel as if you are going crazy because you have these unexplained voices inside your head. You may also be misdiagnosed because of the voices. Auditory hallucinations (voices) are common symptoms of a variety of other psychiatric disorders, including schizophrenia and bipolar disorder (also known as manic depression). Once you learn that what you are hearing is actually the communication of the others within you, you may feel relieved.

> *Sit quietly. What is going on in your head? Do you hear conversations? Chattering and arguments? This is one of those questions that seems like a trick one to me. How do you know that you are hearing voices if you have always heard discussions and yelling? At first when I was asked about hearing voices, I didn't understand what I was being asked. I always had conversations going on with all different voices in my head, so it was not unusual. When I heard that most people did not hear conversations or yelling, I was scared and thought I was crazy.*

Headaches

Headaches are a frequent complaint among people with DID. Often the headaches are severe and are unaffected by typical remedies such as aspirin. While the exact cause of the headaches is unknown, there does seem to be some relationship between headaches and the forced appearance of alters. It's also possible that these headaches are caused by internal conflicts between alters. Although not much is known about why the headaches occur, it does seem that when they do occur they are intense, severe, and don't go away easily.

Referring to Yourself as "We" or "Us" or by Different Names

Without even being aware of it, you may be telling the people you know that you have DID. Using plural pronouns such as "we" or "us" to describe or refer to yourself is a sign that others may be existing within you. Similarly, calling yourself by a name other than your birthname or nickname is also an indication that you may have multiple personalities. Just as you would like to be acknowledged and called by your proper name, so do the others within you. Your alters may have you refer to yourself in one of these ways so that they feel as if they count (which they do). Talking about yourself as a plural is actually more accurate than referring to yourself as "I," because it includes all of you, not just the one personality who is speaking at that moment.

> *I spent all of my life referring to "the body" or saying that "the" head hurt instead of "my" body or "my" head. If I got funny looks I would listen to what words the other person would use and then use their language to describe the pain.*

Feeling That You Are Sharing Your Body With Others

Because DID is based on the idea that an individual has more than one distinct personality, people with DID will without a doubt experience the sensation that there are others living within their body. Feeling as if there are many of you sharing one body is completely normal if you have DID. As you learn more about yourself and the others living inside of you, you may develop strategies for determining who gets to be in control of the body and when this occurs.

> *Now, you need to know that if you have DID, this has been going on since you were little. When you first start learning about this, you think everyone sees the world the same as you. As you learn more about how you function in life and*

how others experience life, you will begin to realize that your experiences are not the same as those around you, unless they also have DID.

ACTIVITY 1.2: WHAT SYMPTOMS DO YOU HAVE?

This activity will help you to identify some of the particular symptoms of DID that you may experience. This is a first step in beginning to understand how DID affects you, and it will be helpful to you later when you are learning how to better manage some of these symptoms. Do remember though that having all or any of these symptoms doesn't necessarily mean that you have DID. You may also want to discuss this activity and what you experience with a therapist to help you determine an accurate diagnosis (if there is one) and how to best treat your complaints.

Place a check next to each symptom you experience. Blank spaces have been provided for you to write in any additional symptoms or experiences which you feel are appropriate.

_____ experiencing dissociation

_____ feeling zoned out

_____ feeling like you're leaving your body

_____ losing track of time

_____ being unable to remember large chunks of time (hours, days, etc.)

_____ forgetting important events (meetings, dates, etc.)

_____ finding things you didn't remember doing, buying, etc.

_____ losing things (keys, checkbook, papers, clothes, etc.)

_____ experiencing rapid shifts in mood

_____ having rapid changes in the personality who is out

_____ feeling depressed

_____ being tired all of the time

_____ having suicidal thoughts or feelings

_____ feeling anxious or stressed out

_____ being unable to stop thinking about the trauma you experienced

_____ trying to avoid things that remind you of the trauma

_____ having nightmares

_____ having difficulty sleeping

_____ experiencing flashbacks or feeling like you're reliving the trauma

_____ feeling hypervigilant

_____ hearing voices or conversations in your head

_____ experiencing frequent and intense headaches

_____ calling yourself "we" or "us" or by different names

_____ feeling like you share your body with others

_____

_____

_____

※

Types of Alters

Most people who have DID have at least several different personalities. Each personality is typically referred to as an alter or alternate personality. Alters may vary in terms of age, gender, and sexual orientation, much in the same way that members of a family differ. Each of these personalities will be distinct from one another and may have differing interests, talents, abilities, and functions. And as different as these personalities are from one another, there are some common types of alters found within individuals with DID.

The Host

The host personality is the one who is "out" the majority of the time. The host may or may not have awareness that other personalities exist. Generally hosts will use their birthnames and will be the personality that most other people know. Although the host personality's identity may include information that is true for the "original" personality, such as name, place of birth, age, and position or role in the family of origin, the host personality may actually be more of a conglomerate of various alters. However, over the course of time, the host alters take on an identity and style of being which is all their own, thus forming their own distinct personality. Just as all individuals grow and develop and create an identity for themselves, the host personality does the same.

> *Maybe they came out with the term* host *cause it is like you are having a bunch of company—they just keep staying. That way you can remember that each one of you is important and hosting is a good thing. You, the host, get to help everyone learn their way around.*

Children

Almost all people with multiple personalities have child alters. These alters may range in age, gender, language abilities, and emotional styles. Some child alters simply love to play, and that is their primary function. Others may feel terrified most of the time and cry, scream, or tremble when they are out. Most child alters will have some issues with trust and may have a difficult time learning that some people and situations really are safe. For this reason, it may take a while before child alters appear in front of others. However, you may find evidence that the child alters have been out without your awareness. You may discover drawings, toys, or even the written words of a child around your house. Until you realize that there are others sharing your body, you may be very perplexed regarding the traces of children around your home (unless you have kids and then you may simply think that the toys and drawings are theirs).

> *Our kids sure didn't used to want any big ones around. It was too scary. We have different little ones who have things to do. Some are just there to watch. During the day it is okay, but at night it doesn't let you sleep much. We have ones that used to pop out at night and want to draw and play and eat*

candy. Then they would let the rest of us finally go to sleep. These little ones wanted to stay up until it got light outside. Too bad that was when we had to get up and go to work.

Sad, Depressed, or Suicidal

Because most cases of DID can be traced back to severe abuse or trauma of some nature, it makes sense that at least some of the alters would have problems with depression. Depression may be evident in various ways, ranging from general feelings of fatigue and hopelessness to more severe symptoms, such as the wish to die. Sometimes the alter who is depressed will go so far as to try to commit suicide. It's important that these personalities realize that by killing themselves they also kill the rest of the system. Although it may not seem like it to the person with DID, there really is only one body and if anything happens to that body, all of the personalities are affected.

At times, we have felt so bad that we thought about hurting ourselves. We would get real sad and feel as if things would never get better. But there was always one of us who would keep us going. It helps to have others, like a therapist, around to talk with for support.

We have one that only wants to sleep. We don't know if it is because we were afraid to sleep and after many years of being awake and scared it has finally realized it is okay to sleep or if this one has the job of trying to make things go away by sleeping. Anyway, this sleepy one is still tired.

Numb

The feelings associated with being abused are incredibly powerful. So powerful, in fact, that for people with DID an elaborate system is created to make the feelings more separated and less intense. The main component of multiple personalities is the ability to dissociate, or rather, to zone out or become numb. Numbness is useful because it allows you to separate yourself from feelings which would potentially interfere with your ability to function. Generally, individuals with DID will have one alter who, in particular, is quite adept at being numb. This personality is called on to perform when the emotions present on the inside are in danger of becoming overwhelming.

*Our numb one gets us through school, work, and more things
than we know. Her name is Nada and when we get way
overwhelmed she takes over and keeps things going. So, maybe
we aren't real talkative or friendly or open when Nada is in
charge, but we are getting things done.*

Communicator/Manager

Every individual with DID has at least one alter who is exceptionally good at communicating with those on the inside. You may
think of this alter as a sort of manager of the other personalities.
Because the communicator/manager has awareness of at least most
of the other personalities, this alter is in a good position to help those
personalities share with each other and sometimes with those on the
outside. The communicator/manager is able to keep everyone on
track and to ensure the safety and well-being of the other alters. The
communicator/manager may also keep some of the inside activity
and conversations away from the personality who is out so that that
personality is able to function. Just like a manager of a corporation,
this type of alter controls and directs the other personalities in their
jobs and activities. But unlike a typical manager, this alter can guide
the thoughts and emotions of those inside.

*It is fun to be the one in charge! Somebody has to take over
and make sure things run right. We like doing that part.
Mostly we know everything that goes on inside now, so we
can help all of us work together. We have been told in the
past that it isn't nice to say we are the best but ... (we
didn't say it!). We also have one who became the secretary.
Probably from being at work, a little one saw that people take
messages so she decided she wanted to help by taking messages.
Just like at work, the messages sometimes just got lost.*

Protector

Protector personalities come in many forms. Some may be
human, some animal, some even fantasy creatures. Protectors have
very specific jobs within the system—to guard against possible harm
and to protect the others from memories or triggers of past events
which could be disturbing. The protectors are very vigilant and may
even remain awake while the others are sleeping.

We have several big ones inside who protect us and keep us safe. They are Tom, Dee Dee, and the old lady. They watch over everything. At first, the little ones ran from them. This made it hard to help the little ones be safe. Just because there are protectors doesn't mean that everyone inside knows that the protectors are good. We had to teach the little ones that Tom and Dee Dee are good and would not hurt them. Now the little ones go to them when they are scared. We also have an old lady who likes to learn. She protects the little ones by coming out and learning about everything around. She keeps people around us answering questions so that they don't have time to think about hurting us.

Persecutor or Demon

Not all of the alters are helpful. In fact, most people with DID have alters who represent the trauma and abuse which they endured. These alters, the persecutor or demon alters, are personalities which are formed from the original trauma. Because of the abuse inflicted on those with DID, as well as the overt and covert messages sent by their abusers, many with DID believe that they are bad, dangerous, or evil. It's fairly common for abusers to tell children that they are "bad" and deserve to be punished. The children then internalize these messages and begin to view themselves as bad or evil and may even go so far as to perpetrate violence upon themselves. Generally, these persecutor or demon alters are kept deep within the system and are rarely allowed to emerge.

Animals and Objects

Not all alters are human. Some alters can take the form of animals, inanimate objects, or even fantasy beings. For some with DID, humans come to represent threats and become associated with great fear. Because of this, some people with DID will have alters that take the form of an animal or some other object because these are viewed as safer. Alters who are animals or objects can serve many functions, including protecting others, performing tasks, or making the inner world more safe or enjoyable. For instance, it's perfectly possible to have an alter who is a lion who serves to protect the others from possible danger. Or perhaps an alter might be a tree, which could offer shelter to the others.

We have a mousy that has a job of getting out of little spaces. This was because one of the ways we were hurt was by being put in a small space. Mousy could always find a hole and sneak out and then we can run around and breathe.

The ant is also one we have. Ant is funny—well, just cause it's an ant. But what ant does isn't funny. Ant comes when real ants bite us. We hate ants. Ant bites us like the real ants. Ant knows that we're getting bit, so it is better if we have one of us do it so we can control the hurt. This way, others don't hurt us, we hurt ourselves.

What Does It Mean If You Have DID?

What DID means to you depends entirely on how you choose to view it. You may be relieved to find out that you have DID, as it helps to explain a variety of behaviors which you may not have previously been able to understand. Or you might feel devastated to learn that you have DID, because you feel ashamed, embarrassed, or completely crazy. Or you might simply accept that you have DID and let this diagnosis have no impact on your current life. What is most important is that you learn how to deal with the meaning and impact of DID in your life and that you learn how to manage your life so that you can function, grow, and be satisfied and happy with your life. This book will focus on many of the ways you can better understand yourself and learn ways to be satisfied and happy with yourself and your life.

ACTIVITY 1.3: WHAT DOES DID MEAN TO YOU?

Now that you've read most of this first chapter, it's probably a good time to evaluate how you're feeling and what you're thinking. Maybe you read this chapter and have decided that you definitely don't have DID. Or maybe you've come to the conclusion that you might have DID. Either way, you have probably had some strong reactions to what you have just read.

If you haven't done so already, get yourself a journal or note-book you can use throughout this book. You don't need to share what you'll be writing with anyone (unless you want to). The idea of the journal is for you to be able to record some of what you're thinking and wondering and experiencing so that you can help process some of what you read and so that you can refer back to it later (some activities in future chapters ask you to do this).

Once you have a pen and a journal, take a few minutes and sim-ply write about what DID means to you. What would it mean if you had DID? Would you be better able to understand and deal with your life? Do you think that a diagnosis of DID makes you sound insane or psychotic? How does DID and or its symptoms help explain things that you've experienced? What questions about DID or its symptoms do you have?

You may find that this exercise takes you a long time to com-plete. You may even want to spend several days thinking and writing about DID and what it means to you. As you begin to understand the role of DID in your life, you'll be better able to learn how to cope with it and have a generally healthy, happy existence.

How Common Is DID?

The number of individuals with DID is almost impossible to accu-rately determine. Factors including shame, embarrassment, and fear prevent people with DID from coming forward and acknowledging this diagnosis to others (even to psychotherapists). The best estimates (and these are only estimates) of DID indicate that there are some-where between several thousand people and several hundred thou-sand people in North America who are living with DID. One thing is for sure, if you have DID, you are definitely not alone!

Common Misconceptions about DID

Although most people have heard of Multiple Personality Disorder (now called Dissociative Identity Disorder), many do not really know what this term means. Partly because of its portrayal in the media, a great number of individuals have the wrong idea about people who have DID. There are several common misconceptions about DID and those who have DID.

Misconception 1: DID Doesn't Really Exist

Some people, professionals included, do not believe in DID. The majority of these people believe that people who say that they have DID are lying and are simply fabricating an elaborate story for some type of secondary gain (usually attention). This misconception is particularly harmful because it makes the person with DID second-guess their own sanity. Also, it causes those with DID to have to justify their existence and prove who they are to others. If you think about how difficult it would be to be consistent and elaborate in the presentation and characteristics of another personality, you can see how erroneous this idea is. DID exists and it's probably more common than you would think.

Misconception 2: DID is Created with the Help of a Therapist

DID is typically developed through repeated, severe trauma at an early age. Unless you have a therapist who is repeatedly traumatizing you, this does not seem likely. Therapists generally help you to identify and label your psychological and behavioral characteristics. Like all people, sometimes therapists can be wrong and there are occasions when an individual will be misdiagnosed by a therapist as having DID. However, in most cases therapists are only reflecting back the information the client presents. So, if a therapist diagnoses someone as having DID, chances are they are correct.

Misconception 3: Having DID Means That You're Crazy

Having DID simply means that you have multiple personalities. Some or all of these personalities may be completely sane, functional beings. However, given that DID stems from severe trauma, it's likely that some of the alters may have been impacted by this trauma and may have some psychological problems. The presence of psychological problems, however, does not mean that an individual is crazy.

DID Treatment Options

There are various ways of treating people with DID. One approach is to have all of the personalities integrate or merge into one. This process, known as integration, is done over a long period of time (usually taking many years). The goal of integration is to allow the person to continually have consciousness of and access to all areas of themselves. In this process, the therapist helps the client to understand the role that each of the personalities has in their life. Once the person has a clear understanding of the alter's functions, they can begin to incorporate and integrate these functions into their own life. During this course of treatment, the individual begins to merge the attributes of each personality into one fully integrated being.

> Karen: *As a person with DID, I am not sure what is means to live with only one. I believe that integration is very appropriate for some people. I believe that it is a decision that everyone needs to make for themselves.*
>
> *There is a certain amount of integration that does occur as you heal. There are some personalities who came out to handle certain experiences or to keep certain memories. These personalities do not have any other role than to remember details. As you remember more of what happened to you, the personalities who have the job of remembering these facts may merge with others who also are not full personalities.*

Although integration may be a long-term goal, it is necessary for people with DID to find ways to live and cope during the present. Learning to live with DID can be quite challenging. Establishing means of communication with the alters is a necessary step in both the process of integration and coping with daily life. Finding methods to build safety and support are also necessary to function well on a regular basis. Much of this book focuses on ways to cope with and live with DID.

There is also the possibility that treatment may not be necessary for some individuals with DID. If people with DID are able to function at a level within their life that they find acceptable, treatment may not be necessary or appropriate. People living with DID do not always need help within their lives. Some people with DID create strategies for living and coping that work well for them without professional intervention. While most everyone can benefit from therapy (even those who don't have an identifiable psychological diagnosis), this does not indicate that everyone needs therapy in order to help them cope or survive. As you read through this book, you'll hopefully begin to make your own decisions on whether or not you want or need to receive integration treatment.

CHAPTER 2

The Underlying Causes
of DID

The contents of this chapter may be disturbing to individuals with histories of abuse, trauma, or ritual abuse. If you think that you may have difficulty dealing with these topics, it would be in your best interest to consult with a therapist or someone else who can offer you support prior to reading this chapter.

You're probably wondering how and why a person develops DID. How could a person develop the ability to create and sustain a number of alternate personalities? Why would someone need to do this in the first place? This chapter will address the process by which DID develops, as well as its underlying causes, which almost always involve some sort of severe trauma.

How Does DID Develop?

In chapter 1 many of the symptoms of DID were presented. Among these was dissociation, the ability to change your state of consciousness and awareness through psychological means (as opposed to doing drugs or drinking in order to change your level of consciousness). It's this ability and need to dissociate that actually allows DID to develop.

DID develops as a means to cope with severely traumatic situations. When you are going through an extremely traumatic event (or events) such as childhood abuse, natural disasters, or ritual abuse, you are forced to find ways to cope with the intensity and terror of the situation. Dissociation, which is a psychological term for what may feel to you like zoning out or separating from yourself, allows you to deal with and survive traumatic situations. DID is an extreme form of dissociation, in which separate personalities are formed and maintained. DID is useful in that it allows for alternate personalities to be present at various times. For example, one personality may have been developed in order to be present during the trauma, allowing the other personalities to, in effect, escape the situation. As DID develops, the different personalities take on more specific and pronounced roles, each creating their own lives, ways of being, and ways of relating to the world.

Dissociation

Surely you can remember a time in your life when you've caught yourself not paying attention to a conversation going on around you or driving past a street you had planned to turn onto. It's likely very easy for you to think of many times you were simply "tuned out," daydreaming, or not paying attention to the task at hand. Everyone has done this at some point or another.

Everyone dissociates to some degree. It would be impossible to attend to or focus on everything which is happening to and around you. When people dissociate, they experience a change or alteration in their consciousness, memory, and—sometimes—identity. During a dissociative episode, you may feel detached from your body or as if you are watching yourself in a movie. It may also seem like you're floating or like you've left your body. You may even be able to dissociate to such an extent that you have actually created separate identities, with separate lives, abilities, and maybe even differing physical characteristics. It is this psychological phenomenon of dissociation that allows you to develop alternate personalities.

ACTIVITY 2.1: HOW MUCH DO YOU DISSOCIATE?

This exercise will provide you with information regarding the role dissociation plays in your life. Higher scores indicate more extreme levels of dissociation.

Rate yourself on the following questions. Use this scale to indicate your response, entering the appropriate number on the blank line preceding each question.

1	2	3	4	5	6	7	8	9	10
never				sometimes					very often

____ I feel detached from my body.

____ I feel as if I am watching myself (as if in a movie).

____ I lose track of time.

____ I find things in my possession that I have no recollection of buying (or obtaining in some manner).

____ I am unable to remember important events in my life.

____ I am unable to remember large chunks of time.

____ I feel as if people, things, and the world in general are not real.

____ I can't remember if I actually said or did something or if I just thought about it.

____ I become so absorbed in reading, watching television, or daydreaming that I don't notice if someone is talking to me or trying to get my attention.

____ Sometimes people tell me that I've done things which I have no memory of doing.

As was mentioned before, all people dissociate to some degree, and dissociation is a very useful mechanism to deal with overwhelming situations.

Add together all of the numbers you have entered. Your score will be between 10 and 100. The closer your score is to 100, the higher your level of dissociation. Scores of 80 and above indicate extreme levels of dissociation. Scores below 30 indicate low levels of dissociation. Scores between 30 and 80 could be considered average. Again, there are no right or wrong answers or scores here. This activity is simply designed so that you can see the role dissociation plays within your own life.

Although DID develops from a heightened ability and need to dissociate, not everyone who dissociates will develop DID. While dissociation is a necessary component of DID, it is not the only factor involved. Just because you dissociate a great deal does not mean that you have DID. You may simply dissociate more than most people. The development of DID has to include the creation of distinct personalities; without this, DID cannot be formed.

Here's one example of how dissociation can work.

> Karen: *It took every bit of energy I had to get through work every day and then be with my stepchildren at night. By the time I had a chance to "be," the little ones were out crying, playing, being mad, and feeling terrified that I was going to have to die because I started talking about what happened. Every time I would get scared Nada would come to the rescue. She would totally numb everyone out and make sure that we got through the day at work. When the little ones would finally come back and Nada would leave, I could feel again. I also knew that I would slip away soon and Nada would take over again because of the work I was doing in therapy.*

What Causes DID?

Trauma

At some point in each person's life, they are likely to be hurt. Sometimes they may be hurt physically, such as if they were to fall off a bike and break a bone, and sometimes they may be hurt emotionally, such as when they deal with the death of a loved one. Most people will be hurt in either or both of these ways many times throughout their lives. While each of these events may be unpleasant, painful, or highly distressing, most would not be considered traumatic. Trauma occurs when people are hurt, physically and/or emotionally, in ways that extend well past the realm of expected or typical experiences (and will often produce long-term psychological consequences). For example, you may know of people who have been in serious automobile accidents and who have lost some of their abilities to recall or remember things. They may even have no recollection of the actual accident. Because the event was so terrifying, painful, damaging, and traumatic, the effects of the accident are severe.

As was mentioned before, all people dissociate to some degree and dissociation is a very useful mechanism to deal with overwhelming situations. Dissociation allows you to escape and protect yourself from the intense psychological or physical distress which accompanies traumatic events. The more severe the trauma, the greater the need to find a way to cope and defend yourself. Sometimes when traumatic situations are so intense or continue over a long period of time, the need to defend and protect yourself becomes so strong that you have to use extreme measures to do so. These extreme measures include using dissociation to such a degree that you actually form alternate personalities, each with different skills and abilities to help you endure these horrendous and terrifying situations.

Although it may be possible that an individual could develop DID without having gone through some sort of trauma, it is not likely (it is rare to discover a case of DID that does not involve some type of trauma). It is also not likely that a person would form multiple personalities from a single traumatic episode. Most people who have DID have been through severe, repeated, intense trauma (the issue of the ability to recall this trauma will be addressed in a later chapter). The following sections will address specific types of traumatic experiences, which are often associated with DID.

Sexual, Physical, and Emotional Abuse

If you have Dissociative Identity Disorder, chances are you have survived some type of sexual, physical, or emotional abuse. Most individuals with DID have been abused in one or more of these three ways. In some cases this abuse may have occurred within a cult or similar setting in which rituals or satanic worship were present (this will be discussed in the next section). However, in most situations the abuse occurred at home or in other familiar settings like school or a friend's or relative's house.

Many forms of sexual abuse are fairly easy to recognize, such as rape and being forced to perform other sexual acts on others. However, there is a great range in what could be considered sexual abuse if you include those behaviors which cross the lines of sexual appropriateness. Fondling, inappropriate kissing and touching, and being made to watch sexual acts could all be considered forms of sexual abuse. While some of these types of sexual abuse may be less recognizable as such, they can be equally damaging as those which are more readily identifiable.

Physical abuse always involves some form of unwanted physical contact. Hitting, slapping, kicking, beating with objects, and spanking are common forms of physical abuse. Other types of physical abuse may be even more severe, such as burning, cutting, stabbing, and even shooting. Physical abuse does not need to result in noticeable injury to the body in order to be psychologically damaging.

Emotional abuse is difficult both to identify and to define. Generally, emotional abuse involves a repeated pattern of verbal or behavioral interactions which result in the victim feeling badly on a psychological or emotional level. Emotional abuse may be something as simple as your parent calling you stupid on a repeated basis or as involved as the emotional atmosphere present in a family in which violence and alcoholism exist. Being consistently ignored or having your needs neglected may also be viewed as forms of emotional abuse.

When you were being abused (regardless of the type of abuse) you had to endure tremendous amounts of physical and emotional pain. In order to survive you had to develop some impressive strategies for coping. If the abuse that you went through was repetitive and severe, it's likely that the ways in which you took care of yourself and defended yourself against the abuse were also severe. Since you were unable to escape the abuse physically, you had to learn to escape the abuse you were subjected to psychologically. This is the reason for developing an extreme ability to dissociate. The formation of other personalities or alters during these dissociative episodes marks the development of Dissociative Identity Disorder. DID is really a unique and effective method of coping with situations which are terrifying and damaging both psychologically and physically.

The little ones of us that held all the bad stuff that happened didn't come out for a long time. We knew that we would be in bad shape if any of the little ones who had been hurt started to tell what happened to us. The little ones were always here, it is just that those around us and the one who managed to get through the days didn't know she had so much company. There were the ones that were on the outside who were nice and knew how to behave. Those of us on the inner inside hid because we didn't want the big one to know what happened. We kept all of this from her so she could function. Well, it seemed like she was doing okay, at least she wasn't in pain and feeling crazy all of the time.

Ritual and Satanic Abuse

Abuse of any type is often difficult to fathom. That some individuals purposefully harm others (often children), physically and/or psychologically, is nearly unbelievable in and of itself. However, when you consider that ritual and satanic abuse involves groups of individuals intentionally inflicting abuse, and even sometimes sacrificing the lives of others, it is no wonder that skepticism of these practices abound. Disbelief and skepticism aside, ritual and satanic abuse exist and the effects of these types of abuse are often severe, and can result in intense psychological difficulties, DID, chronic physical problems, and even death.

A good definition of ritual abuse comes from the Los Angeles County Commission for Women (1989). Their definition states:

Ritual abuse is a brutal form of abuse of children, adolescents, and adults, consisting of physical, sexual, and psychological abuse, involving the use of rituals. Ritual does not necessarily mean satanic. However, most survivors state that they were ritually abused as part of satanic worship for the purpose of indoctrinating them into satanic beliefs and practices. Ritual abuse rarely consists of a single episode. It usually involves repeated abuse over an extended period of time.

While each specific instance of ritual or satanic abuse will differ, there are common characteristics found within these abusive situations. If you have survived ritual or satanic abuse, you may find that you recognize some of these characteristics. You may also remember things which occurred that are not discussed here. It's important that you don't doubt your own experience. Just because your experience is not listed in this text does not mean that it is not real or valid.

Many types of ritual or satanic abuse involve the use of religion. Sometimes religion is used as a front for the group of individuals inflicting this form of abuse. Because of the secrecy and ceremony attached to many religions, use of religious environments provides a cover for the abusive activities found within. There have been many stories of children who have been sexually, physically, and emotionally abused by groups of adults, while they were supposedly attending after-school religious programs. Although these children were in the religious setting when this ritual abuse occurred, the religious education which they were supposedly receiving was a guise that allowed the abuse to occur in a fairly unsuspected and protected environment.

Religion is also heavily involved in satanic abuse. In these situations abuse occurs within the context of worshipping Satan, and similar religious practices, such as some pagan rituals and witchcraft. As part of these satanic ceremonies, abuse in the name of religion is often quite severe, horrific, and bizarre. It is not uncommon for individuals who have survived these experiences to report having been sexually abused by many of the group's members as part of satanic rituals. Also, ceremonial sacrifices of animals and humans (often infants) are frequently reported. Some individuals tell of experiences such as being buried alive or placed in an already occupied coffin during these rituals.

Tracy has worked with several clients who described ritual abuse that took place within their churches. These clients told remarkably similar stories. In each case, the client, who at the time was a young (five- to six-year-old) child, was taken from a class taking place at their church and brought to a separate room or building on the church grounds. Within this setting, these children were forced to lay on an altar of some sort, gagged, and bound. An elaborate ceremony would begin and include the recital of prayers and the lighting of candles; sometimes the ceremony would include drumming or chanting, and often the sacrifice of an animal or human occurred. At some point during the ceremony, the children on the altar would be sexually abused by individuals wearing robes. Following the ceremony, the children would be led back to their classroom and threatened, being told not to tell anyone about what had just occurred. Occasionally, these same children would be coerced into performing some of the actions in the ceremony, such as sacrificing an animal or performing a sexual act with another child.

Within satanic and ritual abuse particular, days and holidays are likely to show increases in ceremonial practices and abuse. Such holidays include: Halloween (October 31) and the days surrounding this holiday; summer and winter solstice (June 21 and December 22); nights in which there is a full moon; days corresponding to Christian holidays (Christmas, Easter, etc.); and times specifically relating to satanic rituals (January 17 and February 2—satanic revels, April 21 through May 1—preparation for sacrifice and the grand climax). During these periods the intensity and frequency of abuse is heightened.

Both satanic and ritual abuse involve the use of ceremonial instruments such as certain types of knives, swords, and other weapons. Use of ceremonial garb and props are also common. Robes, frequently black or red in color, often accompany the ritual episodes. Props, such as altars, chalices, cages, scepters, and satanic symbols like pentagrams, images of Satan, and satanic masks are also frequently present.

Many forms of abuse and torture are specific to ritual and satanic acts. As previously mentioned, sacrifice of animals and sometimes even humans has been known to occur. Animals which are specifically related to satanic worship such as goats, snakes, and cats are those most commonly sacrificed. As bizarre and horrific as it may sound, it is not unheard of for members of these groups to offer humans for sacrifice, sometimes offering their own infants or children for these rituals. Adults, either from the group or abducted from the outside, may also be killed or injured in these sacrificial ceremonies. Sacrifices do not always result in death. In some cases certain organs, limbs, or bodily fluids (such as blood) may be viewed as a sufficient sacrifice to appease the group leaders and members.

> *The worst trigger time for us was when a therapist was talking about coming out of her home and finding a dead rabbit on her door. She knew that it was from a client who was diagnosed with MPD and was still involved with a cult. As she was talking about what happened to her, all of these other voices and feelings starting coming out. We were crying and trying to hurt ourselves. After that episode we felt more crazy than ever. We did not know what a dead rabbit had to do with anything and felt that the best thing would be for someone to lock us up.*

Ritual abusers thrive on control of their victims. Control is often exerted through both physical and psychological methods, being initially established through a variety of means. First, the physical and sexual abuse which most victims endure assists in implementing feelings of fear and powerlessness. When you feel scared and powerless, you have little or no control (and this is often the case in reality). At these times when you are feeling weak, scared, and vulnerable, you have little choice but to comply with the demands of those around you.

Sometimes drugs, alcohol, or psychological methods such as hypnosis or induction into trance may be used to alter the consciousness of members. Through the induction of an altered state of consciousness, members may lose the ability to defend themselves (physically and psychologically) and may become more vulnerable to abuse by others. They may also be unable to recall the events which occurred during this state of altered consciousness. People who experience this may have been drugged or abused, and it is possible for them to have no memory of this experience.

Several individuals Tracy has worked with have described experiences of being taken to the site of the ritual and being drugged. Some were able to remember what occurred during the ritual abuse, while others had no recollection of the actual activities, though they did have physical evidence that something had happened. Sometimes these individuals would return to consciousness only to find that they had been cut, bruised, or sexually assaulted.

Many individuals who have been through satanic or ritual abuse have been forced to perform abusive acts on others. This form of coercion is a psychological method of controlling the group members. Often, the member who is made to engage in these abusive behaviors is physically threatened. These threats usually take the form of "Do this or you will be punished (or injured or killed)." The coerced members, who may be children, usually respond by performing the act, thus ensuring their own survival. However, despite the physical survival of this individual, the psychological damage resulting from injuring another can be severe. If you have had to hurt someone in order to keep yourself safe, you probably feel guilty, shamed, and as if you are bad or evil. If you feel this way, try to remind yourself that you did what you had to do to survive and that under different circumstances (if your own life or safety wasn't being threatened), you wouldn't have done what you did. Behaviors founded in survival are not evil—they are simply necessary.

Threats and other forms of psychological intimidation are used to keep group members from discussing their experiences with non-members. Children who are abused are frequently told that if they tell anyone else what has happened to them, they, or members of their family, will be killed or injured. After witnessing such horrific trauma during the ritual or satanic abuse, the member must take this threat seriously.

Some of Tracy's DID clients tell stories of having to injure or abuse other children as part of a ritual. For these people, the act of hurting others is at least as psychologically damaging as being abused themselves. Most of these individuals experienced great shame and guilt over harming someone else. Some were forced to cut other children in order to satisfy the demands of the adult members. Some were told that they must perform sexual acts on the others. It's common that the lives and safety of individuals subject to ritual abuse are threatened if they demonstrate any signs of hesitation to perform sexual or violent acts on others. The same threats are often used to keep these individuals from discussing the group's activities with anyone else.

You may recall a time when you were told that you must not tell anyone else what happened. Since you are reading this book, you have probably reached the point at which you are out of any real danger of retaliation and realize that it is safe and important to share your experiences with others. It almost goes without saying that ritual and satanic abuse generally involve forms of sexual and physical abuse. As mentioned previously, physical and sexual abuse can have tremendously negative side effects on those involved. The physical and sexual abuse performed within ritualistic settings can be particularly damaging because of the numerous perpetrators. As you probably have realized, ritual or satanic abuse can produce profound psychological as well as physical consequences. That you have DID probably has a great deal to do with the severe abuse you endured as a child.

Factors Affecting People Living with DID

As you may have already noticed, living with DID presents you with a unique way of being in the world. The traumatic experiences you endured as part of developing DID, as well as the consequences of having DID, have given you a unique perspective and a means of existence that are different from that of singletons. Because you have DID, you are forced to deal with factors in your life that most people do not. Factors such as memory problems, memories and flashbacks of the trauma you endured, shame and secrecy about having DID, and various types of addictions are common occurrences for people with DID. This chapter will present and discuss many of the factors which affect individuals who live with DID. Hopefully by reading this chapter, you will be able to make sense of some of the things you deal with and realize that you are not alone in your experiences.

Memory Problems

Most people with DID have difficulty with their memory. You may lose track of events which recently occurred, forgetting where you parked your car, for instance. Or, you may not be able to remember things from the past such as large chunks of your childhood. Given that multiple personalities are a function of the ability to dissociate, it's no surprise that memory problems plague those with DID. It may be particularly difficult for you to keep track of time. You may find yourself always running late, missing important appointments, or even not being able to remember what day of the week it is. Remember, you have many others sharing your body and your time and without total co-consciousness, or the ability to know what all of the alters are thinking and doing, you're probably going to have some trouble keeping track of many things. While these difficulties with memory may be hard for you, they are completely normal given that you have multiple personalities.

ACTIVITY 3.1: HOW IS YOUR MEMORY AFFECTED BY DID?

It may be helpful for you to examine the ways in which your memory is impacted by having multiple personalities. Being able to see the difficulties in your memory will give you a start on learning to manage your life better. Hang on to your answers from this activity, as they will be helpful to you when you get to chapter 5 and you are learning actual techniques you can use to better manage your life.

Use the following scale to assess some of the ways in which your memory is affected by having DID. In the blank next to each statement, place the number that best represents the impact of DID on your memory in that area.

0	1	2	3	4
never	rarely	sometimes	occasionally	often

_____ I lose the keys to my home or car.

_____ I misplace important papers or documents.

_____ I forget appointments I have made with people.

_____ I lose track of time, sometimes for minutes to hours.

_____ I have trouble remembering big pieces of my childhood.

_____ I forget where I park my car.

_____ I get lost going to familiar places.

_____ I start doing something and then forget what I'm doing.

_____ I can't remember something that I just did or said.

_____ I forget names of people that I'm sure I know or have met before.

_____ _____

_____ _____

_____ _____

_____ _____

Most of these statements represent problems with memory that almost everyone has from time to time. However if your scores are particularly high in one or many areas, you may be discovering some of the ways in which DID affects your memory.

Memories of Trauma

Chances are that you or one of your alters will have memories of the trauma or abuse you endured. Your memories can take many forms and may or may not be available to you directly. For instance, your child alters may have clear recollections of what happened, but may not allow those memories to be accessed by the host personality because they fear it will be too upsetting or difficult. You may also find that what you can remember about the abuse is vague or dim. At times you may even question whether or not abuse or trauma occurred. Even though your recollections of the trauma may be hazy, once you gain access to those who were present during the events, you may find that you no longer need to question yourself. In other words, although you may have been dissociating during the trauma and may for all intent and purposes have left the event, someone was there, and it's this personality who will have the memories of the trauma.

You may be able to access the memories of trauma if you are able to communicate with the alters who hold these memories and if they are willing to endure the distress associated with remembering these events. What you do remember is likely to be distorted to some degree. This is not to say that the abuse or trauma did not really happen. Instead, your memory, just like everyone else's, is subject to some error. For instance, when Tracy was younger, her parents owned an old brown Grand Fury station wagon. For all of her family's outings they would use this car. One day, many years later, she came across a photograph of this car. The car in the picture was blue, not brown like the car in her memories. So, although she was able to accurately remember the basics about the car, a few of her memories were a bit off. Inaccuracies in memory are completely normal. As you recall some of the events which took place in your own life, expect to be wrong about some of the details of what happened, but also know that your memories for the overall events are probably quite accurate.

Types of Memories

You have memories that come from each one of the five senses. Sight, sound, taste, smell, and touch all leave their imprints on your memory. Since the trauma or abuse you endured was most likely encoded by all five senses, your recall of these events will occur through each of these senses. You may have pictures in your mind of what happened to you as a child. These pictures are related to the sense of sight. You may have memories of things that were said to you during the abuse such as, "If you tell, I'll kill you." This is a type of auditory memory (having to do with your sense of hearing). Through your sense of taste you may be able to recall certain foods or flavors that were present during the trauma. Your sense of smell, which is closely associated to the sense of taste, also holds memories of odors which were present during the original trauma. Lastly, you may also have memories from traumatic experiences that are of a tactile nature, from your sense of touch.

Each of these types of memory are susceptible to being triggered by similar input. You may see a store display of lit white candles and your visual memories of similar candles, lit during a ceremony in which ritual abuse took place, may surface. Your sense of sound, touch, taste, and smell may also trigger memories in similar ways.

Many people describe having body memories. Body memories are basically tactile memories, or memories of touch. These can arise without warning. There may be certain touches that make you extremely uncomfortable; you may know that you want to run out of the room when someone hugs you or pats you on the back, but you may not understand why. Generally, body memories do not have links to the senses of sound or vision; your body may be remembering, but you have no visual or audio memories that accompany these tactile memories. Without understanding that these are actual memories which are appearing in a way that is new or different, you may feel like you're going absolutely crazy. One reason why body memories occur without the presence of the other sensory memories, such as visual memory of the events that caused the body memory, has to do with the age at which the abuse occurred. Abuse which took place at a preverbal age (before you could talk) is more likely to be stored as a body memory. This is because you didn't have the necessary skills to encode the information through the sense of sound—the words had no meaning.

Your varied sensory memories of the abuse can impact each other. So, although your auditory memory may trigger you when you hear something that was said to you during the abusive event, the rest of your senses can then be activated and other sensory memories may arise.

Sometimes your memories will be so strong that you will feel like the event is actually taking place. When this occurs it's called a flashback. During a flashback, you feel as if you are reliving the event. Flashbacks can be very frightening and can make you act in ways that seem strange to those observing you. For instance, you may be having a flashback in which you are hiding under a table and screaming "No!" in order to try to avert your abuser. During this flashback you may be performing this act in your mind, or you may actually be trying to find a safe place under a table or desk at work. So, to the observer, a flashback may look like you're simply spacing out, or it may look like you're participating in an event that is not actually taking place (e.g., speaking to people who aren't present, etc.).

Once you are able to identify some of the triggers to your memories and flashbacks, you will be able to control them much better. There may still be times when you are caught off guard and find yourself reacting to a memory, but the chances of this happening are much less when you can name what it is that's causing the memories.

※

ACTIVITY 3.2: UNDERSTANDING TYPES OF MEMORIES

Now it's time to understand how the five types of memories—auditory (sound), visual (sight), tactile (touch), olfactory (smell), and gustatory (taste)—are relevant to your own life.

Think about situations that you know you may be overreacting to. In your journal, record as many of these situations as you can. Once you have them recorded, try to answer the following items. Write your answers in your journal.

1. What are the triggers that made you overreact?

2. What kinds of sounds are likely to trigger reactions or memories? Do you overreact to loud noises? Whispering? Drumming? Chanting?

3. What kinds of smells trigger your reactions? Do you find yourself starting to have difficulty concentrating when you smell certain scents?

4. Are there certain ways that people can touch you that make you react? Are there places on your body which trigger memories or reactions? Do you feel like you will explode when someone just touches you on the arm? Your legs? What happens when someone you know and love touches you sexually? Does this trigger strong emotions?

5. Are there any tastes which can affect your reactions? If so, what tastes?

6. What kinds of visual images trigger reactions? Does watching movies or seeing pictures of violence make you feel out of control? How about watching an adult act affectionately toward a child?

7. Are there times that you have had people ask you what is wrong because you are acting abnormally? Why were you acting the ways you were during those times? Was it watching a scene in a movie or hearing someone yell? Could it have been an activity you were engaging in?

8. If you can, identify what these triggers remind you of. This may be difficult for you if you have not yet dealt with the

original issues of trauma, and you may decide to wait until you've done some work in this area.

By understanding how you remember, you will be better able to identify some of the possible triggers which may lead to flashbacks and/or emotional distress. Once you can identify these triggers, you will likely be able to avoid or control these areas.

Splitting

Splitting refers to the process of rapidly changing identities. Generally there is one personality who is in control at the moment. At different times different personalities decide that it is their turn to come out. Since you are all sharing the same body, only one of you can really be out at any given time. Sometimes you can be in control of who is out, and at other times you may feel like a revolving door. The control only comes after you learn who all lives in your system and you have some communication internally. However, which personality is out can change quite quickly. When you are in this process of swiftly changing who is out you are splitting.

Splitting generally occurs for one of two reasons. First, splitting can happen because you are triggered by something, a reminder of past abuse or some type of information, that causes an overwhelming emotional response. In this case, the splitting reflects the internal chaos and seeming lack of control. You may find that some of the child alters begin popping out and showing their responses to the triggers, perhaps crying or screaming or simply feeling terrified. Interspersed with the appearance of the child alters, some of the adult alters or the ones who have more control may come out to try and handle the situation.

We have the most trouble with splitting when we are triggered by something or when someone is mad at us. One time we were talking with a friend who knew we hated loud noises. Out of the blue, he hit his hand on the desk. Next thing we knew, we were on the bathroom floor crying hysterically with all of the little ones coming out to have their say. It took us a while to pull together enough to have the big one come back and return to the room. Once he finally understood that loud noises make us react it made life much easier.

The other times that we have everyone out are when someone is mad at us. The only people that it is difficult with are people very close to us. If the person who is mad is just a friend it doesn't matter and we don't react in the same way. If it is our partner, Tracy, then every little one inside has something to say. These reactions begin with one yelling, "Well, you did something to us," while another thinks that she is going to be hurt. Another one knows that we have to kill ourselves and another is trying to figure out what happened. Since we have difficulty tracking time, it makes arguing difficult because we never know when things happened and sometimes who has said what.

Splitting is the way we learned to deal with trauma and it took us a long time to realize that if people close to us get angry we will still survive. We have now come up with agreements on what to do when people are mad at us. We listen to what they have to say and then wait until the big one can answer them. Our good friends do know all of us but we know they feel awful if the little ones come out because they got mad at us about something. So we inside agreed that it is best just to let the big ones handle it. Sometimes we wait until we are away from other people and then the little ones can talk about what happened. This way big ones get to keep friends because the little ones won't make them feel like they have to always be on good behavior.

Splitting sometimes happens simply because several alters want to express themselves and have some time to be out. This makes perfect sense if you view DID like a family. You probably couldn't imagine having a family in which some of the members were never allowed out of the house. Since the body is like a house for the personalities, sometimes they will want to be out and be able to freely express themselves and their interests. Many of the inside ones have great talents and abilities and they simply need time and access to the body and the outside world in order to use them.

Sometimes you will be aware when you are splitting and sometimes you will not. Some people with you can tell you when your are splitting by watching your behaviors and seeing who is out. Of course, that person would have to be aware of the DID, or else they might think that you've become psychotic or something. Perhaps once you realize you are splitting, you can explore the reasons why this is occurring and decide if this is problematic for you or not.

Shame and Secrecy

Shame and secrecy can affect you similarly to a natural disaster, such as a flood. First, you feel a few drops of rain, which don't initially seem that bad, and before you know it, you have a river flowing right in front of your eyes. At first, the impact of shame and secrecy may seem minimal; but as shame and secrecy continue, they're power becomes incredibly strong and, like a flood, they can overwhelm and destroy.

Because of the way in which DID is portrayed in society, you are likely to feel a great amount of shame and embarrassment over having multiple personalities. Generally, people with DID are seen as crazy, dysfunctional, and even dangerous and the media portrayals of these people typically don't contradict these views. But, as you know, DID doesn't have to be any of these things. You may be able to function quite sanely (as much as anyone ever does), and you need not be dangerous in any way.

Being raised in this society, you have probably in a sense been brainwashed into believing that having multiple personalities is something of which to be ashamed. And because of your feelings of shame, you're likely to keep your DID a secret.

In addition to the general views of society, shame may also stem from the original trauma that you went through. Many people who are victims of abuse or trauma feel very embarrassed, ashamed, and even partially responsible for what occurred. You may feel as if you should have been able to do something to stop the abuse from happening, and because you couldn't you may think that you helped to cause the abuse. These feelings and the attached distorted thoughts may make you feel really badly about what happened to you as a child. These feelings also tend to replicate the original abuse; if you were feeling ashamed of being abused, you may now be feeling ashamed of having DID. Although your feelings about this may be strong, they just aren't true.

You may also have been convinced that if you ever tried to tell anyone about what happened to you, you would not be believed. You may have been told by your abusers that any people you did tell would think you made up things or that they would just ignore you. Often this is what does happen when you talk to people about what happened to you—people think you made it up. This can lead you to believing your abuser. It is in the abusers' best interest to make you feel like you are the problem and that you caused it. Shame keeps you from feeling like you can get healthy and from telling your story.

In order to help alleviate some of the resulting shame, it's important that you take a minute or two and challenge these beliefs. Drive by a playground or a school and take a look at a child who is about the same age that you were when you were abused. It'll probably be difficult for you to imagine that child in any way causing a situation which leads to abuse. Just like that child, you couldn't have caused or prevented the abuse or trauma which you've survived.

While the sources of shame and secrecy are fairly obvious, some of their effects are not. Shame and secrecy can lead you to become more isolated, depressed, and scared. If you think about it, very few people have the courage to stand up and point out what they are most ashamed of. Instead, most people will try to isolate themselves or hide what they don't want anyone to know. In terms of DID, you may keep your other personalities from coming out around others. You may try to overcompensate for some of the difficulties which go with having DID, such as frequently losing objects and having problems tracking time. You may even go so far as to lie about having multiple personalities, simply because you're afraid of the responses of others.

There is no doubt that having DID can be very isolating. Finding others who have multiple personalities or even people who understand this phenomenon is difficult at best. You may feel like you're the only person on earth who is in this situation. Hopefully the mere presence of this book will assure you that you are not alone. Simply because DID is rare does not mean that there aren't others like you. In fact, there are many like you, but due to feelings of shame and embarrassment, they, like you, probably don't tell many people about having multiple personalities. Once you can view DID for what it is—a way of surviving a horrendous situation—it will be easier for you to reduce the shame and embarrassment you feel about having multiple personalities. Also, speaking with others who understand or have DID will give you a perspective that might even make you feel proud. You are a survivor and you are very special (see the Resources section at the end of the book for ways to help you cope with DID).

Karen: *When I began to be aware that I was a lesbian, I knew that it was viewed by many as being something unhealthy. I had often heard that being gay was a way to get attention or somehow impact others. I never dreamed of growing up and being "one of those gay people" society hated. I never wished that I could face various types of discrimination. After I realized that being a lesbian was who*

I was and that I didn't have to hide, it was one of the most freeing times of my life.

One of the reasons I wanted to do this book was to recognize that having DID is not bad. It is a result of bad things that were done to me. I am very lucky to be alive today. When I first came to understand who all I really was in the world, I was embarrassed and ashamed. I knew that some people would reject me and think I was crazy. It has taken me many years to become comfortable with the fact that DID is part of my life, just as being a lesbian is a part of my life. While I might wear a T-shirt around town that says, "We're here, we're queer, get used to it!" I'm still not ready to wear a shirt that says the same about having DID. Maybe some day!

Addictions

Addictions are fairly common for people who have multiple personalities. Just as dissociation itself is a method of dealing with intense emotional or physical experiences, addictions are another way of reducing the amount of psychological tension and discomfort. Addictions take many forms, including, but not limited to, addictions to drugs, alcohol, gambling, shopping, food, sex, excessive exercise, and even eating disorders.

Addictions work by replacing the negative emotions you are experiencing with some kind of distraction. Sometimes addictions can change your physical state as well as your emotional state, as in the case of drug and alcohol addictions which actually alter the chemistry of your brain.

All addictions basically follow the same cycle. You feel bad emotionally, so you get it in your mind that you'll do this addictive behavior. Once you start thinking of this behavior, doing drugs for example, you are distracting yourself from your negative feelings by focusing on something else, the drugs. At this point you may begin to feel excited or tense, which is a reaction to your focus on the addictive behavior. Next, you actually perform the addictive behavior and you immediately feel some relief. The addictive behavior allows you to release some of the emotional tension and distress you've been feeling.

You may also have a physical response to the behavior. Drugs, alcohol, nicotine, caffeine, and even exercise all have the capability of changing the chemistry in your body or brain, which will result in making you feel differently on a physical, as well as psychological, level. However, after the psychological and/or physical changes dissipate, you start feeling badly again. Only now, you may feel worse because you have engaged in a behavior which you may regret or feel ashamed of. Additionally, you may feel worse physically depending on the type of addiction you have. For instance, after doing too many drugs, you may feel hung over or out of it, or you may be going through a physical response to withdrawal from the substance. Additionally, once your negative feelings return, you will probably want to start the whole cycle all over and return to the addictive behavior.

Some of the addictions you may have are ones that others don't notice. You may be a workaholic. This is one addiction that is often supported in this society, partially because employers get so much work from these employees. This addiction also develops because if you stay so busy that you do not have time to think, you also do not have time to feel. If you look at your life and realize that you have two jobs and are going to school, perhaps in addition to managing a relationship and a family, you may be a workaholic. This addiction, like other addictions, keeps you from dealing with yourself and your feelings.

Many people who have survived abuse suffer long-term psychological effects of that trauma. Often the abuse leads to repeated bouts with depression, anxiety, anger, and other negative emotions. Because most people who have DID have experienced tremendous amounts of trauma and abuse, it makes sense that they would also experience difficulty tolerating these intense negative emotions. For this reason, many people with DID also have addictions, which help them to cope with these overwhelming psychological states.

Some people with DID have certain alters that engage in addictive behaviors. For example, while one alter may not drink or smoke at all, another may be a full-fledged alcoholic. One alter may be bulimic and another may enjoy gambling. Or perhaps, you have no knowledge of any personalities who have addictive behaviors, but find yourself waking up feeling hung over every Sunday morning. In other words, it's likely that you engage in some sort of addictive behavior, whether you have awareness of it or not.

> We were/are what you might call a chocoholic or a sweet
> freak. Either would be very accurate. We are picky, though,
> about the type of candy and the kinds of ice cream we eat.
> What we are not picky about is when to eat these things:
> breakfast, lunch, dinner, snacks—you name it—it is always

time for chocolate! We knew we were in trouble when we had chocolate for breakfast, grabbed some M&Ms to get through the midday tireds, had a hot fudge sundae for lunch, and ate a few more M&Ms to stay awake through the afternoon. When we had that fresh dark chocolate cake with dark fudge icing for dinner, it was the perfect day!

We ended up having to stop eating sugar totally for six months so we could get back under control. But we managed to get something we always wanted—a puppy. We had a deal with our therapist that if we didn't eat sugar for six months, we could get a dog. It was worth it. Now we have a rule that we have to eat real food first—foods that outside people would call real. Not our inside little ones—their food groups are chocolate, ice cream, cake, and milk (only with M&Ms or chocolate cake).

We know that if we are eating candy first thing in the morning and looking for those peanut butter cookies for lunch that we had best slow down to see what is going on.

Self-Inflicted Violence

Self-inflicted violence (SIV), also known as self-injury or self-mutilation, is fairly common among those with DID. SIV is best defined as the intentional harm (when you hurt yourself on purpose) of your own body without a desire to kill yourself.

Many people who engage in SIV behaviors do so by cutting themselves with sharp objects, burning themselves, hitting or bruising themselves, pulling out their own hair, and even going so far as to break their own bones. SIV, like any addiction, is a method of coping with extreme emotional distress. It may be surprising to you, but SIV is more common than you might think, with roughly one to two million people in this country engaging in these behaviors.

Self-inflicted violence follows basically the same course as any addictive behavior. Bad feelings exist, thoughts shift to self-injury, and tension occurs. However, unlike most other addictive behaviors, prior to the actual act people engaging in SIV will usually dissociate to a further degree. This dissociation allows for the person who is self-injuring to psychologically block the pain associated with damaging the body. The cycle following the actual self-injurious act continues to follow a typical addiction cycle, which includes a feeling of relief and release and eventually the return of negative emotions.

As you know, dissociation is the psychological mechanism which lets you form and maintain multiple personalities. Both abuse and dissociation are highly related to SIV. Thus, it makes perfect sense that self-inflicted violence would also relate to DID.

For most people, SIV serves many functions, including providing a manner of communicating, a way to release overwhelming negative emotions, and a general method of coping. However, for those with DID, self-injury has some additional uses. Sometimes, SIV will be used to prevent an alter from coming out. The physical sensations experienced during an act of self-injury may be enough of a reminder of reality to inhibit the presence of certain personalities. Similarly, SIV can also be used to elicit the emergence of a specific identity. One alter may be in so much emotional or physical pain that it becomes necessary for a different identity to take over, and this change in identity may be implemented through the use of self-injury. Thus, SIV can be used as a way of controlling dissociation and the presence of certain personalities.

Additionally, just as violence sometimes exists within typical families, violence can occur within the family inside you. Many individuals with DID have at least one alter who is angry, violent, and abusive, and these alters may take their rage out on the others. The important part is to realize that if you have an alter who is hurting your body, there is a reason. It may be that one alter has the role of keeping you from talking about your past. Anytime you are going to therapy you may start cutting yourself. It could be that after you have talked in therapy, you hurt yourself because the alter who is trying to keep you quiet is showing you that you have to not talk.

You may have an alter that wants to make sure you realize that things were done to you as a child. If you begin to doubt that you have DID, you may have an alter who decides to hurt the body so that you will always remember that you were hurt. Sometimes SIV is a reliving of the original harm that was done to the body.

SIV may also occur due to the thoughts and conversations between your alters. Occasionally, you may find that one of your personalities will direct other alters to injure themselves. Depending on the strength of this identity, the result may be that you actually do harm to yourself in a physical manner by engaging in an act of self-inflicted violence.

While it is completely possible for you to stop hurting yourself, it takes some work. When you decide that you want to stop injuring yourself, it will be very important that you get support and possibly therapy. The more help you have, the more likely you will be to succeed in this endeavor.

ACTIVITY 3.3: YOUR ADDICTIVE BEHAVIORS

Almost everyone has some type of addictive behavior. Whether it's candy or caffeine or even a person, everyone at some point in their lives will continue to include these things in their lives even though they know it's not in their best interest.

This activity is designed to make you more aware of your addictive behaviors. Chances are, you'll be able to identify one or more areas in which you may be addicted. Once you can name these addictions, you're in a better position to evaluate and possibly change them. Remember, not all are life-threatening addictions. While spending too much time on the internet may interfere with your relationships with your friends, it's not likely to kill you.

Using the following scale, rate how often you use the items or engage in the activities listed below. Some blank spaces have been provided for items which are not listed but you feel apply. You may want to have each of your alters perform this activity, because some may perform these behaviors more than others. Place your rating(s) in the space next to each item.

0	1	2	3	4
never	rarely	occasionally	often	always

____ candy   ____ exercise   ____ self-injury

____ alcohol   ____ running   ____ internet

____ caffeine   ____ dancing   ____ telephone

____ marijuana   ____ reading   ____ television

____ narcotics   ____ gambling   ____ creating art

____ amphetamines   ____ shopping   ____ driving

____ _____   ____ _____   ____ _____

Once you have rated yourself on these items, take a look at all of the items you marked with a 3 or 4. Would you consider yourself addicted to these things? Would you be able to give up the use of these items with relative ease, or would it be very difficult for you to not use these things?

Chances are that at some point in your life you will discover that one or several of your alters do have some degree of addictive behaviors. It's important that you understand the function of addictions, as well as how these behaviors play out in your own life. Once you are able to see what addictive behaviors you engage in, you can begin to control them or replace them with healthier alternatives.

Any of the addictions you may have are coping mechanisms that you have developed in order to survive. It is important to find someone to talk with about these behaviors. Given the trauma you've probably survived, it is no wonder that you want to numb out and not remember the pain. Unfortunately, none of these addictions will help you get healthy. You can develop a plan with your therapist on how to begin to gain control over your behavior. It is important to replace addictions with something positive so that you do not just learn a new destructive thing to do.

PART II

Living with DID

CHAPTER 4

DID Explains the Life You Never Understood

Singletons, or people who don't have DID, simply cannot comprehend how it feels to share their mind and body with many others. In this chapter, we will try to depict aspects of the ways in which people with DID experience their lives. You'll likely find that sections of this chapter mirror your own life and offer confirmation that what you've experienced for so long is actually typical for someone with DID. You may also discover that you have some ways of being that are unique to you and that aren't described in this chapter. Don't worry, though; differences are what make each person unique, special, and human.

> When I first started realizing that there was a possibility that I had DID, I thought it was the end of my life. I thought for sure that I would lose my relationship, and that if any one knew that I was DID, I would also lose my job. I spent half of my day a zombie and the other half denying that there was anything different about me. I was also terrified that if my friends found out I would really be alone because they would think I was crazy. I knew I was crazy, so it was the least I could expect from them. If I could just keep anyone from finding out, I knew that I would be fine.

I spent the first year being ashamed of who I was and waiting for the moment when I would lose my entire grasp on reality. When all of this became too overwhelming, I would go into denial and try and figure out how a person could create all the symptoms I was experiencing. I came up with great reasons for my constant nightmares—scary movies, of course. Only one problem: I never do and never have watched any type of gory or scary movies. So then I knew I must have seen these types of visions on TV. Same problem: I would not watch scary things on TV. Eventually, I ran out of excuses and accepted that what happened was the result of having been abused.

Realizing That You Live with DID

If you're like most people who have DID, it has taken you a long time to figure out that you have multiple personalities. You may have spent the majority of your life assuming that your behaviors, thoughts, and feelings are similar to most people's. Or, perhaps you went through years of psychotherapy, only to discover that you had been misdiagnosed as having schizophrenia, bipolar disorder, or some other psychological disorder. There are many paths you could have taken in determining that you have DID. Regardless of how you came to this conclusion, you now know that you have multiple personalities and that this is something you've probably been dealing with for most of your life.

I came to realize I was really a we in a rather strange way. I had been talking with a friend about her family and how they had hurt her as a child. This talk went on for several hours that night. When I went to bed, I was falling apart. I started crying and suddenly one of the little ones came out and told my friend that I could not trust my family. They were the ones who had hurt me, and they would lie, so I had to be careful. The little ones that came out asked her to make sure that we were not around the mean ones in the family, ever.

Several months went by before anything was said about this incident. In the mean time I was having flashbacks and body memories that were totally confusing. I felt the flashbacks were just totally crazy. I had no idea what I was reacting to. I wasn't sure where the memories or body pains were from, but I knew they were not being created by anything in the present. I would feel pains in my legs and end up with my legs crossed so tight so that nothing would separate them. I would even stand that way. I would feel the sensation of someone cutting my skin, but knew it wasn't real. At times the little ones would come out and cry and scream and try to pull the skin off the body because it felt like bugs were biting us.

Then I would come back to the answer that I was just nuts. I was sure that I had made up everything that was going on and that I just needed to figure out how to stop this bad habit. During this time, I would end up hiding under the covers at the bottom of the bed, crying in terror, trying to pull off my skin. My partner would sit with me and spend time trying to calm me down. The next day I would get up and go to work and not realize what I had been through the night before. Often we would not even talk about the situation because it felt like there was really nothing to say. But I believed that nothing had happened to me as a child and that this was just a crazy way to live in the world.

I finally started confronting and struggling with the possibility that I could have DID. At that point, I couldn't deny anymore what was going on. I tried to just say it was anything other than DID. I knew that I had to be ill, because I had all of these pictures and feelings and I knew that I had to have made them up. I did know that I had Post-Traumatic Stress Disorder, as I read the diagnosis and could accept that answer. Even though I met the clinical criteria for DID, I was certain this was an error. This was a serious charge and it was easier for me to accept any other diagnosis except that one. In order to really look at being a person who had DID, I had to look at how I got there. It was all too much to try and understand, even though I was living with the results of this diagnosis every day.

I spent months in therapy trying to come up with other answers. I spent every day trying to think of other options and would see my therapist and try to get her to join me in my denial. She let me sit with my explanations and would ask if I had ever seen movies that showed things like what I was living through, and I would say no. Slowly, she allowed me to prove to myself that all my excuses were excuses. While *this was helpful, it didn't change the fact that I was still embarrassed and ashamed of what I was going through.*

During this time, I was still working more than full time and being a step-mom. No one at work knew what was going on, and very few friends knew the real struggle I lived with every day. I spent more time alone, not wanting to socialize with people. I was amazed that somehow work got done and so did everything else. I may not have been real social (this is not one of Nada's skills—she's the robot who gets things done), but I was functional. When things were too bad, I would take the day off and stay in bed crying.

Every time a new little one would emerge to talk or cry, my friend would freak, thinking I was more ill than we previously knew. It got to the point where we were not sure we wanted her to know that there were different ones out.

After several years, we both got more used to the fact that little ones and big ones would come and go. She often knew before I did who was hanging around and which little one wanted to say something.

It has taken me a long time to accept having DID. When I was afraid that I was going to lose my job, I had to stop and realize that I had been the same all the while I had my job. I was often ashamed and more often believed I was crazy. I now know that I have lived this way all of my life. I just wasn't aware of how I lived. Living out the expression "know thyself" can bring many surprises.

Finally Understanding Your Actions

Realizing that you have DID may be a great relief, as it can help to explain some of what you've been going through over the course of your life. Knowing that you have multiple personalities may allow you to understand some of the behaviors, thoughts, and feelings you've experienced. Each person perceives and responds to the world in their own unique way. However, having DID can greatly affect the ways in which you relate to the world in general. For instance, you may have difficulty remembering large chunks of time, or you may hear voices talking inside of your head. While these experiences aren't typical for most people, they're perfectly normal for someone who has multiple personalities. Learning that you have DID may help you understand what you've been doing all of these years.

> *We were, and still are, great for finding chocolate. Chocolate is the best invention ever. No matter where we were, we would begin the search for chocolate. Whenever we found that there was chocolate someplace, we would not let the big one have much food, so we could save room to eat what we wanted—chocolate. One time we got caught by the big one's partner at a friend's house, scarfing up this box of chocolate. It was for snacks and we knew that we had to get it quick or someone would take it away.*
>
> *Our big one's partner leaned over and said really quiet that it may be time to pass the candy on. We were not happy about this. When she said that, our big one took over: She realized she had candy in her hands and that her mouth was stuffed full of candy, so she tried to swallow some of the chocolate and explain that it was really good candy. Our friends just stared but didn't say anything, because we were known as the major chocoholic. So, we were never invited back to that house again—who knows why!*

ACTIVITY 4.1: DID AND YOUR LIFE

Since first learning that you have DID, you have probably become aware of how it explains some of your behaviors. This activity will help you to explore what it has been like for you to realize that you have DID and to identify some of the things that you do that may be due to having multiple personalities.

In your journal, write about your experience of realizing/learning that you have DID. This may take you quite some time. Learning that you have DID is a major life event and you may want to spend a while reflecting on this event before you begin to write. Use the following questions to get you thinking about this experience: When did you find out? How did you find out? Was the determination made by a therapist or other mental health professional, or did you come to this conclusion by yourself? How did you feel when you found out? Were you relieved? Frightened? Angry? What did you do when you learned of your multiple personalities? How has your life changed since you first realized that you have DID?

Now for the second part of this activity. Take a few minutes to reflect on your behaviors, thoughts, and feelings prior to learning that you have DID. In your journal, make a list of everything about you that didn't make sense to you before you realized you had multiple personalities and that can be explained by the diagnosis. For example, maybe you have always had difficulty keeping track of time, and you would sometimes look at the clock to find that hours had passed and you had no recollection of this period of time. This type of situation is very common for people who have DID, and in this way, learning that you have DID helped to explain this behavior. Now see how many things you can think of that DID helps to explain.

Realizing that you have DID can be seen as something positive. You now have more of an understanding of your behaviors and of people's reactions to you.

Learning That You Don't Process Information The Same as "Singletons"

"Singletons," or people without multiple personalities, process incoming information in a particular way. They have one personality who tracks and stores incoming information. Sometimes this information is lost, forgotten, perceived incorrectly, or never received at all, thus causing difficulties in memory or general processing. However, all of this occurs within one particular mind.

People with DID process information somewhat differently. Conceptually, each one of the alters has a separate mind and an individual way of relating to the world (this is only conceptual, because in reality there is only one body with one brain, even though it may feel or seem like each of the alters has a body and brain of their own). But, because the mind is perceived differently, it actually processes information differently.

Most people pay attention to what is occurring around them through a selective filter. This filter blocks out unwanted sensory input and allows the brain to perform its functions adequately. There's just no way that the brain can pay attention to and process all of the information around each person. For singletons, this filter limits what information is sent to the brain for processing by blocking information that isn't deemed to be interesting or important. People with DID have many personalities, each with their own interests and ideas of what is important. Because of this, the amount of stimuli that is attended to and subsequently processed by the brain is much greater for people with DID, as opposed to singletons, who only have the interests of one personality to contend with. In this way, those with multiple personalities are unusually adept at attending to and taking in their surroundings, because so much is interesting or important to them. You may have noticed that you are able to handle much greater amounts of information than your singleton friends. You may be able to attend to many things simultaneously, while your friends without DID are able to focus on only one or two things at a time.

As a person living with DID, there are many things that you have probably assumed that everyone does. You may have thought that everyone had alters who knew not to come out around others. As you grew up, you may have realized that people had reactions to what you did or said, so you probably learned to change your behavior. The adult in your home may have told you to quit acting like a child and to act your age. If you received these clear messages that you were not "acting correctly," you may have learned to keep the child alters inside when you were around others.

> At times, we actually snuck out, but people always excused what we did for one reason or another. People always noticed we were different, but sort of let it go because they didn't know what to say (at least that's what we think).

You may have experienced strange flashback-like pictures your entire life, but may have never understood them. People living with DID often have symptoms of the disorder for the majority of their lives, but do not realize that they are unusual. From the perspective of people with DID, as with people in general, it is common to conclude that if their life is a certain way, it must be similar for everyone else. It is not until the people who have DID begin to talk about their process that they find that it is not the norm to see bloody pictures or want to end their life when the topic of family is discussed.

Seeing the Uniqueness of Certain DID Characteristics

Growing up with multiple personalities, you have come to view the world in a certain manner. You may have assumed that everyone loses their house keys several times a week. Because this is how you have lived your life, you simply assume that others live their lives in the same fashion. In reality, though, having DID gives you a unique way of experiencing the world.

Hearing voices or conversations inside of your head is very common for people with DID. You may have grown up believing that everyone heard voices inside their head, but the truth is that most people don't. While almost everyone does have an internal monologue inside their mind, these thoughts come across quite differently than the voices in your head that you hear. The voices or chatter that you experience probably sound like actual conversations, in which you are sensing and perceiving audible talking. In other words, what you hear is similar to several people talking in a room, rather than an internal monologue in which there are one set of thoughts coming from one personality.

In addition to the chatter in your mind, you may also have found ways to block out incoming noise such as imagining other noise in your ears. Until you told others who don't have DID about this, you may have thought that everyone had this ability. The sounds that you imagine may sound like strong wind, your amplified heartbeat, or even fluttering. You may have learned this talent as a method of blocking out particular sounds, noises, or words associated with the trauma you went through. For instance, the person who abused you may have whispered things in your ear that were too emotionally overwhelming for you to hear, so you imagined another noise in your ears to protect you from the abuser's words.

Another characteristic that many with multiple personalities have is the ability to escape difficult situations by using mental imagery. When things get overwhelming or frightening, you may picture yourself turning into a bird and flying away or becoming an animal and burrowing underground as a way of protecting yourself. Although people without DID may use similar forms of mental imagery, the way in which it is experienced does differ from how it is experienced by those who have multiple personalities. Those without DID generally understand that they are employing these techniques as a way to reduce tension or anxiety and view these images as having been created to symbolize a safer way of being. People with multiple personalities actually experience this imagery as real and may fully believe that they or their alters are changing physical forms.

Growing up with and living with DID, you may also have come to believe that everyone loses track of time and has great difficulty remembering things. While most people do occasionally forget things or lose track of the time of day, most people without DID don't experience these problems to the same degree that you do. Dissociation greatly distorts reality and causes major problems with memory. Also, because each of your alters has certain things on which they are focused, your ability to remember and to track time will change with the appearance of each alter. So, while it may be very important for one of your alters to remember a business meeting, another may not care at all. The interests and abilities of each of your alters will definitely be a factor in your overall ability to remember and to keep track of time.

For many people with DID, real feelings are rarely experienced. They will be able to tell you if someone is happy or upset. They may also have some feelings, but may not be able to identify them. The process of disassociation allows the feelings to be kept away from the person, as the feelings are kept by various alters. This process is what allowed people with DID to survive the extreme abuse they likely underwent as children.

If you know someone with DID, you will probably see them expressing feelings. This is also because people who were severely hurt memorize everything in their environment to figure out how to stay safe. Often, people with DID have learned what emotions look like from watching those around them.

> *I thought everyone just acted. I was a quick study and learned what to do in different settings. I also knew how to act so people would not notice me. I knew that there were times that people were happy and if you were happy the face had a certain look. This was true for all of the emotions. I knew what they were called and when it would be appropriate to have them. I didn't know that these emotions were feelings and actually had a connection to the inside. I learned what to do when my grandmother died from watching the other people. I was only numb. What I know now is that I was numb because I could not handle the feelings. It wasn't until I was in my late thirties that I even had a clue of what those concepts really meant.*

ACTIVITY 4.2: HOW YOU DIFFER
FROM OTHERS

This activity is designed to help you see how you differ from people who don't have multiple personalities. Remember, differences are not wrong or bad, they simply mean that you have a style that's unique.

In your journal, make a list of all of the ways that you are unique from those people you know who don't have DID. Some of these differences are likely due to DID, and some may not be. For instance, you may have a wonderful romantic relationship, while those people you know who don't have DID may have bad relationships. This is still a difference, so be sure to list things like this. After you've completed this list, go back and place a "D" in front of those items which are clearly due to your multiple personalities.

By the time you finish this list, you might be surprised to see how many differences you've found. You may be even more surprised when you look over your list and find that many of the things you listed really don't have to do with DID. Understanding that people are going to be unique regardless of the presence of DID may help you feel a bit better about yourself and the fact that you have multiple personalities.

Working on Communication Problems

Living with DID can be challenging at times. One of the major challenges is the difficulty in communicating clearly. There are two main ways in which communication problems occur. First, the communication difficulties may be between you and people without DID. Sometimes those without DID may not understand what you are experiencing and may misinterpret your words or behaviors. For instance, one of your very young child alters may be talking with one of your friends and your friend may not be able to make sense out of what you are saying. Deciphering what any two-year-old is saying can be challenging, but when this dialogue emerges from what seems to be the body of an adult, it can be even more confusing and can lead to definite communication problems.

The second way in which communication problems are likely to surface is in your ability to communicate with your alters. You may not even be aware of all of your alters, let alone be able to communicate with them. Typically, there is one alter who acts as a liaison between all of the others (including you). Until you are able to establish co-consciousness (an awareness of and ability to communicate with the other alters), you are likely to have problems communicating with the others. There are many ways to improve co-consciousness and to decrease the difficulty communicating with your alters, and these will be presented in chapter 5.

> *My family always said that I didn't make sense. They often suggested that if I got drunk maybe they would be able to understand me. I had friends who were usually able to understand what I was trying to say and would translate so other people could also understand me. As I began to work in different jobs that required me to explain issues or supervise people, I found that I had trouble with people understanding me. I have learned to slow down when talking to people and try to remember to not talk about more than one issue at a time. I also have learned that if I am tired, I will have a hard time trying to communicate. If I am really tired, it is better for me to just go home. At those times, I will use words that are close to what I am trying to say and put the words in a strange order. I know that when I start getting blank looks, I might as well give up trying to explain things because I just confuse people more.*
>
> *I used to do talks at work and in school and somehow managed to make sense. I just had no idea what I had said. People would come up to me after the presentation and tell me how much they liked what I said, and I just hoped they wouldn't ask me to repeat any of it. I eventually got brave enough to ask someone to go with me so they could tell me what I said and if I made sense.*

Living Life as a Committee

Imagine that you are running a small company and that each decision you make about the company has to be approved by a board of directors. You would need their approval in order to send out a memo, purchase supplies, meet with prospective clients, and even to open for business each and every day. Sound a little draining? Well, this is what living with DID is like. People who have multiple personalities are forced to live life as a committee. Each personality has a say in what takes place, and in some circumstances, consensus must be reached before an action takes place.

Without this committee, any one alter would be able to take control and make decisions that could potentially disrupt how the other personalities are living their lives. For example, some of the child alters may desire to not go to work and to stay home and play for weeks at a time. And, while playing doesn't sound too bad, the consequences of not working could be serious. The opposite could also occur, in which the one who works may want to do nothing but work, leaving the others little time for sleep and entertainment. As you can see, working together and acting as a committee helps to prevent these potentially serious consequences from occurring.

You may be wondering who gets the final say on these decisions. The answer to this is simple—it depends what is being decided. Decisions about work and functioning as an adult typically get made by those personalities who are acting in those roles. Decisions on when and how to play and ways to spend free time may be made by any or all of the personalities. Just like in a company, some tasks are more critical than others, and while anyone can decide to photocopy a document, only some have the keys to the safe.

Communication is critical when living life as a committee. It will take a while before you're able to communicate clearly and easily with your other personalities. You may not even be aware of all of your alters at this point. Chapter 5 will give you some suggestions for ways to get to know your alters and learn to communicate with them better. The bottom line, though, is that you have to practice. To go back to the analogy of a company, in order to be a successful employee, you have to go to work. And, while you're at work, you have to learn how to deal with and communicate with those around you.

Once you are able to communicate with your alters, you may want to have meetings with everyone present in order to help you make decisions. During these meetings, it's helpful if everyone is present, so they can all offer an opinion about the situation at hand. Again, holding meetings is a skill which develops over time as you increase your awareness of your personalities.

The big one always gets to be in charge. At first, we all
wanted to be in charge. It was fun to be out and have time to
play. But we had to learn that if the big one wasn't in

charge, we wouldn't get the fun things, like candy and ice cream. We decided that it was important for us to keep working, and that meant that we had to agree to stay away during work time. We now know that it is important to let her do the work that needs to be done. We also know that when the little ones stay and try to take over, we will have to spend hours looking for papers they hid or other stuff they didn't care about. When we were having bad days with flashbacks and stuff, we would all meet and agree to let the big one do what needed to be done. When we got home, we could come out and talk or draw about what was going on.

We have one, well, had one, who used to come out to keep things moving. Nada's job was to go to work, go to school, and survive. People would comment on how quiet we were; they thought that we didn't know things. What they didn't know is that Nada was the one who was given the job of keeping the body functioning. She managed to get through work, school, and whatever crises that occurred. She really had no feelings and spent her time keeping all of us quiet— so that we could still work—and making sure that things happened. People said we had no sense of humor (well, it was true about Nada). She managed to get everything done regardless of how much there was to do. Many people around us had no idea how we got anything done, let alone working a full- and part-time job, going to school, maintaining a relationship, and writing a master's thesis. Her role was to keep us safe by doing everything that needed doing and keeping us from being seen.

She never told anyone who she was, until one day after we had been in therapy for a while the ones that began to feel got mad 'cause she was always out. The feeling ones knew that if we could feel bad we would eventually also begin to feel good things. As soon as any feelings started to come out, she would hide all of us so she could do her job and nothing would get in the way. One day one of the little ones told our therapist about Nada and she was MAD. She told us that we were going to fall apart and that we broke the big one. Nada told us that she was the one who kept the body going, she allowed us to work and go to school. She was the one who came out when we were growing up so that no matter what went on at night we would always be able to get through the next day.

Nada learned how to act by watching others. If someone died she would watch and see what people did and then imitate. Nada just never let any of us feel. We knew that there were words that had different faces with them—mad, sad, happy—we just didn't know that anything happened beside the face changing.

When we heard Nada tell the therapist that we broke the body, we were scared. We knew that we still had to have someone go to work every day and act like things were fine no matter what a mess we were. We knew we did not want to hurt anyone, especially the big one, who we knew had to get money so we could get candy. We were really scared 'cause we were only trying to help. What we found out was that we didn't break the body, it was fine. Nada just thought that if anyone knew about her we would be in trouble.

As we learned what each of our jobs were when we were little, we found better jobs for the little ones to do. The one who wanted to dig circles to practice the bad stuff now gets to plant flowers and veggies. We also have all the little ones help us draw, 'cause they like that and they got to make pictures of the bad stuff. Because they were afraid we would forget what happened, the little ones would keep showing us pictures of cuts and bleeding. Our therapist helped us make a museum and we put all of the pictures in it. Now they know that we don't have to keep seeing the bad stuff, because we will not forget what happened. When they remember the bad stuff we tell them it is in the museum. Now we have time to have all of us draw fun stuff for fun books.

Nada is still around and makes sure that we keep doing our job. She just mostly does it from inside now. If we get too tired, she will still come out to keep things moving. We also have some fragment little ones that have joined with other little ones [this can happen as the responsibilities of an alter, such as holding a traumatic memory, are alleviated].

Even if your focus in therapy is not integration, alters nevertheless do integrate on their own or take on lesser roles in your life. Some people describe the loss of an alter as though the alter has died. Often, it is that the alter has joined another one because its job is done. The goal of people who are working toward integration is to have each alter merge with the host or primary person. The alters never die, they just join together to become a more focused and powerful host personality.

ACTIVITY 4.3: WHO'S ON YOUR COMMITTEE?

In this activity, you will explore how each of your alters add something to your life and serves various functions. The first step of this activity is to generate a list of all of your alters. Once you have their names, spend a few minutes jotting down some of their characteristics—their ages, things they like to do, favorite foods, purposes they serve, and anything else you can think of.

Now, just as if you were forming an organization, see if you can make a flowchart listing everyone and showing how information and decisions are handed down. Who is it that controls most of the decisions or is the president of your committee? Is there a vice president who oversees everyone else? Is there a secretary who takes messages or communicates information to everyone? Is there a manager who looks over most of the alters and has some control over making sure everyone's needs are met?

If you're unable to do this as a chart, see if you can simply explain the functions of your alters. Be sure not to leave anyone out, even if you're not positive about what they actually do.

Remember that as you identify who is in each role, you have to make sure that no one is left out. It is also helpful to have an adult to help keep the little ones safe. You can see who you have inside that can help with this role. Sometimes you may have an older one who is in charge and helps to keep you out of trouble. You may have some alters who like to get drunk or take off from everyone they know. Once you know why they are getting in trouble, you may be able to help them find other ways to handle their problems.

Coping with Organizational Problems

There are certain organizational problems that occur because you have multiple personalities. Because you have many people all living in one body, things can get a bit crowded and confusing at times. If you ever went on a class field trip as a child, during which there was one teacher trying to control thirty energetic children, you might be able to relate. Basically, your body is a container for many others and each of these beings has their own desires, interests, and ways of being. Whenever you have to share such limited supplies (the body) with so many people (the alters), you're bound to have confusion and other organizational difficulties.

You may also have trouble organizing your life because you have too much to do and too little time in which to do it. You and your body are in limited supply, yet the interests and commitments of your alters could keep you busy twenty-four hours a day. Until you learn how to balance the desires of your alters, you will feel rushed, tired, and as if the days are never long enough.

> *We have a bunch of us who live inside. We like it a lot. We have a set of twins we call the screamers (guess why). One screamer has many inside like them, but mostly they just scream as one. These ones came because of the pain. They never let the noise out and only scream inside. They are afraid that if anyone ever heard them we would be killed.*
>
> *We also have Tom and Dee Dee, who are the big ones inside. At first we didn't like them at all. We didn't like any big ones—they were for sure not to be trusted. Over time, we have watched them and watched them watching us and know that they would not hurt any of us. They are too good.*
>
> *There are a couple little ones who were badly hurt and are not right in the head. They came out when everything was a mess, but now they also have a safe room and Tom and Dee Dee watch them to make sure they are okay. Some talk funny and Oppie just runs and cries. It is a problem cause Oppie can't run or walk very well so when he is out it is a bit hard on the body. We let Tom and Dee Dee work with those ones to help them feel better.*
>
> *Some of us are gay and some aren't, some like boys and some like girls. Some don't want anyone near us and hate it when someone wants to give us a hug. We have a couple of mean ones, but everyone who knows them laughs at them, we guess because the mean ones aren't as mean as they think.*

Unexplained Missing Items

Difficulty remembering is quite common for those with DID. One of the ways in which memory problems manifest themselves is through frequently misplacing important items. You may lose such things as your house or car keys, wallet, valuable documents, or even your eye glasses. While this may be quite frustrating, it is also quite normal if you have DID.

You may lose things for several reasons. First, some items are lost just because you forgot where you placed them, the same way they are for people who don't have DID. No one has a perfect memory and each of us, at times, will simply misplace something important. Occasionally forgetting or losing something is simply part of being human.

Having DID does play a big part in misplacing items. Sometimes you won't be able to remember where you put something because you weren't the one who put it there—one of your alters did. Think of your alters as your family. You place your wallet on the kitchen table and walk away. Your sister later finds your wallet on the table and decides she should move it to your dresser so it will not get lost. However, your sister forgets to tell you that she put your wallet in your room. So, when you go to get your wallet, you discover that it's missing. Only by searching the house or asking those around will you be able to find your lost wallet. In order to find things that you have lost, it's helpful for you to first communicate with your alters and ask them if they know where the items are located. With help from your alters, you may be surprised at how easily you're able to find what you lost.

On occasion, your alters may purposely hide things from you. They may do this as a way of communicating with you, perhaps telling you that they haven't had enough attention or time being out. They may also be hiding things from you as part of a game, in which they find it entertaining to watch you search for what is lost. Regardless of why the objects are hidden, you can see how important communication with your alters becomes. Talking with your alters about losing or hiding your things can help solve many of these problems with unexplained missing items.

> *I developed many coping skills (though I didn't realize what I was coping with) and found that I had many ways to get by. Because I lose things pretty easily, I have the largest key collection of anyone I know. I have given sets of keys to my friends, I have them hidden at work, in my briefcase, and in my drawers at home. By preparing for when I lose things like keys, I found a pretty good way of coping with my bad memory.*

See, when the big one would decide that she was not DID, or whatever the outside singletons call us, we would remind her. Okay, so sometimes we did do it by hiding things, but after a while she had to admit we were there. One time she was mad 'cause she lost her checkbook over and over and over again. It was one thing when she didn't know anyone at the bank, but now she does know people and gets mad at us if she loses the checkbook. She doesn't want people to know about her losing stuff. We now have other ways that we can get her attention besides hiding things. She also believes that we are here now and she quit trying to pretend she was a singleton. We also found that if we don't hide things she has to find, we can have more time to do other fun stuff.

How to Manage Living with DID

Meeting the Ones Who Share Your Life

Before you can meet those who share your life with you, you must be open to the idea that you have multiple personalities. The hardest part is the first step—acknowledging that you have many alters (or whatever term works for you). You may or may not be aware of when your alters are out. You may have noticed, however, that people think you said or did things you do not recall doing. Or perhaps you frequently find yourself dressed in clothes you were sure you didn't put on (after all, you don't look good in fluorescent orange polka dots). Or you may find that you've purchased things that you don't remember buying (you really did need that new car anyway).

Once you have identified that you have DID, you can begin to make sense out of your life. You may not yet know the exact details of who or what is sharing your life with you (let alone what they do when they're out), but you've taken the first step in learning more about them and about living with DID.

As you meet those who share your life you may have many reactions. You may be comforted by meeting these other personalities. Or you may be surprised by the number of others who share your life, body, and mind with you. As you develop co-consciousness and learn more about each of these personalities you'll likely be amazed by the diversity found within you.

By now, you probably have some idea that you have others that share your life, body, and mind. They are all part of you. Most times the alters who are part of your system do not want to own the body—they just want to borrow it. Eventually, you will want to be able to have a way to communicate with your different alters and to set up strategies to help you handle tough situations.

Again, since everyone is unique, the process of meeting those inside may be different than the way we describe it. As you learn who is inside and what each alter does, you will begin to understand how to work together. Each of your alters may have different purposes. Some may exist so that they can hold on to bad memories. They may have experienced one thing that they hold for you so you don't have to live with it. As you begin to do your work to heal, you will learn that it is not helpful for you to keep secrets. You'll begin to learn about the ones who came into being just to help you survive and cope through the trauma you endured. It's important that you remember that you have already survived the worst. Each of the little ones that took the bad memories did so to allow you to keep functioning in life as though nothing was wrong.

Once you begin to discover each of your various alters, you'll become aware of their purposes or jobs, and you may be able to understand some of the things you do. The goal in understanding your system is to learn to have each alter communicate with you. This is called co-consciousness. As you begin to understand why the little ones are afraid, you can help them realize that you are really safe and that what they are experiencing is old feelings. The more you know the other ones inside, the more you can also understand why some may do things that are harmful.

Alters that drink do so to keep away from the pain. Those that do drugs also are trying to numb the hurt. If you feel suicidal, it could be because one of the alters was told to self-destruct if anyone started to ask questions. Or it may be an anniversary of a bad event that happened, and in order escape the memories or flashbacks, that alter may think it is better to be dead than remember that time.

The list of who could be inside you is infinite. It may take you a long time to discover all of those in your system. It might take you even longer to figure out what role they serve and how they act. The first step in this process of discovery is to learn who is inside. You can ask your therapist or friends if they have talked to any of your alters. They maybe able to help you by describing the ones that come out in their presence. If you have co-consciousness, you will have some awareness of what goes on when the others are out. Sometimes it is hard to remember all of the details that were shared when the alters were out. A therapist can be helpful with this part of meeting your alters. Even if you don't remember your sessions (you may sometimes feel like you have just walked in the office and then suddenly realize that it is time to go), someone within you had time to talk or be out. You can have your therapist relay the information or take notes for you so you begin to understand who is there and what each alter has to say.

There are ways that you can begin to meet your alters on your own. One way is to get a journal, write questions to the others, and see if one of them begins to answer your questions. You may try drawing and see if any of your alters come out to draw.

> We began to learn who lived inside by drawing pictures. We asked the ones who wanted to do so to draw what they looked like. It took a while for them to draw themselves. Then, we had a day when we went through papers and magazines and had any of the ones who didn't draw themselves pick out pictures that looked like them.
>
> One of our little ones wanted to make everyone tell her who they were. She would just get mad and yell (inside at the others), asking them to come out so the big one could meet them. This method of being pushy may work for you, but it didn't for us. The unknown little ones just stayed hidden. The ones that did not come out decided that they would have more fun not letting the one who yelled find them.

You'll find that each of your personalities will need different levels of management. As you get to know your alters, you will discover that each has very different needs and ways of being. Some of your alters may never come out, some may come out often, and some may only come out at select times and places, such as at your home. Some of your personalities may be practical jokers, some may be angry, some may be sad, and some may have very specialized functions like protecting you from possible harm. You may have some alters that only come out when things are bad. They may come out when you get mad at someone or someone gets mad at you.

> For a long time, if we got upset at home all of the little ones would start to come out. It would feel like we were stuck in a revolving door that had different ones popping out as we spun. It made it hard to have an argument because we would end up not even knowing what the point was of the discussion. We would try hard to listen to the big one be upset, but then we got scared and came out to try and stop the discussion. We were afraid that the big one would be hurt, so each little one would line up to talk to the person who was mad at us. It made it hard for other people to be mad at us because the little ones would come out and say that they believed that if they hurt someone's feelings, they should be dead. So one would plan how to die, another would plan to move, another would become a tree, and the list went on.

As you meet each alter and understand what they feel, you can begin to find ways to help support them. It is very confusing to experience all of the changes, because each one that takes over is different. Your body feels different with each one coming out. If you have someone else who sees what happens, you can ask them to help explain to you what they saw. It's hard to know exactly what is going on when you are caught in the revolving door. The more you know about each alter, the better your life becomes. You know how to give support to each one and understand what will upset each one.

You will probably have some that you don't like because they were created to do something bad. What is hard to realize is that when young children are being hurt, they will often identify with the abuser in order to feel some sense of control. So one alter may be the abuser internalized. This internal one believes that by trying to hurt the body, no one else will get to do harm to the big one. This is not a logical process. These alters came out because they believed that if they could act like the mean people, they somehow could protect you. It is important for you to honor each alter's role, because their sole reason to exist is to keep you alive. If you are reading this, then they did their work very well and used the best skills they had in order to help you survive. Understanding what they did and why they did things will help you find ways to allow them to continue helping you, though in more effective ways.

ACTIVITY 5.1: MEETING THOSE IN YOUR SYSTEM

Although it may take you a while before you know all of those inside you, it's helpful to keep track of those you do have awareness of. In activity 4.3, you generated a list of each of your alters. Next to their names, you recorded information about their ages, things they enjoyed, their favorite foods, and their other characteristics. Now, go back to that list and revise it to include any alters you've recently discovered. Once you've done this, try to write down information about how you are able to communicate with them (if at all). For example:

> Barry: first identified 6/3/94 by my therapist; about four years old; comes out when he's scared and cries; have not yet established communication or co-consciousness with Barry.

You may want to include more information, and you will definitely want to keep revising this activity as you discover more about those inside you. Knowing and listing each alter not only helps you keep everyone straight, but it allows them to see that you know that they exist and they count. Also, knowing how you communicate with each alter can increase your co-consciousness and be helpful in planning strategies for communication.

Identifying and Meeting Your Needs

Learning to identify and meet one's own needs is hard enough for those with one personality, let alone those who have DID. While almost everyone has their own particular set of needs, humans have some common needs which must be met before they can work on their other needs or desires. First, they must have their biological needs met; this involves ingesting food and water, which ensures their survival. If you have survived this long, you must have this need pretty well taken care of. Well, at least you have come up with something that will get you through. Next, people have to make sure that they have safety, both physically and psychologically. People who have been traumatized or abused often have difficulty feeling safe, and in some cases will repeatedly find themselves in unsafe or abusive situations.

Third, there is the need to feel loved and to love others. You may also experience this as the need to belong or affiliate with others. Living with DID can be very isolating. You may limit your interactions with others so that they do not discover that you have other personalities. You may only let others know superficial things about your life. By hiding who you really are, you are not able to be a whole and complete person. If you don't allow others to know who you really are, you are preventing yourself from being loved and accepted by others, and you are unable to love and accept others fully. Trust is a fundamental part of any relationship, whether it be a friendship or a romance. By not trusting others with the fact that you have DID, you are not allowing yourself to fully enter into relationships with others. This will prevent you from meeting your needs for love and affiliation.

Very related to the need for love and affiliation is the need for esteem. Learning to respect yourself and others develops as you learn to accept yourself and the presence of your other personalities. You may have some inside who do feel good about themselves and are very self assured; when these ones are out you feel strong. You may have some others who still feel that they are worthless and not much good. It is good to start to allow the ones who are strong to keep that sense. You can find out what these ones do best and then trust that they will be good at whatever that may be.

> Well, some of us had to learn we were not really the best (of
> the insiders). For a while, it was everyone wanting to be the
> best, the most liked, the most fun. Then we had a therapist
> who had a chat with us to say that we were all good, and
> that we had to quit trying to have some be the best (okay, so
> it was us, Rosalee et al., who were always the best—we just
> let others also join us now).

You have some that were created to be strong, and they are the ones who gave you the courage to live. You also have the ones that carry the message that there is something wrong with you. This feeling is often stronger than other feelings and has surely taken its toll on your sense of self-worth. You may feel damaged, bad, worthless, or incompetent. It will take you some time and a good amount of work to see that you are worthwhile and that you can achieve most anything you set your mind to. You are a survivor, and with that comes some confidence in yourself and your own abilities to navigate a difficult path through life.

While all of these global needs—the need to fulfill your biological requirements, the need for psychological and physical safety, and the need to love others and be loved by others—are important, it's also essential that you learn to identify the exact nature of your individual needs. So, while each of us may desire love from another, the way in which this need is represented differs. For instance, getting a hug from a friend may be a sign of love for you, while receiving a verbal compliment may be how another individual feels loved. Identifying your needs is the first step in ensuring that they are met. If you don't know what pleases you, chances are no one else will either. Think of it this way: Imagine going to a restaurant, looking at the menu, and asking your server to decide for you what you're going to eat. If you were to order for yourself, the chances of getting something you enjoy would be much greater. Life is simply a big smorgasbord. Once you figure out what you want or need, you can try to obtain those things. Sometimes you'll be successful and sometimes you won't be (there might not be any cupcakes around, even though you know that's what you really feel like). As long as you keep identifying what you need and asking those around you to try and meet those needs, you'll be in good shape.

Activity 5.2: Identifying Your Needs

This activity will help you begin to explore your own needs and how you can meet them. In the left hand column, you'll find a list of global needs. Underneath each of these items, spaces have been left for you to fill in the specific needs you have which relate to that particular global need. To the right of the spaces are more spaces in which you are to describe exactly how these needs can be met. If you have trouble coming up with needs or ways to meet them, think of the things that you enjoy or that bring you pleasure and try to work backwards. Surely those things must be somehow meeting your needs. If you need more room, feel free to do this exercise in your journal. An example has been provided for you.

	Global Needs	Ways to Meet Specific Needs
Biological Needs	*food/ice cream*	*go grocery shopping once a week*
Physical Safety		
Psychological Safety		
Loving and Being Around Others		
Being Loved by Others		
Self-Esteem		
Esteem for Others		

Building Safety in Everyday Life

As mentioned in the previous section, safety is an incredibly important need. People all have to find ways to feel safe, both physically and psychologically, in order to function optimally in this world. If people don't feel safe, they will live their lives in constant fear.

Although people who have DID have survived great trauma, there continues to be a focus on and vigilance for unsafe situations. Now that you are older and have the ability to identify bad situations, you also have to learn to trust your reactions. You may be somewhere and meet someone and feel fear and a great desire to get away. Honor that feeling, and later when you have a chance to think about what went on, you can see if your reaction was appropriate, or if it was too extreme for the situation. Often, your perceptions may be very accurate. It's important that you recognize that, because of your past, you have a very strong sense of how to read people. The hard part of this skill is that often when you were growing up you were probably told that what you knew to be true was not true. These messages from the past may make you feel confused now, as you may have trouble deciding what you can trust and what you can't.

> *Mostly we do know that our reactions are right. We can tell when someone is mad, even when they say they aren't. We also have learned that one way to trust ourselves is to ask people if what we are feeling is accurate or close to what is going on.*

Having safety within your life is incredibly important. If you are currently involved in an abusive relationship, you and your alters will suffer. Your alters, particularly the little ones, know that in their experience, people are not safe and neither is the world. If they start to emerge in an unsafe situation, they will react in ways that will surely disrupt your life. The alters have many behaviors that developed in an attempt to keep you from harm as you grew up. These behaviors can be destructive in your adult life. In order to allow your little ones to grow and adapt, they must feel safe and know that the world now is not the dangerous, traumatic world in which they were developed. If they learn that the big one (you) is not in danger, and that they do not have to try and keep you quiet, the little ones will be able to grow and learn more helpful skills. If you try to meet them while you are still being hurt, it will be harder for you to find safety, because the little ones will always be in terror.

If you are in an abusive or dangerous relationship, we hope that you get support from a therapist or a friend to understand that you do not deserve to have anyone harm you at any time. As a child, you could not leave bad situations. You could not leave the person or people who treated you badly. You had no choice in whether you lived with someone who emotionally or physically hurt you. If the person who harmed you was someone other than the people you lived with, you still were not able to stop the mistreatment. No person has the right to hurt you, make you have sex when you don't want to, or threaten you. This is abuse, and if it is coming from your partner or someone in your household, it is also called domestic violence. As an adult, you have power you did not have as a child. You can actually leave a bad situation as an adult. Although it may not be easy, you can physically remove yourself from harm. The little ones do not realize that the behaviors they used to perform to try and keep you safe when you were younger will not help the same way now and will make it harder for you to live your life.

If you are not in a situation in which you are being harmed, it is important to realize that you are safe now. If someone threatens you, you can call the police. You can get up and leave a situation that is uncomfortable. You never have to allow yourself to be humiliated or harmed. As easy as this sounds, it is one of the hardest concepts to understand. Often a person who has been hurt expects to be hurt again. Although this may not even be conscious, there is a sense that someone or something can get to you and harm you. It is helpful to realize that now you can leave a bad situation and that no one has permission to hurt you.

If you feel uncomfortable or threatened around particular people, your reactions could be warranted. As a person who grew up in a bad environment, you learned to closely observe what goes on around you and what people are doing. At the same time, while you were learning to be hypervigilant, you were probably told that what you knew was wrong. If someone was hurting you and told you it was your fault, even though you knew that you had not done anything wrong, you may have felt that you were crazy and that they were right. Both reactions are self-destructive, because you learn to falsely believe that you cannot trust yourself or that you are just plain bad.

In order to keep yourself safe, it is important that you acknowledge that your intuition is something to be trusted and believed. You may often have a better understanding of the situations you walk into than singletons because of your skills in assessing your environment.

Understanding Your Reactions with Family

Many people who have multiple personalities came from homes that were dysfunctional. Because of this, many individuals with DID never learned how families are supposed to function and have never experienced a healthy, supportive family. Thus, if you have DID, visiting your family or even the families of friends can be quite disturbing. You may expect or even experience the same kinds of disruption and dysfunction that you encountered as a child.

If you find yourself around those that treated you poorly or are visiting family that may have been with you when you were harmed, you will probably feel disturbed and upset. This is normal in this circumstance. You learned to dissociate to get away from bad situations. At times you may find that being around those who were there in your life at the time you were hurt will cause you to go back into old patterns of behavior. You may find that being in the place where you were hurt can cause a similar reaction. It is always hard to change that internal response to bad places, especially when other people there do not remember or admit to being part of your experience. Since there are times that the harm was done by family members or in family space, it may be especially hard for you to visit your family if they live at the same place.

If you were harmed by a family member or at your home, yours was more than likely not a healthy family. Often, the mode of communication in such families is to ignore anything bad. If a person tries to change their behavior in the family by trying to talk about the past, you may notice that the subject is changed, the speaker is ignored, or people just get up and leave. This may be an unconscious reaction on the part of other family members, as it could simply be the way they lived their lives. Of course, if you are the one trying to have this discussion and no one is acknowledging your feelings or experiences, it will be especially difficult for you, and you may feel tempted to question your entire reality.

It is helpful to have a safety net set up for yourself if you plan to return to the place where the unhappy experiences occurred. Remember, you not only have the big one's reactions, but also the reactions of all of the little ones who may still not be sure that it is safe or that things have changed. You may find yourself once again feeling like you have no control and permitting other people to treat you any way that they desire.

Safety can be established in a variety of ways. It's important to remember and remind the little ones that you are an adult and you do have control over your own life. Having control means that you can leave a bad situation at any time you choose. It also means that you can talk to family members and ask that they change their behaviors.

Additionally, having an established support system will help you feel safer. There is something incredibly powerful in being able to call up a friend while you are visiting your family, tell them a story about how your family is currently acting, and get feedback that validates your own experience. Even having a friend say something like, "Your family really is nuts. Why don't you come home now?" can be really empowering. Using your support system as much as you can will make you feel more sane, more safe, and will help you to remember that you have an adult life away from your family.

Activity 5.3: Creating Safety

This activity is designed to help you identify ways in which you can feel more safe in your body and in your life. This activity suggests several methods you can use to create safety. Some of these methods are actual activities which you can do to create safety in your everyday life, and some are simply suggestions for what to do when you feel scared. For the activities, write down your responses in your journal. For the suggestions, after you have tried them, write about your responses. Did the suggestion make you feel less afraid and more safe? How could you improve this plan? When you are feeling scared or insecure, remember to review these exercises and your answers.

1. Make a list of things that make you feel strong in your life. Come up with at least ten ways that you feel strong. Be sure to include things like the fact that you are an adult, and that you can call the police if you need to. Carry this list in a place where you can find it easily (such as a purse, pocket, or wallet), so when you start feeling scared or lost you have a way to remind yourself that your life has changed and that you're going to be okay.

2. Set up and record a list of people in your support system. You should do this before you actually need them, so that if you are in trouble you know how to reach people who understand you. These should be people you know and trust and who know that you have multiple personalities. Make arrangements to call someone collect if you need to, so that you always have someone to talk to even if you have no money. You may also want to record the numbers of crisis lines or hospitals so you have these available to you when times get really rough.

3. Always carry things with you that remind you of who you are now in your life. These can be pictures, journals, sea shells, stones, stuffed animals, or whatever helps you remember that this is a very different time in your life, and that you are no longer a defenseless child.

4. Create and record a plan on how you can get home if you need to. Sometimes you may find yourself in a situation that you want to leave. It's best if you always have some way of getting out of there and getting home so that you feel some control over your life. Find and keep with you the number for a taxi, a bus schedule, and/or the telephone number of a friend who is willing to pick you up. Even if you don't use it, you'll know that you can leave situations you feel you need to, and you'll feel more safe and secure.

Often just knowing you can get away is enough to help you feel safe. But it is helpful to go in knowing that you are in control and can leave at anytime.

> *This is helpful for any time you think that things might make you upset. We went to a conference on DID and really thought it would not bother us. So we walked in and listened to people talk about general stuff and it was fine. We forgot that in this place they would also talk about things that create DID. We tried to stay and listen but we could not keep the little ones in and ended up in tears and panicking in the bathroom for the rest of the day.*
>
> *Now we make plans to give us options so we don't have to be so scared all the time. It also helps because we now try to think about what could freak us out and plan out ways to handle the overwhelming feelings. As hard as it is to read*

about bad things or see bad things, somehow we have a radar that detects them and we just end up there. There could be one article during an entire year in the paper talking about ritual abuse and, wouldn't you know, we always happen to see it. We may be in a city where we don't know there is one art display done by people who were hurt, and somehow we end up inside the gallery. We still will get overwhelmed by looking at the terror of people being hurt in art or drawings.

Some of this goes back to remembering that DID came about because of what happened to you. If you try to pretend that nothing happened (like we used to) you will find yourself being freaked out much more than you need to be. With a little bit of planning for and checking out situations you are going into, you can prevent being taken off guard and finding yourself splitting all over because the situation is so similar to your experience. Now we ask people about movies to make sure they are not about child abuse, because we know that if we watch this we will be up all night being freaked. If we forgot to ask what the movie is about and it is child abuse, we just get up and leave, which is much better for us.

Learning to Feel Safe in Your Body

If you have been traumatized or abused, learning to feel safe in your body is no easy task. You probably think of your body as a very unsafe place, a place where great trauma and pain occurred. You learned to dissociate in order to get away from being in your body. Now as an adult, it's time to reconnect with yourself and your body and realize that you can feel safe without having to dissociate.

Ugh, we never wanted to own one of those things (bodies). We each would just borrow it so then we could give it back. Yup, if we were out and talking about the body, it was because it was someone else's. For a long time, we thought we each had a body inside and knew that if someone took an Xray of the body, we would get to see how many of us there were. After much discussion with our therapist, we finally agreed we just had one body to share. We also found that because no one really owned the body, it was pretty easy to have it run into things. We didn't pay attention to what was happening, so next thing we knew we walked into the wall and hit our head. We did reduce the number of bruises we had when we began to live more in the body.

There are probably many ways in which you express the lack of safety you feel. You may feel threatened by the gentle touch of another. Or perhaps you don't look at yourself in mirrors, because your own reflection raises tension and fear.

(You also might have a very different picture of you than what is looking back—depending on who is out!)

It may be that you even do things to neglect or injure yourself because you dislike or fear your own body. You can probably think of many more ways in which you show your feelings of fear and lack of safety.

There are several ways of beginning to feel safer in your own body. The first step in this process is to start living in your body. While your ability to dissociate and to leave your body has helped you to survive, it has also prevented you from experiencing a sense of your physical self. It's essential that you learn to reconnect with your body and remain present in your body, even though it may be scary. This process is much more difficult than it sounds. It will take a great deal of effort and concentration to make this happen. You will have to be committed to yourself and to improving your sense of security.

(If this is just the beginning of your looking at this body thing, then we bet you have no clue what we are talking about! We sure didn't understand what people were saying about bodies at the beginning, either!)

ACTIVITY 5.4: EXPLORING BODY AWARENESS

This activity offers several suggestions for ways to increase your body awareness. It's important that you try each one and write about your experiences in your journal. You may want to describe how your awareness changes, how your body feels, what is difficult for you, and generally what this process is like for you. Try each of these activities several times and see if your awareness and your experiences change.

1. Sit on a comfortable chair, close your eyes, and see if you can tell where you end and the chair begins. Spend a few minutes just feeling the support of the chair underneath your body. You may want to use your hands to explore some of the aspects of the chair. What does the chair feel like? What do you feel like? Can you tell where you end and the chair begins? Try doing the same activity using a hard or uncomfortable chair to sit on. Does your awareness differ? Write down or draw what you feel or experience.

2. As you go through your day, take three minutes every three hours and just notice what it feels like to put your hands on the arms of a chair. If you sit there for a while, can you still tell the difference between your hands and what they are resting on? If not, try moving your hands or your fingers slowly against the material on the arms of the chair and describe what it is like.

This was a hard one for us. We just became part of whatever we sat on or touched, and the only way we could tell the difference was if we moved our fingers or hands or legs; then we could tell what was us and what wasn't.

Ways to Increase Awareness of Your Body

One of the biggest challenges of anyone who was hurt physically is learning to reclaim their own body. Your body has many sensory and physical memories and feelings stored in your brain. This is why you have "body memories," and you feel things that did happen but are not happening now. If you were also abused sexually, you have to relearn how to own your body instead of having the feeling that it is out of your control.

It is also hard to learn about your body if you are never consciously in it. For people who have grown up feeling their body, this concept may make no sense, but if you have no awareness of your body, you probably feel like you don't actually live in it. Before beginning to work on your body, it will help if you go back to the previous exercise and remember when you were hurt and remind yourself that the abuse happened a long time ago.

> *We believed that it was the body's fault that we were hurt. If we didn't have one, no one could have hurt us. From a very young age, we decided that it was better to let the body do its thing and we would do ours. That meant if a mean person was hurting the body, we would go somewhere else and leave the body being hurt. Now we know that we just stopped feeling anything in the body. Often, we didn't know whether we were sick, because we just dissociated from the body whenever we didn't feel good.*

One way to begin to increase your awareness of your body is by touching your body and noticing what it feels like. You can do this in a quiet, safe space where you have some privacy. You may feel uncomfortable at first. If you like, you can begin with less threatening areas such as your feet or hands. If you have ever had a foot or hand rub, you may know how wonderful it feels after you get to relax a little. Learning about your body and increasing awareness of your body allows you to realize that touch is not all bad.

Bodywork

Bodywork or massage therapy may be of assistance in improving your awareness of your physical self. Of course, you may need to work up to this. Allowing anyone to touch your body can be frightening and may raise issues related to past abuse or trauma. However, working with a professional to focus your awareness and help keep you from dissociating can be quite helpful.

> *We were always hurting our back, so we decided to see if massage would help. We knew the person who gave us massage, so we felt safe. We had friends who would get massages and talk about how wonderful it was and how much it helped them relax. We would come out of a massage with our shoulder a little less sore, but feeling ready to tear down the walls. We could not relax and would spend the night awake freaking out. Needless to say, we gave that up. We wanted to have the same reaction that other people did, to feel relaxed and calm, but all we knew was that it made us agitated. We gave up on massage for a long time because it*

*just made us worse emotionally, and we decided we would
live with the sore shoulders because most of the time we could
ignore the pain.*

*After we had been in therapy for a while and knew about
having DID, we wanted to see if we could try again. By then
we were not sure we wanted anyone near us, but we wanted
to be able to lift things and work on projects without hurting
our back more than we already had. We were lucky that we
had a friend who taught bodywork at a local school and knew
some very skilled bodyworkers. We were able to find one
person who helped us learn to become aware of our body and
later we found another person who helped us learn ways to
live in our body.*

Tips for Dealing with Bodywork and Bodyworkers

1. Call a bodywork school in your area and ask if they can refer you to someone who is skilled in bodywork. Get several names so that you can interview people.

2. Meet all of the people recommended so you can talk to them about yourself. It is easier to do this before you decide to have them work with you. This way, you don't have to space out to allow someone to work on your body. It is easier to decide if you feel safe with someone when you are not dissociating and are actually "there" when you meet them.

3. Find out if the person has ever worked with people who are DID. If they have done work before, find out what their experience was and what type of work they did.

4. If they have never worked with people with DID, ask them if they have had experience working with people who have been physically and sexually abused. If you like the person and they have not worked with someone like you before, ask if they have somewhere they can get supervision to help with the work.

5. Make sure that you do not neglect to discuss your having DID with the bodyworker. This is essential, because you do not want to end up in a situation where someone is not aware of what is happening or is just starting out doing bodywork and could trigger feelings that overwhelm you.

(Now we know that this was what happened to us, because we didn't know about the past and we didn't know what to expect.)

6. Have the little ones or some of the other alters meet the bodyworker prior to the actual bodywork.

   We always came out because we wanted to make sure we wouldn't freak them out if they were working on our back and suddenly one of us popped out. We like to know what people's reactions are so we know if we will be okay. We watch them and see what they do.

7. It is good for the bodyworker to have a sense of humor. Also you can tell them ahead of time anything they should know, like who is okay to drive.

   One time our little one came out during the bodywork and decided that she would drive home. The bodywork lady was not so sure because she didn't know this one. This was Rosalee and she usually was in charge. She can drive, but many of the others can't. Anyway, this day she was out and chatting away. When it was time to go, the bodyworker asked where the big one was and Rosalee said, "Oh, she is here, but it is okay, we will drive today," and she did. She told everyone she was 121 years old so she could drive! Guess it worked, 'cause she did drive well and still does—at whatever age she is!

8. Talk with the bodyworker about what clothing you want to wear during the massage. There should not be any problem with you keeping on a T-shirt or tights (or any kind of clothing, for that matter).

9. Respect your little ones and make sure they tell the person what is going on for them as you get a massage. Some days they may not want to have anyone touch your stomach or legs. It is important that you trust the bodyworker enough to know they will listen to your request.

10. There may be times that you just do not want to have anyone touch you and you need to cancel your work. You get to decide what works for you. You can always go back in the future when you feel that it will help again.

It is also important for you to work with your bodyworker so you stay present when they are working on you. You can discuss ways to help bring you back to the present if touching a certain area makes you dissociate. If you are dissociating during the bodywork, it is possible for you to not realize where you are and feel that you are being traumatized again. It is also possible for the bodyworker to push too hard in an area and cause bruising because you are not aware of what hurts. Breathing can help keep you in touch with your body, if you focus on the air going in and out of your lungs. Sometimes it also helps if you can follow the touch of the bodyworker in your mind. It is interesting to see what areas you can feel and what areas seem to be missing. If you really get into this you can go to the bookstore and get one of those coloring books of bodies that they give to biology students.

> We like to know what goes on with everything, so we wanted to see how come it hurts on the back of our neck when our arms are touched; we just ask all sorts of things. We sort of remember what the muscles look like, so when the bodyworker is working on a certain muscle, we know where it starts and ends and try to figure out how we hurt that one!

Another way to begin to reclaim your body is to have your partner work with you. You can talk about what kind of touch feels good and what does not. You also may want to do this when you are not being sexual, because that way you have the freedom to explore touch without that fear that all touch must be sexual. This can give you safety and fun while you learn about your body. You'll begin to see that you can say no to things that do not feel good and enjoy the touch that feels nice. Sex and sexuality will be discussed in more detail in chapter 10.

Distinguishing the Past from the Present

As the little ones or alters come out, you will find that they have been frozen in a time during which life was not a fun. Instead, their world was one of trauma. In order for them to help you and become a part of your life, it's important for them to realize that there has been a major time change. The bad things happened in the past, and it is hard for them to understand this because they do not know that the clocks have moved forward. They were small when they spent time out and are still small now. Their experiences have been frozen and their perceptions of the world have not yet changed.

ACTIVITY 5.5: DISTINGUISHING PAST FROM PRESENT

Often it is hard to distinguish the past from the present, especially when you are experiencing intense feelings or flashbacks. One of the first tasks is to begin to look at how old you were when you were hurt or experienced trauma. The goal of this activity is to help you find ways to tell that it's a different time in your life than when your little ones came into being. There are various suggestions presented here. Try some or all of these ideas and write about your experiences in your journal. You may find that one of these works particularly well in helping you to distinguish past from present.

Step 1: Select pictures, either real or from magazines, that remind you of your life when you were young. Did you have a pet? Did you have a house or an apartment? Do you remember your room or other possessions that were important to you?

Take these pictures and make a collage of this time of your life. Then, on this collage, write down the year you are representing with the pictures. Next to that year, indicate how long ago that was. For instance, if your collage represents 1965, and the present year is 1998, then write down that year and by it's side write down thirty-three, indicating that this was thirty-three years ago. You may also want to write down your age then and now.

Next, find pictures which represent your life now. Again, you can use either photos or magazines to collect these pictures. Do you have a favorite chair? Is there a place you go that you enjoy, such as the park or beach? Do you swim? What are all the things that are different in your life now than when you were little? Do you drive? Do you take the bus places? What are the things about you that have changed? Is your hair different? Are your clothes different? Are there things you do now that you could not do when you were little?

Place these collages side by side and examine the differences. Write about these differences, what you observe, and how you feel in your journal.

Step 2: Make a paper chain that has one link for each year of your life. For the years that you were experiencing the trauma, use one color for the rings on the chain. For the years that have passed since that time, use a different color for the rings. Use another color of paper to make the rings for the years when you began to understand that you are someone who is living with DID. Write about what you observe in your journal.

Step 3: Create a timeline and put it up on your wall. First, put up a long strip of paper (or bunch of sheets connected together) and on the far left side, write the year in which you were born. As you progress along the timeline, write in anything that was significant in your life that you remember (such as changing schools, moving, joining a club, death of family members, etc.). Over time, you can fill in memories that come up for you in therapy.

As you meet each alter, you can collect information about their age, the things they like, the things they hate, and other details. Put this information on the timeline at the age they are now. For example, if the alter is six years old and you were born in 1960, put the alter's information down on year 1966. As you enter all the information on the alters, the experiences you remember begin to form a picture of your life.

When you reach the present year, make sure that you list all of the good things that occur in your life now. You also should go back and add in all the things that are happy and have improved over the past few years. This will help you and everyone in your system remember that you are not in the old, hurtful situation anymore.

The goal of each of these options is to find something that you and your alters can understand about when things happened and how much time has expired from past to the present.

Managing at Work and School

Not everyone who has DID works or goes to school. Some people will not be able to do work or handle the stress of school, depending on what their lives are like. Other people who have multiple personalities are able to hold down a job or work on a degree and sometimes do both. Some people with DID spend their lives raising their children and being parents. Usually it is hardest to manage life when you first begin to meet all the ones who live inside. Until you can get communication between your alters, you'll probably have difficulty tracking time and understanding what is going on at certain times. Some people will have difficulty when trying to simultaneously work and deal with issues related to having DID. For these individuals, volunteer jobs may be a good option (if their financial situation allows) because they generally involve fewer demands and less stress. Working or being at home is much easier for you if you have DID because you are able to allow yourself to be who you really are and the only people who are around you are generally those who know about your entire life and the DID. In this situation, you don't have to monitor or worry about the appearance of your alters.

There are a number of issues which are likely to arise in a work or school environment. You may have difficulty controlling which of your personalities is out throughout the day. If you have sick time and have a job from which you can take time off occasionally, it may be a good idea to save the time for when you really can't keep it together. Sometimes just leaving work and going home to take a nap will help you focus and get in control of things. You may need to take a few days off if you are having bad flashbacks. It is easier not to have to try to stay present while your little ones are freaking out. These breaks can make all the difference in you getting your work done and concentrating on difficult things.

You may have to come up with rules for work. It is not a good idea to have your little ones out at work unless you have an office that you can go into and lock (unless the people you work with know about you having DID). You can let your alters play after work and give them a treat if they don't cause trouble during the day. Once you explain to the little ones that if you do not work you cannot pay for candy, ice cream, pet food, or whatever is most important to them, they will realize that it is better for them to work with you. If you just need a break, you can go for a walk and have your little ones come out and talk then. Seeing people talking to themselves as they walk down the street isn't a completely abnormal occurrence, and no one has to know you are talking to many others who are having very active conversations.

Sometimes our little ones would start to talk inside about people in a meeting. They would begin to describe someone or what was happening and we would have to just make sure

*that our face remained the same and we didn't start laughing.
Later we would share the story with friends who knew us and
the situation—the little ones' stories of what occurred were
usually right on.*

You may also have to agree on who gets to pick out the clothes
and fix your hair in the morning. You may have one little one that
loves to wear clothes that are six sizes too big. If you have a job
where baggy clothes tend to stand out and employees don't wear sag-
ging pants, you may decide that alters can pick clothes on the weekend or after you get home from work or school. Talk with the little
ones so they understand that the big one gets to make all the decisions about work and school. If they have things that will help in
either situation, let them know that it's okay to talk about them
inside, but that the big one still gets to handle the situation.

If you have trouble keeping track of things, have a meeting with
those inside so that everyone can figure out how to work together.
You may have one place that all mail goes, one place for new work,
one place for things that need to be done, etc. You may still find yourself with a mess which you can't quite figure out, but you and the
alters will know that you have to get it cleaned up. Organizing work
or school activities is easier if you have some rules. Imagine if each
alter got to put things wherever they wanted—you would never be
able to get organized and stop finding such a mess on your desk. If
you do tend to lose things, make copies and put them in different
places.

*One thing we found was that since people at work knew we
lost things, they would think we wouldn't notice if they just
slipped more work in later—wrong! We know when we have
seen something, but we just don't remember where we saw it.
It's rare that we see something and not remember it.*

You can have someone who is good at organization help you to
set up systems, and then you can work with your alters so they help
keep the system. You may even have a neat freak alter who likes to
organize inside, but as soon as things are set up, the others play a
game in which they get to make a mess. You can also let the little
ones know that the more time they have to spend trying to find
papers or homework, the less time they will have to draw or play.
They should understand that concept pretty well.

Managing Addictions

Addictions serve the purpose of keeping you away from feelings that are overwhelming. These addictions can cover every area: eating, drinking, drugs, sex, work, gambling, shopping, or any other compulsive activity that you can't give up or cut back on that is harmful to you. The addictions of a person with DID serve the same purpose. You just may have more addictions because different alters may have different interests. It is important to look at the role of the addiction in your life. If you drink a great deal, you may begin to explore when and why this occurs. Discuss with your therapist the specific issues involved to determine if you have a problem.

If you have one that likes to work, you also need to look at what is gained from always working. It could be that it keeps you out of the house. It may get you so exhausted that you can fall asleep at the end of the day. Working is also a good way to keep your focus on those around you instead of your own problems. This is a hard addiction to come to terms with because in our society many people like to see others working hard. It is only recently that more people are beginning to realize the toll excessive work takes on people.

The behaviors that could be addictions are, in many cases, things you may do without harming yourself (such as eating, exercising, etc., which are things that are good for you when you do them healthily and in moderation). They are only a problem when they become overwhelming in your life or put you in danger. It may take you time to explore this area, as it can be difficult to distinguish when these behaviors are okay and when they're excessive and harmful. You may have a social drink with friends and not have a problem with alcohol. You may also have another alter that does have a problem with drinking and is not able to stop. Certain behaviors are a problem even if you only do them occasionally. Taking or selling illegal drugs can get you into trouble with law enforcement. Sexual addictions, which include practicing unsafe sex or engaging in sex for money, can cost you your freedom or even your life. It is helpful to understand the role the addiction plays in your life before you try to stop it. It is also better if you have another behavior you can replace it with that is better for you, so that when the times arise when you want to go back to old behaviors, you will have something to do instead. If you always go to the bar after work and have four or five drinks before going home, look at what purpose this may serve. Is it socializing with friends, getting numb so life's problems don't matter, or avoiding your problems at home? Once you know what the behavior helps you do, you can begin to understand why it is so important in your life.

Rarely can people stop addictive behaviors without some type of support. There are groups, internet sites, and crisis lines that can provide support for you when you feel that you may relapse. When you have DID, you also have to come up with a way to help the alters who engage in the addictive behavior understand what happens when they do these things. If you have an alter that drinks a lot and then drives, it is important to help them understand how dangerous this is for you and everyone else. This alter may not be interested in living and not care if they get killed in an accident, but they may not want to hurt anyone else. You can then help them to understand that if they drive drunk, it is very possible to kill others who did not do anything at all. See the Resources section at the end of the book for places to get help with addictive behaviors.

If you have one who keeps wanting to hang out in dangerous areas that are known for drug dealing or violence, you can talk with them about what they are trying to do. What do they get from being in danger and do they really understand the danger of being in these places?

Having DID makes it hard to control some of the addictions, because one alter may understand the risk of what they are doing and another may not care. It is important for all of the alters to understand that the big one is ultimately responsible if any alter hurts someone else or does something illegal. Usually your big one will help keep you and others around you safe.

One of the reasons some singletons are afraid of people with DID is that there are stories about those with DID hurting others. The only people we know who get hurt are the people who are living with DID. In reaction to trauma, most people with DID who were harmed want to make sure that they do not repeat this behavior by hurting others. The biggest risk people with DID have is that they might hurt themselves. Often, one or more of the alters is depressed or suicidal, believing that death is the only way to escape the harm. This is why it is important for you to find ways to have your little ones know that life is not the same as it was in the past.

If you have a problem with addiction(s), set up a support system that includes appropriate recovery groups. If you know that there are certain times of the year or certain dates (because of your history of abuse) when you are more likely to become suicidal, plan ahead. Make sure that you are around other people during those times. If it is not possible for you to arrange this, talk with your therapist about other strategies to help you get through the bad times. Often you'll find that crisis lines, support groups, friends, books, and/or your therapist can be of great help.

Managing Self-Injurious Behaviors

As mentioned in chapter 3, many people with DID also engage in self-inflicted violence (SIV). These behaviors occur for many reasons and may take many forms (see chapter 3 for more information). Management of self-inflicted violence can be rather difficult if you don't understand the dynamics of why you injure yourself or if you don't have proper support.

When you have multiple personalities and you are injuring yourself, you may be trying to punish yourself, replicate the abuse you underwent as a child, or control a dissociative episode. Although each of these reasons for inflicting self-harm may have a slightly different goal, the basic function of each is to help you cope. Similarly to other addictions, SIV provides you with a way to make your life seem more tolerable and to give you some sense of comfort. It may be that injuring yourself prevents you from feeling your emotions. The bottom line is that inflicting self-injury may help you temporarily feel better.

Any behavior that produces desired results will be difficult to give up. For this reason, it's important that as you begin to manage your self-injurious behaviors you get plenty of support. You will find that there are times when you really feel like hurting yourself. Having available support can help you refrain from injuring yourself and can assist you in coping in more positive ways.

Ending SIV is not easy, and it's also not something which can be sufficiently addressed in a small section of a chapter (as this is). If you're seriously considering ending SIV or finding ways to better manage this behavior, your best bet is to find a qualified therapist to help you with this issue and to read as many books as possible on this topic. You'll find that there are some pretty good self-help guides concerning SIV available at your local bookstore or library (one of which happens to be written by Tracy Alderman, Ph.D., one of the authors of this book).

Activity 5.6: Managing Addictions and Self-Injurious Behaviors

As with any addiction or behavior that you are trying to stop, it's essential that you have options to that behavior. So, instead of hurting yourself, you could go to a friend's house, go to the movies, take a bath, make cookies, or do something else that is soothing or distracting. Instead of having a drink, you could go to the gym, talk on the telephone, look on the internet, etc. This activity will help you identify options to these troublesome behaviors.

In your journal, create a list of all of the things you could possibly do rather than engage in your addictive or self-injurious behavior(s). Make sure to list everything, even if some of the things on your list are as potentially damaging or dangerous as the behavior you're trying to avoid. Having all possible options available to you will simply give you more choice and more control in how to refrain from this behavior. For example, you may list things like exercise, sex, going out for coffee, swimming, drawing, eating candy, and so on.

Once you have created your list, make a photocopy and carry it with you at all times. You never know when you're going to need an option to your troublesome behaviors.

As you learn more ways to handle the pain and realize that times have changed, you will begin to discover more about the joys of having DID. It is a process that you will survive, and when you start to shed the grief, you begin to feel the fun in life. In order to do so, though, you have to find out how to work with your system and begin to change the negative messages you have been given about yourself. You will someday realize that it was not you that was bad or ill, it was the people who hurt you. Only people who are sick hurt children or have sex with them. It is not the children who cause this to happen to them, no matter what the adult says. Remember, if an adult will do something to injure or harm a child, that same adult will very easily lie to you.

C H A P T E R   6

DID Adds Variety and Strength to Life

Most often, DID individuals are portrayed in a negative light: as disturbed, impulsive, dishonest, and even dangerous. Although some people with DID may have many or all of these characteristics (just as someone without DID may also have many or all of these characteristics), most people with DID lead balanced, productive lives. In fact, most individuals who have DID appear perfectly "normal," hiding their alters and performing in ways that would not signal distress to others. Despite its bad reputation, there are actually many positive aspects of having DID.

Creating Your Own Entertainment

Individuals with DID have an incredible inner world. While one alter may be hard at work or reading a book, many of the others on the inside are busy playing, talking, or doing any number of things. Just as each of your friends has their own interests and hobbies, so do your alters. Because of all this internal entertainment, someone with DID is rarely, if ever, bored—there's always something going on!

We decided that it would have been best if those of us with DID had been given an extra six or eight hours of time a day, along with the energy to keep going. We always run out of time. We have too many things we like to do. We have ones who draw, play music, build things, fix things, make things, take pictures, write music, and read; when we have time and energy we like to hike, camp, travel, study and learning about everything and anything.

The best time of all is when everyone gets a chance to play. If we have a day or two when we have no work and no other people around, we have a blast. Well, until we have to clean up after we have all been busy with everything every-where. We guess it is rather messy. You should see the look on our partner Tracy's face when she comes in after we have had some time in the house alone. She just takes one look around and knows that everyone has been out playing. It is funny—things are everywhere.

One DID client Karen worked with talked about the activities she was involved with as a child. Lucy described going on picnics with her family and taking off to find things to do. She said that it did not matter if she was with others or was alone. Her parents would be involved in a game with Lucy's brothers, and she would walk into the woods to find a creek to explore. She could spend hours just turning over rocks and watching things swim. Her brothers would play with her for a few minutes, but they would soon leave to get someone to direct the next activity. Lucy had as much interest in the woods as she did in the museum or in attending school. Her alters each had their own interests and helped Lucy use her inner world to entertain herself.

ACTIVITY 6.1: HOW YOU ENTERTAIN YOURSELF

This activity can help you to see just how much you do entertain yourself. By the time you finish this exercise, you'll likely have a much better understanding of the ways that your alters help to make your world imaginative and fun.

1. Make a list of things that you have done over the years. If you can recall your different activities in school, list them. If not, list all the activities you do presently (i.e., swimming, writing, drawing, walking, etc.).

2. Make a list of the topics in which you are interested. If you are having difficulty, it may help to think about which classes you would take if you could learn anything you wanted.

3. What things would you do to your home if you had the time and the money? For example, would you want to tear down a wall and add skylights? You may be interested in doing this, though you know that you could not because your partner wouldn't be as enthused as you are. You do not need to consider right now whether those around you would agree with your ideas; just think about what you would like.

4. Are you interested in travel? If so, make a list of where you would like to go and why.

5. If you had a free day (or week or month), what types of things would you want to do?

6. If you like to read, list the types of books you enjoy and titles or authors you'd like to read at some point in your life.

After you have finished this exercise, you will probably begin to see the extent of your ability to entertain yourself with all of your various interests. These lists that you have created will also be helpful to you when you're looking for something to do. Simply return to this exercise and see what you've listed.

Creativity

Creativity isn't a concept unique to people living with DID. There are many creative people in the world, and many do not have DID. When you think of the way DID is formed and how it functions, however, you may notice that it is a really creative process in and of itself. In order for children to develop DID, they have to be creative. It is common for children to talk to their dolls or stuffed animals and even have their toys perform plays. In children with DID, the play becomes their entire reality.

When a child is being hurt by a parent or other adult, the child automatically believes that there is something wrong with them, because children have no other way of understanding the actions of others. If the adult continues to abuse the child, the child may develop another personality to take and feel the abuse. After the adult is done hurting the child, the host personality generally returns. Each time the adult begins to hurt the child, the created personality will come back out in order to take the pain. This complex method of protecting oneself is quite an imaginative and creative process.

Many with DID are also highly creative and artistic in more traditional ways. If you have DID, you are probably well-versed in many forms of the arts. Perhaps you draw, write, or play musical instruments (or you may even excel in all of these areas). It may be that you have no formal training or education in the arts and still have immense skills in these areas. Creativity is simply an outlet for expression of emotions, thoughts, memories, and even physical sensations. Since you have so much internal energy (just ask those inside), creativity is an excellent way to process some of your experiences.

> We had someone suggest that we just do one thing at a time. That made us really crazy 'cause everyone inside wanted to have their project done by the body. It's a drag that we all have to share just one body, but we do. Sometimes we think that if we had a set of arms for each one of us, we would really be cooking . . . or maybe we would just be making a mess . . . oh, we guess two arms aren't so bad.
>
> We love to do too many things. We love to learn everything: one wants to understand physics, another is interested in archeology, another wants to build computers, another would like to design solar-powered machines, and others want to make paper, weave, paint, learn how to take salt out of water, make better insulated houses, create a social norm change for stopping violence, bring people together to have summits on why religions cause wars, figure out how to invest in the stock market, take apart and rebuild our house, learn how to do plumbing, figure out how people learn, research the effect of pollution on our world, study the stars and planets, explore how life could be sustained in space, find out how economists really predict the future, study laws and their impact on people, find out how to stop the increase in putting people in jail, study all the different diseases and

treatments, and the list goes on. Maybe this is why we could be considered overachievers.

Overachievement

Overachievement is another benefit of DID. Most people with DID are classic overachievers in a variety of fields: for example, business, education, athletics, and creative endeavors. Given the vast pool of skills and knowledge found among the alters, it's no wonder that the potential for achievement is so great.

Overachievement may also occur as a side effect for the need to distract yourself from your internal world. When things inside of you are feeling chaotic (maybe your alters are fighting or scary memories are emerging), it's easy to distract yourself through immersing yourself in school or work. Thus, by trying to avoid internal commotion, you may become an overachiever and accomplish things that few people would dare dream.

In many ways, overachievement is something that is reinforced by society. Although overachievement is usually viewed positively, it can have detrimental effects. When you work to the extent that other parts of your life are suffering, you may be working too much. For example, Kelly was a client of Tracy's who had DID. Kelly had three different jobs, one of which was full-time. Because she worked so much, Kelly didn't have time to date or even to socialize with her friends. This left Kelly isolated from others and able to avoid any meaningful relationships, of which she was very fearful. Kelly was able to use work and her achievements as a way to avoid forming relationships with others.

If you are always working, you also have no time to be quiet and think about yourself. Whenever you engage in one activity just to avoid another, you're stepping into dangerous territory. In this way, overachievement and excess work do have their downfalls and can be harmful.

When we were younger, life at home was pretty bad, so we began to do everything we could to stay out of the house. We were in band, orchestra, choir, Girl Scouts, cheerleading, and when we were in high school we got even more involved. We were in the science club, drama club, debate team, future business leaders, marching band, two orchestras outside of school, and the choir. We also baby-sat several days a week and would clean houses occasionally. Because we had poor

*grades, our teachers in high school told us we would never
get into college and we would never graduate from college
(little did they know). It took us years to realize that we
really were workaholics. This is often an addiction that is
rewarded in our society.*

Intelligence

Dissociation and the ability to create and sustain different personalities is a high-level psychological mechanism performed to prevent the experience of trauma from being physically and psychologically overwhelming. It takes a highly intelligent individual to implement such a strategy for survival. Research has supported the idea that people with DID have higher than average levels of intelligence (Ross 1997).

Because of what you may have been told as you were growing up, you may not even recognize or believe that you are intelligent. You may have come from a home in which you were told you were stupid or worthless, or where you were associated with other negative attributes. The truth is that you survived based on your intelligence. You were bright enough to use a very sophisticated psychological skill in order to help you cope. Despite what you may have been led to believe, you really are smart.

*When we were in high school, we did not do well in school
and were often told we would not make it into college. We
had an English teacher who told us we would never pass an
English class in college. We did manage to get into college
and even got into several master programs. Maybe the
teachers really didn't know us at all!*

Brad's partner Ruth has multiple personalities. He states, "Although Ruth and her crew would never admit it, she really is brilliant. One of the cool things about her being DID is that she can look at things from many perspectives. I think that this helps her understand difficult situations and be really effective at solving problems. She loves to learn, and the amount of things she knows is amazing. One minute she'll be explaining to me the basics of plumbing, the next she'll tell me about ways to reduce violence, and the next she'll help me understand how to use watercolor paints in ways I've never imagined. She really is a renaissance woman. Someday, maybe she'll figure out just how intelligent she is. After being told that she'll never succeed in school or anything else, it will take some time before she can accept that she's really quite remarkable and brilliant."

Exceptional Insight

Keeping in mind that most DID is borne out of long-term severe trauma, it's not surprising that individuals with DID learn to be extremely vigilant of their surroundings. This vigilance, or attention to details around them, was a very useful strategy in your survival of the trauma you experienced. If you knew what was going on around you, you could devise ways to escape (if only in your mind), or, at the least, you could learn what to expect in given situations. This fantastic vigilance, paired with exceptional intuition, helps lead to incredible insight for the DID individual.

Perhaps you had the experience of knowing when a friend is upset over something when no one else is able to tell. Or perhaps you are able to sense when people are being dishonest with you. Maybe you can even use your creativity and insight to resolve a problem or offer advice to those around you, finding that your friends rely on you a great deal for help and support. Regardless of how you use this insight, it is a skill you have that likely surpasses the perception and insight of many singletons (Ross 1997).

> We love to people watch. It is amazing what you find out from really observing others. We somehow manage to pick up on things, and we can never figure out how we know things. This is an excellent skill that keeps us very well-informed. The challenge with this is that sometimes those around us come to rely on us being so intuitive that they prefer for us to figure them out, rather than figuring themselves out.
> Often, we are more accurate about picking up on feelings of others and of the person's experiences than the person is. This is a bit frightening. We decided that this information is best kept to ourselves, because otherwise people want to know how and where we find out things. Sometimes we are wrong. We have learned, though, that we are usually right.
> Listen to yourself. How often have you been told in a situation that something is different than how you perceive? Later, you may find that you often come to find out that your perceptions were extremely accurate, and you may regret that you listened with your ears instead of your body.
> Remember, your body rarely lies. Trust your intuition.

Variety of Interests

Given all of those who share your body, it's no wonder that you have a wide variety of interests. Some of your alters may like cooking, some renovating houses, some art, some reading . . . the list could be endless. Imagine that you and all of your alters are like one big family (in many ways you actually are). Each family member will have their own distinct interests and skills and will devote time to pursuing these areas. You and your alters are very similar to this typical family, with each of the personalities resembling siblings and having their own unique interests to pursue. Your vast interests can keep you busy, entertained, and connected to others who share those interests.

Humor

A great sense of humor typically accompanies DID. Humor is used both as a coping mechanism and as a manner of expression. Humor can also be used to help you deal with difficult events (sometimes people laugh when they really feel like crying). Sometimes you'll find things that you do to be funny and, at these times, it's helpful to laugh. For instance, you may catch yourself talking aloud to those on the inside, and this may amuse you. You may also find yourself laughing aloud at some internal dialogue that your alters are having (remember they also have good senses of humor). There are surely many areas within your life in which you can use your creative talents to demonstrate humor. By acknowledging and honoring your great sense of humor, you're likely to amuse yourself and those around you.

> We never thought of ourselves as funny, well, until we all got a chance to talk. Now, we have to make sure we keep our comments inside. We do entertain ourselves. We also can entertain those around us, but we try to be quiet about it. Sometimes things just pop out, and we start laughing. Then the big one takes over and gets back to being whatever it is she is at work (we call it dull; we think she calls it professional). Have you ever sat in a meeting where people just seem so full of themselves and their self-importance in the world? We always have to make sure that nothing is said

outside, but inside we sure wonder what world would find them important.

We then begin designing spaceships to send them to this world. Our hobby is figuring out what games people are really playing in these meetings. It is funny: you see one trying to build their case, another trying to stir up trouble, and another trying to get close to whomever they think is in power. You know what we mean?

Next time you have to go to a meeting, let your big one sit there, and all of you inside start watching. Take notes, and when you get out you can share them with the big one. Sometimes it is the only way to survive the meeting.

Varied Fashion Statements

Just as each of your alters has different tastes in hobbies, foods, and friends, each will probably have different tastes in fashion. One of your alters may enjoy wearing jeans and sweatshirts, while another may prefer dresses. You may have some that like women's clothes, while some wear only men's clothes. You may surprise some of your friends by your revolving wardrobe and taste in clothing. It's actually very useful to not limit yourself to one particular style of clothes (like most people do). You will always be on the cutting edge of fashion (provided that your closets are big enough).

We like to keep people on their toes. Actually, it is just fun to wear whatever you want whenever you want. Okay, so there are limits. Sometimes we get to play and dress butch, femme, sloppy, or whatever. This lets each of us pick the clothes we like. When we have to go to special things, we let each one pick the outfit—tux, dress, costume whatever. It is all fun. We do have a few, though, that can only pick play clothes. At times, these alters have gotten us dressed in the morning, and fortunately we have someone around who checks us before we head out. When we are the only one home in the morning, and our partner has left for work we just think about outfits that we have worn on other days that people have said go together. This way we know what really goes together. If the little ones are up in the morning, they can pick only from these work clothes.

Ability to Survive

Although some people see DID as a psychological problem, it can also be viewed as an exceptional tool for survival. Being able to dissociate is a skill which was necessary during the trauma and allowed you to distance yourself enough from reality so that you could endure horrendous situations. Dissociation and being able to switch personalities is a tool that continues to help you survive even now. There are days when your memories or flashbacks probably become overwhelming and threaten to disrupt your daily functioning. However, because you have DID, you are able to draw upon the resources provided by your other personalities, which allow you to function and survive those difficult moments.

> *We were lucky enough to have a skill that kept us alive during experiences that we would not have otherwise survived. We knew we could do many things at once and easily move from one intense situation to another without needing to transition.*

Often, people who are not DID cannot move from a crisis to another situation easily. For example, if someone has just remembered that a family member had hurt them while they were little, they may require time to absorb this information before heading into a meeting or class. This person may not be able to return to a meeting or continue with their tasks that day.

A person with DID has learned how to move from an extremely traumatic experience to another environment without taking time to transition. The person who is living with DID may go straight from a therapy session that explores the trauma they endured as a child to a business meeting, without being at all distracted during the latter.

Managing Multiple Tasks

How many times have you read a job description or announcement that requires the employee be able to handle multiple priorities at the same time? What the ad could be saying is, "People with DID apply here!" If you are someone with DID, you have been self-trained from a young age to have many different experiences simultaneously. You learned this skill because you had to have each alter handle their separate tasks at the same time. You may have one who watches everything around you all day and one who watches everything all night. You may have another one who goes to school and does the homework. You may have one who helps you negotiate a fight in your home and gets you out of trouble. Each one of these tasks may go on within several minutes, but you can manage to get all of them done in a way that not everyone could.

There are other times when your child alters may also lose track of what they're doing because another alter comes out and has a great, new, fun idea of something for you all to do. If this happens to you, take the opportunity to think about what all of you are trying to do at the same time. This is one of the skills you have developed as part of having DID.

Mandy, a former client of Tracy's, has DID and is employed as a vice president of a company. On a daily basis, Mandy has to perform a great number of tasks, some for her job and some for her personal life, which includes raising two young children. Mandy believes that having DID is a great asset to her roles as a professional and as a mother, because it helps her to be able to focus on many different things while still doing each exceptionally well.

Enjoying Life

You may be thinking, "You've got to be kidding." But honestly, what you learn as you heal is that life is not something you have to avoid. You do not have to wait until each day ends so you can merely get through the next one. As you begin to separate the past abuse from your present situation, you'll realize that even though you may not feel great at the moment, it is not as bad as you were feeling when you were abused as a child.

You also may go through a time when you feel tremendous hurt, pain, shame, and depression. These are the feelings that your alters have been trying to protect you from for years. The problem with this isolation of bad feelings is that you cannot feel any feelings if you block the bad ones. As you begin to allow yourself to feel the bad feelings, you will also begin to feel the good feelings of being alive. When you first begin to feel, it is usually not a joyful moment, because they are rarely, if ever, feelings of intense happiness or pleasure. The first feelings that begin to surface are the ones of hurt and pain that you have blocked from your awareness for years. But eventually, the joy you will feel will be worth the painful feelings you first have to experience.

When we heard people talk about feeling happy and enjoying things, we understood what they meant but really didn't get how they felt. We still remember the first day when we couldn't wait to get up and see the flowers outside and were happy to know that the next day was here. It is hard to explain to people who always experience emotions in their lives, but for people with DID, simply having feelings is a revelatory experience.

Now, even when we feel bad, we enjoy being alive. It is fun to feel happy and a relief not to wake up dreading every day. Enjoying life is realizing you can change what happens to you every day by doing something different. If someone is mean to you, you can leave. If you really are not wanting to do something, you do not have to do it.

Life has just gotten better every day since we began to heal. For us, healing doesn't mean that all of the little ones will go away. Healing means that we can go through each day, and when we get triggered by something from our past, we can soon remember that it is just that—a memory from the past. For example, if we read an article about a child being abused, and the little ones inside get scared, we can talk to them and separate the old feelings of terror from the reality of what we are feeling now. We still are upset that another child is being hurt, but we do not have to run and hide in terror. This is healing for us.

DID is about survival and survival is about life. By choosing to survive, you are also choosing to live. You have not succumbed to the destructive and negative forces which accompanied the trauma you went through. Instead, you have emerged from abusive times alive, and this is something which should be honored and enjoyed.

The best part of being DID is that we live. We never thought we would know what it meant to live in the body. We knew how to use it, but we did not know much else about what feelings were or how to enjoy life. When we began to accept ourselves, we started to realize that we had problems, just like everyone else. We know that we survived growing up in a world that was not very nice. We learned how to survive in some fun ways. We love becoming trees or birds or the wind. Once we could accept that DID helped us enjoy, we began to have a life!

ACTIVITY 6.2: RECOGNIZING POSITIVE ASPECTS OF DID

In this activity, you will begin to recognize some of the positive things about having DID. You may find this activity difficult at first, because you were probably taught to view DID in a negative manner. For this activity, you will need your journal or a few pages of paper. At the top of the page, list the headings given in this chapter (e.g., "Creating Your Own Entertainment," "Creativity," etc.). Once you have this done, under each heading list as many things as you can. Make sure that you get input from all of the alters; some of them may have positive traits of which you aren't even aware. You may also want a close friend or family member to help you with this activity. Chances are, they will be able to add a number of items to your list. We have provided a brief example for you here (hopefully your lists will be much longer).

Entertainment	Creativity	Overachievement
like to swim	like to draw	have a Ph.D.
like to bake	like to play piano	own a business

Once you are finished, take a few minutes to reflect on all of the positive aspects of having DID. You'll probably be surprised to see just how many good things about DID that you have listed. The next time you're feeling badly about yourself or about having DID, pull out this list, refresh your memory, and you'll feel better in no time!

Coming Out as a Person with DID

Coming Out and Empowerment

"Coming out," or telling others, about having multiple personalities is likely to be a tough decision. There are many risks associated with telling others you have DID. You may lose friends and family, and even your job could be threatened. You may be viewed by some people as crazy or mentally imbalanced. Some people don't even believe that DID actually exists and may accuse you of making up your different personalities and putting on an elaborate act. Any and all of these negative reactions could make you feel worse about who you are and might make you question your reality. With all of that in mind, you may still decide that the benefits of telling outweigh the potential drawbacks and that you want to tell others about your having DID.

Informing others that you have multiple personalities will not be easy. You are likely to feel very scared throughout the coming out process. However, the benefits of coming out to others are well worth the fear. Coming out about having DID is quite an empowering act. By doing so, you will be able to be your entire self more often, allowing each of the personalities to openly exist and be out around others.

Telling others that you have multiple personalities allows you to be whole; you no longer have to hide the existence of your alters. Coming out also allows you to be more honest with others and to increase the connection and intimacy you have with these individuals. Allowing others to know that you have multiple personalities also helps to dispel many of the myths people have about DID—DID does exist, it is real, and people with DID have just as much right to be themselves as everyone else.

Just as singletons each have their own unique characteristics, there is a great deal of variety among those who have multiple personalities. Some people with DID are unable to work because of the results of the abuse. Some people work part-time, and some work full-time jobs. If you have DID, it is not the total of your identity. Instead, it is about how you learned to survive in life. By coming out to others, you can show them the reality of DID. They may be surprised to know that people with multiple personalities live real lives.

One of the reasons that it is empowering to tell others about all of your selves is that you are taking back control. Abusers often gain strength by getting the victim to keep the secret. In cases where the abuse was extremely severe, victims are often told that they would not be believed if the secret was told. As you begin to tell others about your life, you realize that many people do believe you and, with this realization, you can take back control of your life. If you tell someone and are treated poorly, you can leave and know that this person is not someone you want in your life anyway. By exposing the secrets, you are making the world safer for yourself and others. Child abuse damages all of us; it results in significant harm that keeps many victims from living full, happy lives and from sharing those lives with the people who love and respect them. Refusing to keep the abuse a secret sends a message to abusers and potential abusers everywhere that they cannot force their victims into secrecy and isolation forever.

Coming out to others about your personalities also allows you to become a role model for others. You are one of many people who have DID, but because most people are so embarrassed or afraid of what others will do and say, they keep their DID a secret. By being willing to tell others about your personalities, you are showing others that DID exists and that it's okay to talk about it. You are giving others permission to be as courageous as yourself and to openly communicate about DID. You will find that once you open up about having multiple personalities, others will seek you out and tell you of DID in their own lives. You are, in fact, becoming a role model for others.

The strength of shame is immense, and it will keep you feeling badly about yourself. There is nothing shameful about having multiple personalities. You were able to survive because of DID, and without it, you might not be here today. By opening up about having multiple personalities, you are able to loosen the grip of shame and begin to feel proud of who you are. Just as it took amazing courage to survive the trauma you went through, it also takes amazing courage to come out about having DID. As you begin to tell others about having multiple personalities, remember this and give yourself credit for doing something very difficult. After all, you are a courageous survivor of things far more challenging than this.

Telling Others about Having DID

Telling others about your multiple personalities can be incredibly empowering and healing. When the time is right for you in your healing process, you will hopefully begin to tell others about having DID. Before you do this, however, there are some things you should think about first. Considering the risks and creating a plan will make your experience of coming out much more positive.

When to Come Out

If you have any choice over the matter, it's best if you come out only when you're ready. This may not be possible in all situations, as sometimes those close to you may notice the change in your personalities and may inquire about them. However, telling others generally goes a bit more smoothly when it's in your control.

Knowing when you are ready is likely to be difficult. You may feel scared, tense, or anxious when you even think about telling others you have DID. Don't let these normal feelings fool you into believing that you aren't ready to come out. If you wait for these feelings to disappear or decrease, you might just be waiting forever. You aren't going to feel calm when you tell others about having multiple personalities; it's going to be difficult, but it will be worth it.

You may also feel that having DID is not a problem and begin to tell everyone. Although there's nothing wrong with having multiple personalities or with telling everyone around, coming out to others is a decision that should be thought through very carefully. You may even want to discuss this decision with someone you trust before you start acting on it. In a perfect world, having DID wouldn't make a difference to anyone. However, the world in which we live is far from perfect. While telling others about having multiple personalities may be very liberating and empowering, it could also have negative consequences, such as costing you friends or your job. If you do come out and receive negative reactions, try to keep in mind that you're okay, it's just the fear and ignorance of others that causes them to act as they do.

Remember, this is something that you've kept secret for a very long time, and revealing this secret is likely to be difficult. Only you will know when you're ready to tell others about having DID. Unfortunately, there's no one thing to look for to tell you that you're ready. You just have to trust your instincts and the opinions of your alters. Perhaps you can imagine yourself standing on a diving board. You know that you either need to jump or climb back down; jumping is scary, but if you're ready, it is also exhilarating. If you decide to jump, you'll know when to go. And, just like in diving, take a big, deep breath before you jump into the murky waters of what could potentially be a very frightening conversation.

Why to Come Out

We decided to tell! Before you get the billboard on the main street that announces you have DID, you may want to talk with some trusted friends about telling the world. Yeah, we know, by writing this book we are, in a way, taking out the billboard. But in the beginning of our healing, we were very selective in who we told. Over time, we told more friends and realized that the more people we told, the more we could not control who knew we had DID. When we decided to do this book, we wanted to give others something that would help them heal. When we came out as a lesbian, we heard all of the same garbage that people may throw at you when you tell them you have DID: You could be different if you wanted to, you could change, you are ill, and on and on.

Truth is, we are who we are. We have met other people like us who have told only one person in their life—their therapist. Their therapists helped them understand that developing DID was how they survived being a child. These folks have felt like we did at first: isolated, crazy, and certain that they would be locked up if anyone really knew about them. Over time, we have learned to appreciate the strengths that we have because we have DID. We also have learned to

live with the difficulties resulting from this diagnosis. So
telling for us is about healing. We have spent our life walking
our talk. We believe that the majority of people mean well in
life. We treat others with respect and try to be honest with
people. We will never physically hurt another and never
intentionally hurt someone or embarrass someone.

We found that when we talked to other people who
were living with DID it was very helpful. There are many
similarities and many differences among those of us with
DID. When we finally accepted our having DID, we
understood that we were doing nothing wrong by living our
life. The abusers might see this differently, because they would
prefer that we were dead or locked up in some hospital for
being crazy. At times, it would be easier to give up and let
the world treat us as crazy and hide. Then we see the real
nuts who are out there doing harm to people through abuse,
crime, or just destroying people by being hostile and hurtful.
At some point in our life, we decided that we did not want
to live being a victim. We like feeling and living, so we talk
about what happens because of abuse and try to help others
realize they can survive and live. And we will continue
telling.

One benefit of coming out is that you can have closer relationships with the people you love and who stand by you. If you have
close friends or are interested in developing close friends, there will
be a time when your relationship will go no further because many
real parts of your life are secret. Telling others allows you to talk
about your full life, not just the censored version. You may want to
think about who you turn to when you need support. Do you have
friends you can call who understand what you may be struggling
with? It is helpful to have someone to talk with besides your therapist
when you are having flashbacks or are approaching anniversary
dates of bad things. Selectively telling people allows you to gain emotional support from those you tell. One of the most positive reasons
to come out is so you can live your life more honestly and with pride,
and so you can begin to develop deeper connections with others.

One reason to tell others about having DID is so you are not so
isolated. It is important to realize that people you tell about DID have
the same negative socialization about mental disorders as you had,
which is not very optimistic or realistic. It is important to let them ask
questions and provide them with resources and information so they
can learn about the reality of DID. It may take them a while to under-

stand what it means to have DID. You may get questions like, "Who is talking now?" You may know it is the adult telling them about you, and you may feel frustrated that they don't automatically understand this, but it will take time for your loved ones to accept and understand how DID affects your life. In the beginning especially, they will only know that there are different ones who are part of you; they won't be able to understand and identify all of your selves the way you might wish they could. The people you tell will probably have lots of questions for you, many of which may frustrate or discourage you. It's important that you respond to your loved ones with the same patience and understanding that you are wanting from them.

> The question, "Who is talking now?" always threw us off—who do they think is talking? We forgot how hard it was for us to understand ourselves. It has taken us so much work to understand ourselves, it makes sense that it will take others even longer to understand us. People who ask us the question, "Who's talking?" simply wanted to know if it is Karen or another one speaking. We forget that they are not inside with the rest of us, so they can't tell as easily as we can who is out at any given time.

You will probably approach others with the hope that they will accept and understand about your DID (even though they might be a bit confused at first). As confusing as DID is, you may find the reactions of others to be even more puzzling. Remember, you have had much of your life to experience DID first hand. Your family and friends haven't, and they might react strangely or in ways you don't expect or want. It's not uncommon for people to say one thing but be giving you nonverbal messages that indicate something else. For instance, your friend might say that she understands and that your DID doesn't change your relationship with her, but at the same time she may be looking at you like you have three heads. Sometimes what is said verbally doesn't match what's said nonverbally. And because most people with DID are vigilant and adept at picking up nonverbal cues—like people's expressions, gestures, and behaviors—you may find that you get some very mixed and confusing reactions from those you tell about your multiple personalities.

> We were good at reading nonverbal reactions to what we said, so when people we told were saying one thing but clearly feeling another, we would ask them to be honest about their feelings. Sometimes we would ask the people we told if we could call the next day just to check in and see if they were

still okay with us. Telling people you have DID is sometimes a shock to them, so giving them a little time to process this information can help.

Unless you understand your own motives for telling others about having DID, the people you choose to come out to aren't likely to understand why you're telling them and what you may or may not expect from them. You may want to tell someone just because it makes it easier for you talk about your life. You may want to tell someone because you need support in a situation, and it would be helpful for that person to understand what you would like. Perhaps you are thinking of telling some people because you know that if you spend time with them, it is likely that it will come up. If you know why you're telling someone about having DID, and you know what you hope to achieve by doing so, you will be better able to direct the conversation and will be more likely to get what you want from the disclosure.

We decided to tell people about our living with DID when we wanted to develop closer friendships. It was hard to have close friends without telling them why we had a bad day. If the friends were people we spent more than an hour or two with at a time, telling them made it easier to be ourselves.

How to Come Out

Once you make the decision to tell others about having multiple personalities, you'll need to figure out the best strategy to do this. Possibly the most important factor in sharing this information with others is how you are feeling about your having DID. When you tell those close to you that you have DID, it helps tremendously to be able to present this fact without shame or embarrassment. (Just remember, your personalities helped you to survive and cope with tremendous trauma; without DID, you might not be here today.) Your own feelings regarding DID will dictate to others how they should respond. For instance, if you cry and apologize and present your multiple personalities as something to be ashamed of, those around you will probably perceive DID as something negative. However, if you present your DID as simply the way that you are and even indicate some of the ways that it helps you cope and function, others will likely see it that way, too. So, in order for you to have others respect you and be proud of you for who you are, you need to respect and be proud of yourself first.

As you talk with others about having multiple personalities, you should be as direct as possible. If you are evasive or indirect, you'll come across as if you have something to hide. Talk about DID with pride. You and each of your alters are important, valuable beings. DID was a great survival skill. You were courageous and strong for being able to survive the trauma you went through, and you are even more courageous for being able to talk openly about having DID.

Also, having your support system ready prior to coming out to others is really important. Regardless of the reactions of others, you are likely to want your support system close by. You will definitely want to have a friend or therapist, who already knows you have DID, available to discuss how you felt about coming out. (If you don't have a therapist or anyone else who knows about and supports your having DID, you may want to first seek an understanding and qualified therapist.) You may want to talk to people in your support system directly after you tell others about your multiple personalities, or you may need to first process your own reactions or the reactions of the others. Regardless of the purpose, or when you need the help, having someone there after you have come out, especially if you are just beginning to tell others about having DID, will be really helpful to you.

Each person you tell about having multiple personalities will react differently. For this reason, it's essential that you keep coming out to people, even if it didn't go so well the first time. Talking about DID is difficult, but it does get much easier over time, with lots and lots of practice. Keep telling others; it'll be worth it!

Telling Significant Others

Of all of the people you may tell that you have multiple personalities, telling those you are closest to is likely to be the most difficult for you. Coming out to significant others is especially hard, because they're the ones that people with DID (and people in general, for that matter) usually care about the most. You're probably afraid of how they will respond and how their perceptions of you may change. You might even fear that they will leave you if they find out that you have DID.

While you may have a lot to fear when coming out to your partner, you also have a lot to which you can look forward. Telling them that you have multiple personalities can help create more honesty, connection, and communication in your relationship. By coming out, you get to be a whole, complete person around those you care about the most. Your partner will be able to appreciate and love you in entirely new ways, and your relationship is sure to benefit from the honesty and lack of secrecy. And if your partner for some reason doesn't decide to support you or stay with you, you need to realize that it's for the best, because you deserve to be in a relationship in which you are loved for who you are, not for who someone wants you to be. So although telling significant others may be very difficult, the potential benefits surely outweigh the possible risks.

Telling Your Children

If you have lived with your children since they were born, they have probably seen more than you realize. They may not have a name or names for all of your alters, but they may have different ways to describe and understand each one. It is helpful to provide a therapist for the children so they can talk to someone else about DID. They may want to discuss what it's like to live with you, or they may have questions or others issues they want to talk about. Providing your children with plenty of support is really helpful as you come out to them.

It's important to find a therapist who understands how to work with children and who understands DID. Not every child is going to want to understand this issue or want to talk about it. Some children may feel more comfortable if you don't discuss your multiple personalities or if you don't allow your alters to come out around them. Again, these are things that it's helpful to discuss with your children with the support and objectivity of a therapist.

If you notice that your child is acting out in inappropriate ways, such as having trouble in school or having difficulty getting along with others, then it is important to talk with your child about these issues. You may also want to engage in some sort of family therapy to deal with the root of these problems. It's important that you try to find out what's really causing these difficulties, rather than jumping to the conclusion that it relates to you having DID. It may be that your child is having problems that have nothing to do with you.

You may have step children or other children who come into your family after infancy. As the children get to know you, they will be struggling in their attempts to define who you are in their life. If you are not the biological parent, you are in for a challenge regardless of the issues raised by your having DID. Being a step parent is difficult in the best of situations; if you are a step parent who has DID, this will further complicate things. Remember, the children did not choose you to share their life, their parent chose you, and step children are not likely to run to you with open arms. The best thing for you to do is to respect the children's needs and wishes, unless these needs are destructive to them or you. You are not their primary parent (biological parent or parent who has raised the child since birth), so it is not wise to try and set rules with them unless their primary parent is supportive. You may have to negotiate with your partner (their parent) ways to handle various situations.

One teenager Tracy knows said it very well: Teens get mad at their parents anyway. If there is an issue in the family (such as a step parent having DID), it will often incorrectly be assumed that the issue is the root of the teenagers anger or misbehavior; the issue may actually be a secondary problem, while simple teenage rebellion may be the primary issue at hand. DID is an issue your step child may use as cause to reject you—just try and be patient. Step children generally have a tough time learning to trust their step parents. If you can just be supportive and loving, eventually they will come around. If the step children remain distant and angry, it is important to find ways to continue to nurture your relationship with their parent. Otherwise, the children can create enough problems to overwhelm any relationship, let alone one in which one of the partners has multiple personalities.

Telling Co-Workers

The relationships that you have with your co-workers are likely to be somewhat different from the relationships you have with your friends and family. Generally, you'll interact with the people that you work with only on a professional level and mainly at your place of employment. While you may be friendly with some of the people at work, you may consider these individuals your "work friends" and place them in a friendship category of their own. Because the role of co-workers in your life is somewhat limited, coming out to these individuals about having DID should be done cautiously.

You will definitely want to put a great deal of thought into making the decision of whether or not to inform the people at work that you have multiple personalities. While having DID is nothing to be ashamed of or embarrassed about, some people may be too used to their misconceptions about DID to be willing to change. For this reason, you may decide that there are some people who just don't need to know this information. There's nothing wrong with telling the whole world that you have DID, and there's also nothing wrong with not telling the whole world about this.

Perhaps the most important factor in your decision to come out at work is determining why you would want to inform your co-workers that you have multiple personalities. If you find that having DID is an issue for you at work, then it might be important to tell the co-workers to whom you are closest. For instance, if your little ones come out during important meetings, then you might want to let others know that this is happening so that you and your co-workers can formulate strategies for dealing with this issue (like maybe you won't be expected to go to boring meetings anymore). If having DID really doesn't affect you at work at all (it may be that you have only one personality who goes to work and the others never some out in that environment), then you should really consider why you would tell your co-workers and how you could benefit from doing so.

Because DID is still viewed as an oddity and many people do not understand the implications of having multiple personalities, you need to be careful about coming out at work. This isn't to say that you're doing anything wrong by coming out or that you're a bad person for having DID. Instead, it's just acknowledging that many people are ignorant about psychological issues such as this, and they may overreact to learning that you have DID. Use your best judgment and give plenty of consideration to coming out at work before you do so.

Coming Out and the ADA

The Americans with Disabilities Act (ADA) was established to protect individuals with disabilities from discrimination in many areas, including housing and employment. If, by coming out at work as a person with DID, you are fired, you may have some rights under the ADA. Although DID is not necessarily disabling, it is a type of psychiatric disorder. Because of this, you are entitled to protection from discrimination under the laws set forth by the ADA. Hopefully you will never need to consult the ADA or an attorney after disclosing that you have DID, but if you do, know that there are some laws that are designed to protect you against potential discrimination based on your psychiatric condition.

※

Activity 7.1: Plans for "Coming Out"

This activity will help you devise your own plan for how you will tell another individual about your multiple personalities. Although you can never really control or predict the reactions of others, being prepared will help you to feel as if you're more in control of the situation. With this activity, you will plan not only how, when, and where you will tell this person about having DID, but also what you will do following the experience to take care of yourself. Being well prepared can only help make the coming out process go more smoothly for you and for the person you are telling.

In your journal, answer the following questions.

1. Who are you going to tell? (It's best if you choose just one person to tell to begin with, instead of a group of people. You are better able to predict the reactions of one person than several people or a group.)

2. Why do you want this person to know that you have multiple personalities? What are your motives for telling this person? What do you hope to gain from disclosing that you have DID?

3. When will you tell this person? (Be as specific as you can, including both day and time.)

4. Where will you be when you tell this person that you have DID? (Being in a place where you feel comfortable will help you feel more at ease and relaxed when you break the big news. Also, you will probably want to be somewhere private, so that if any of the alters want to come out, they can do so without worrying who else might be around.)

5. How will you tell this person about your personalities? What exactly will you say? (Sometimes it helps to write out what you will say in advance, almost like a speech that you are preparing for. You may also want to include some information on how and why your DID developed. Most people are likely to ask questions related to this.)

6. How do you expect this person will react? If they do react in this way, how will that be for you? How will it be for you if they don't react in the way you are expecting? What other

reactions might that person have? How might those reactions affect you?

7. What will you do to take care of yourself after this event? Who are you able to call or see for support? What things can you do to make yourself feel better?

8. After you have come out about having DID, write about how it went. What would you have done differently? Were there things that you did or words that you used that, in retrospect, were not helpful? What went well? What would you do again? Overall, how was the experience for you?

Since you will be telling others about having multiple personalities, you might want to complete this activity after each coming out experience and review your responses prior to telling others. Eventually, you'll feel much more comfortable disclosing that you have DID.

Therapy and DID

It is confusing to begin therapy for the first time. Some people are taught that if they try hard enough, they can make it through any situation; asking for help is perceived as a weakness. In most families where abuse occurred, there is also a "no talk" standard that keeps people from expressing their concerns over any issues of concern. So, to go to a stranger for help with personal and family problems can seem foreign, confusing, and perhaps even taboo.

You may, however, have reached a point in your life where you realize that you've gone as far as you can on your own in improving your life, and you may still be unhappy. One benefit to therapy is that you are talking with a person who has not had all of the same family rules you were taught, nor do they have the same distorted filters that come from living in a dysfunctional, abusive home. Until you obtain differing perspectives from others, you will always process information in the same way, because that is what you know. To try and change the way you understand the issues in your life, you have to have someone who is outside of your experience. Think about it for a minute: If you decide to talk to your siblings or family peers about what you felt and experienced growing up, chances are pretty strong that they will try to keep you within the family norm—don't talk; don't explore. They also may tell you that the past is over, and expect you to just "get on with your life." The trouble is, if you had an unpleasant childhood that required you to learn coping skills that work for a child, you will find that, as an adult, these coping skills now get in the way of you living your life. For anyone, processing the past is helpful in improving the present and future.

It is possible to not deal with things that happened in your life. It is possible to live day to day without changing your coping skills. There is no requirement for you to go through this process of self-exploration and self-growth. As is true in life with any issue, when you begin to realize that you have no control over addiction or actions and they cause you trouble, you can decide if you want to change. It is important to realize that growing and changing is your choice, not your therapist's or anyone else's.

With this in mind, learning how to live your life in ways that are different and new can be very beneficial. Making the decision to alter your life can give your life a new direction and focus. You can learn how to deal with issues, both large and small, more effectively and effortlessly. Changing, growing, and learning more about yourself allow you to better manage your behaviors and gain control of your life. Change and growth are rarely easy, but they are definitely worth the time and effort you put in.

Making Decisions about Therapy

Many people with multiple personalities are in therapy for years before they actually receive the diagnosis of DID. If you're already in therapy at this time, you may want to read this section anyway in case you have been having doubts about being in therapy. You may also use this section to help you determine whether your current therapist is meeting your needs surrounding DID. If you've never been in psychotherapy, or if you had gone through therapy before for other issues, this section will help you determine if you want to enter therapy for issues related to having multiple personalities.

The first step in deciding whether to enter therapy or to remain in therapy is to identify how you think therapy might help you. In other words, why do you want to be in therapy? Are you looking for support? Do you hope to find a way to integrate your personalities, or do you only want to find ways to make your life be more manageable? Do you want to know if you actually have DID? Are you just feeling crazy or out of control, and feel you need some help sorting things out? You may have a number of reasons why you think therapy would be beneficial. There's not one particular reason that's right, nor is there a wrong reason to enter therapy. However, the more realistic your expectations, the more likely you will be to find therapy useful.

If you enter therapy so that your therapist can magically cure you, make all of your bad feelings disappear, and ensure that nothing bad will ever happen again, you'll be out of luck. Therapists can only guide you in a process of self-discovery and emotional well-being. They are not magicians, nor are they psychic. Therapy can give you a place where you can be yourself, find support, and learn more about DID and how it affects your life. Therapy may even help you find ways to improve your life and enhance your coping skills. While there are many things which therapy can be helpful with, the success of therapy depends primarily on you.

You may also want to determine why you are or aren't thinking of entering therapy now. Did something recently occur that makes you want to reach out for help? Did you just find out that you have multiple personalities? Is this time of year particularly troublesome for you? Is your partner or one of your friends suggesting you get help? Understanding why you desire to be in therapy now—as opposed to a month ago, a year ago, or two years from now—may help you clarify your reasons and decision to enter therapy.

Or perhaps you aren't considering therapy at this point in time. Are things going well for you? Is it simply the pressure or advice of friends that's making you consider therapy? Are you afraid of entering therapy? Do you not have the time or financial means to consider getting help right now? Don't begin therapy if you don't want to or if you're not willing to participate fully. Of course, you'll have to figure out if your reasons for not wanting to be in therapy are simply excuses because you're frightened. Entering into any new relationship is scary, and therapy is no exception. Only you can make the decision if therapy is right for you.

Related to the reasons you have to be in therapy, you should, if possible, also identify the goals you have for therapy. Once in therapy, you and your therapist will probably work together to develop specific goals. However, it's helpful if you go in with an idea of what you expect from therapy. If you aren't sure if you have DID, then you may be entering into therapy to see exactly what is going on with you that is causing trouble in your life. If you are aware or suspect that DID may be part of your life, then you might have a different goal for therapy, such as learning how to establish coconsciousness with your alters. You will spend a lot of time, effort, and expense just being in therapy. If you know what you hope to achieve, it makes the process much more directed and, perhaps, a bit easier.

Entering therapy is sort of like taking your car in to be fixed. If you bring it in and say it's making a funny noise and ask your mechanic to fix it, it's much more difficult, time consuming, and expensive than if you say that it needs a new fan belt. Since you are more complex than your car, you may not know exactly what you hope to achieve in therapy. However, if you have a general sense of how you would like to be able to function or what specific things you would like to achieve through the process of therapy, the experience will be more fruitful.

If you have never been in therapy, you may be wondering just what does happen when you go to see someone. Do you have to lie on some couch and pay money to have a person sit there and look at you suspiciously? For most people who have experienced trauma, this picture would keep them out of therapy forever. Don't worry, there are only a few therapists who use this style of therapy, and you can decide if this would be comfortable for you.

> *When we went into therapy, it was because we felt crazy about our life. We had two jobs (working a total of sixty hours a week) and went to school. We were writing a master's thesis and were involved in a long-term relationship. We started to plan what other things we could do, and realized this was a bit crazy. We knew what therapy was, but we'd never been in to see anyone. We also knew we had done all we could to make life better, and it was still a mess.*

When you are at a point where all you know is that you need help, it's sometimes hard to determine where to go for help and what kind of help you might need. Prior to choosing a therapist, think about what is going on in your life. Make a list of things that are not working for you: difficulties in relationships, struggles at work, feelings of loneliness or depression. Think back on your past: Do you know what your family was like growing up? Were people supportive of you? Were you criticized or demeaned a great deal or ignored by the adults in your life? Do you feel that you are doing okay in your life? If you can, think about what you would say about a friend who was in your same situation. Would you describe them as successful? Would you think that they should be proud of their work? Sometimes stepping back and pretending you are looking at someone else makes it easier to see the reality of your life, especially if your view of yourself is inaccurate or distorted.

Therapy demands a great deal of motivation and commitment. You are the one who will undergo intense emotional experiences; your therapist is simply a guide. Because of this, therapy is not always fun, and you won't always feel good when you leave your therapist's office. It takes a great deal of courage, commitment, and motivation to keep returning to therapy for the duration of the process. With issues of DID, therapy is often a long-term process. You may be in therapy for years before you're able to achieve some of your goals. While you should see some progress along the way, it may be difficult to maintain your motivation for such a long period of time. Without a doubt, there will be times when you want to quit. However, just keep in mind that healing is a process, and that you will get through it eventually.

ACTIVITY 8.1: CHOOSING THERAPY

In your journal, answer the following questions relating to your choices about therapy. These questions should assist you in your decision to remain in or enter into therapy (if you already have a therapist, these questions may help you clarify if you're on the right track and if your current therapist is right for you). After completing this activity, you should have a pretty good idea of whether or not you want to be in therapy, as well as what you hope to achieve by participating in therapy.

1. What issues or problems do you want to work on in therapy? Be as specific as you can. For example, instead of saying that you want to work on issues related to your multiple personalities, be more specific and say that you want to work on creating coconsciousness between your alters.

2. Are you able to deal with these issues on your own? What has happened in the past when you dealt with these issues by yourself or with others (including past or current therapists)? There are many problems that you can solve by yourself or with the help of some trusted friends. What is it that makes these issues require professional help?

3. How do you think that having DID will be dealt with in therapy? Do you expect that the therapist will focus on integration rather than on coping skills for current problems?

Do you think that the therapist will believe that you have multiple personalities?

4. Why are you seeking therapy? Did something happen recently that made you want to get professional help? Did you just find out that you have multiple personalities?

5. What are your goals in therapy? Are they realistic?

6. How motivated are you to be in therapy? How long will you commit to this activity?

7. Are you at a point in your life where death seems better than living with the feelings you have? (If you answer "yes" to this question, call someone today. If this is a weekend and you are at an extreme low, call a crisis line and talk to someone, or have a friend stay with you until you can contact someone.)

8. Do you have funds to go to therapy? It is a commitment to your future, but it is generally not free. If you have a low income, you may be able to see someone through a community agency that is less expensive. The cost of the therapist is not the measure of their effectiveness in their work. More important is their understanding and experience in working with DID.

Finding a Therapist

Once you've made the choice to seek therapy, you'll want to find a therapist who is right for you. Finding a good fit between therapist and client is difficult at best. It's even more difficult when you're dealing with issues related to DID.

There are many ways to begin locating a therapist. The best way generally is to choose a therapist through a referral from someone you know and trust, like your medical doctor or a friend. This way the person giving you the referral will have a sense of who you are and can match your needs with a respected therapist. A second, though riskier, method of finding a therapist is through the Yellow Pages of the telephone book. Depending on where you live, you're likely to find many names of therapists. The problem with using the

Yellow Pages is that you have no idea about the quality of the therapist. Simply because certain therapists can afford to place a big advertisement does not mean that they are good therapists. You're much better off looking for a referral from someone you know.

In your process of finding a therapist, you'll likely learn that therapists come in many varieties. Most therapists will have some graduate training in psychology, social work, human behaviors, or medicine. The therapist's exact title will depend on their actual degree or license (Ph.D., Psy.D., M.F.C.C., L.C.S.W., M.D., etc.). Psychiatrists are actually medical doctors and are the only type of therapist allowed to prescribe medication. Psychologists; psychiatrists; social workers; and marriage, family, and child counselors each have slightly different approaches to therapy based upon their training. You may want to ask them about their particular approach or the specific type of training required for their degree.

In most cases, it really doesn't make a difference what specific degree the therapist possesses. Most psychotherapists are able to perform a variety of functions. However, you would be better off locating a therapist who is licensed through a state accrediting agency. In many states and countries, individuals can call themselves a counselor or therapist without having a license and sometimes without having proper training. Possession of a valid license ensures that you, as a client, have some recourse if you are dissatisfied with the nature of the therapy. Licenses to practice therapy are generally designed to protect you and to ensure some type of quality control. While there may be some exceptional therapists who operate without a license, you would probably be better off not seeking treatment from an unlicensed therapist.

Once you have located a therapist who sounds promising, it's time to conduct an interview. Most therapists are more than willing to answer questions related to therapeutic issues. However, as you interview therapists, you should know that most of them will not answer personal questions or queries into matters which don't pertain to therapy. So while it's acceptable to ask what type of degree therapists have, inquiring about their marital status is a bit out of bounds.

Interviewing a therapist is important, as it allows you to get an idea of who you might be working with. It's difficult to find a good match between a therapist and a client. Over the course of treatment, you'll be disclosing some very intimate and personal information, so it's essential that you feel comfortable with and have trust in your therapist. Comfort and trust won't come right away, but after a few sessions you should have an idea of whether or not you can actually work with that therapist. Hopefully, the therapist you've been working with will be willing to talk with you about issues you've raised (such as ritual abuse and DID) without steering the conversation away from those topics. The therapist should also be accepting of who you are and why you have entered therapy, instead of trying to persuade you that DID doesn't exist or that you need to integrate your personalities, if you've stated that this is not a goal of yours. Your therapist should treat you respectfully, be on time for your appointments, and listen to what you are saying. While you're not likely to be comfortable in therapy at this point, you will probably have a good sense of whether or not this therapist is right for you. Interviewing will help you screen out therapists who don't match your needs, without investing a whole lot of time or money.

Many therapists will answer your questions over the telephone prior to setting up an appointment with you. Others may feel more comfortable scheduling a session and answering your questions face to face. Either way, it's important that you have in mind what questions you want to ask. The following questions will help you determine some items which you may choose to inquire about.

How much experience do you have with DID?

This will be important for you to find out. While not all therapists will have extensive experience working with people who have multiple personalities (most won't), the therapist should be knowledgeable about related areas such as child abuse and trauma. Also, the therapist should express a willingness to learn about DID in order to better help you. This is an important point. If you talk to someone who has seen one or two clients with DID, ask the therapist if they took steps to learn more about treating DID, and what exactly they did. Reading a book is a good start, but you may want someone who is willing to get supervision from another professional who is skilled in this area. It is okay to help someone learn about treating DID, as long as you are not hurt in the process. If the therapist tells you that they have worked with people with sexual abuse and the treatment is the same, keep looking. You may end up getting treatment that would help a person heal from sexual abuse, but without addressing issues of coconsciousness and tending to the special needs of child alters; this treatment may simply retraumatize the person who is living with DID.

What is the normal course of treatment for DID?

Because most therapists will not have a great deal of experience dealing with DID, it may be difficult for them to describe a normal course of treatment. However, this question will help you find out how that particular therapist would treat DID. For example, you may learn that the therapist often uses hypnosis, and, depending on your preferences, this may affect your decision to enter therapy with that individual.

What are your views on integration?

As you interview therapists, you'll probably find that many view integration as a long-term goal. Asking this question can allow you to gauge the therapist's eagerness to impose integration; depending on your preferences (to focus on integration, coping, or both) this will help you choose a therapist who respects and supports your treatment goals.

What do you know about areas related to DID (child abuse, trauma, dissociation, eating disorders, addictions, self-inflicted violence)?

Again, you're simply assessing the background and experience of the therapist. The more the therapist knows about these areas, the better.

How well do you work with children?

Since some of your alters are likely to be children, they, too, will need to be in therapy with someone who is qualified and interested in working with kids. It's important that your therapist treat them for who they are and not force the little ones to act like adults and engage in "adult" therapy.

How long do you think I'll need therapy?

This is sort of a trick question, because no therapist can really give you an answer on this. However, in dealing with issues of DID, therapy usually takes years. If you interview therapists who state that they can "cure" you in six sessions, run away fast.

What is your availability?

Depending on how much assistance you need or desire in dealing with your issues, this question may be critical. Find out how often the therapist thinks you should be seen. Also inquire about the way in which emergencies are handled. It's important that you know if the therapist works evenings and weekends, and whether or not they're willing to return phone calls when they aren't in the office. While you may or may not care about these items now, having the answers may come in handy later when you feel in need of support or assistance.

How much do you charge?

Many people are afraid to raise the issue of money with therapists. However, you need to know what to expect. Fees are not an indicator of quality. Some very good therapists may charge very little and some not so good therapists may charge a great deal. Thus, it's important that you find a therapist you can afford. The last thing that you should have to worry about in therapy is how much each minute is costing you. You'll find many low-cost therapists at agencies run by non-profit groups such as universities, medical centers, and some social service agencies.

Is there anything else you think I should know about you and how you do therapy?

This question allows the therapist an opportunity to tell you of things you may not have thought about, such as specialties, past experiences, or specific techniques employed.

There are a great number of therapists in the world. You may have to interview many before finding one that you think will match your needs. It may seem stressful if you are in crisis, but it is in your best interest to choose a therapist based on long-term treatment goals.

ACTIVITY 8.2: INTERVIEWING A THERAPIST

(You may want to make several photocopies of the next two pages so that you can use them when interviewing each therapist.)

List the questions you will ask a potential therapist. Below each question, indicate the therapist's response, as well as any notes which might help you in your decision (their tone of voice, the feelings their responses gave you, etc.). When you are interviewing prospective therapists, keep in mind that you are the consumer, and you are essentially trying do determine if you want to purchase a particular product.

Therapist's Name _____

Therapist's Telephone Number _____

Therapist's Address _____

Date Interviewed _____

In Person? Over Telephone?_____

Question 1: How much experience do you have with DID?

Question 2: What is the normal course of treatment for DID?

Question 3: What are your views on integration?

Question 4: What do you know about areas related to DID (child abuse, trauma, dissociation, eating disorders, addictions, self-inflicted violence)?

Question 5: How well do you work with children? How would you go about treating child alters?

Question 6: How long do you think I'll need therapy?

Question 7: What is your availability?

Question 8: How much do you charge?

Question 9: Is there anything else you think I should know about you and how you do therapy?

Overall Impressions:

＊

Creating Safety in Therapy

Once you find a therapist that you are comfortable working with, you can begin to explore ways to help you feel safe. Understanding what is expected from your therapist is helpful. Part of safety is having a clear sense of the boundaries in therapy. If you know that you have trouble remembering things like therapy appointments (because you have others who would prefer you stay home), and your therapist is strict on charging you if you don't show up, you may want to talk about ways to deal with this situation. Otherwise, you will become angry at your therapist, and it will make it harder for you to do the work. Your therapist may have some suggestions as to how you can more easily remember your appointments.

Another way to feel safer in therapy is to find things that help you feel safe and take them with you. You may have a special stuffed animal that gives you comfort and keeps you safe. Put it in a bag and take it with you. You can also carry pictures or stones that help you remember that this is a different time than when you were first traumatized. It may be that you want to sit facing the door so that you have the sense that you can leave at any given moment. If you are unable to relax for any reason (e.g., because you can't see the door) then talk about how you and your therapist could change the space so you feel safe. You may want to wear special or comfortable clothes to therapy or bring certain foods or drinks (if it's okay with your therapist). Whatever you can do to give you a sense of safety is important. Once you begin to feel more safe and comfortable, you'll be better able to open up and work on important and difficult issues.

You may also feel more safe if you free yourself of pressures prior to or following the therapeutic session. Try not to schedule things right before or after therapy. This will allow you some time to collect your thoughts and process the intense feelings which will regularly be raised during the session. If you have friends who are in therapy with your therapist, make sure that you are not scheduled before or after your friends' appointments. It might be difficult for you to be sociable or polite when you are coming to or leaving a session, and it's not a position that you need to place yourself in. If at all possible, try to allow yourself time to "just be" after therapy. If you can take an hour before going to another activity, you will have a chance to settle down. At times you may need to make arrangements to have someone pick you up after therapy if you are going to be doing work that triggers the little ones. It is important that only the ones who can drive do drive.

We have some little ones who would want to come out and drive. They were the same ones who wanted to push other cars with our car. When they got out we would pull over until we could get one of the ones who knew how to drive to come out.

You may need to talk with your therapist about making sure that you spend the last five minutes of the session getting the big one back, just to make sure that you are oriented to where you are so that you can drive home. If you are still having trouble getting back to yourself, see if you can wait in the waiting room until it is okay for you to drive or until you get a ride. It is helpful to discuss strategies with your therapist early on if you find that it is hard to get back home.

ACTIVITY 8.3: HOW TO CREATE SAFETY

This activity will work best if you and your therapist complete it together. In your journal or on a piece of paper, make a list of all of the things you and your therapist can do to make the setting for therapy seem more safe. Are there special items, such as stuffed animals, that you want to bring with you to therapy? Is there a time of day when you would prefer to schedule your appointments? Is there anything in the office which makes you feel scared? While you may not be able to control all of the things which make you afraid, see how many ways you can think of to make yourself feel more safe. You may want to take this list with you to therapy until you feel comfortable enough to leave it at home.

Allowing Everyone to Come Out

It is helpful to realize that each one of your alters has important things to say. Some just like to have fun, some like to play, and others can let you know what is really going on inside. Each one needs time to play and be out. It is important, however, that everyone inside agrees that the big one has the final say on when the little ones and others come out.

Sometimes it is helpful to understand which little ones know which facts. Some little ones will be able to let you in on why you have been struggling, when all you know is that you have been upset. At other times, the little ones may have interesting insights to share on various issues.

> *We would go see the man who gives us medicine so we could stay awake, and our big one would not let us say anything. We had told him we were DID but didn't talk much about it. One time when we went to see him the big one was not telling him everything that had been going on, so we came out and filled him in on the rest. We knew we upset him some, but the information would not have been there otherwise. (He did call our therapist and told her that we "regressed" in his office—she said, "No, that was just Rosalee!").*

It is sometimes harder when you are first meeting all who reside within you to keep everyone under control. It can help if you set up times each day when everyone knows that they can be out. Otherwise, it becomes hard, because everyone needs time to be out, yet they may try to stay inside because they don't want to cause trouble or get those on the outside mad. It takes a tremendous amount of energy to keep totally contained. By having times that you know you can just be yourself, you can reduce the stress for yourself and everyone in your system.

Your Expectations of Therapy
What You Should Expect From Therapy

Knowing what to expect from therapy may help you to feel more safe, secure, and confident about the treatment you are receiving. While therapists each have their own styles and ways of conducting therapy, there are some standard procedures.

Do Expect Plenty of Questions

Therapists need to ask questions so that they can learn about you and try to help you. Usually when you first enter therapy, the therapist will ask you a lot of questions about your life. They may have you complete a questionnaire or take a survey to gather more information. Most therapists do not initially offer diagnostic tests when you go to see them for therapy (such as the kinds of tests that you see in movies—ink blots, puzzles, etc.). If you have some understanding of the problems you are having, then you will want to make sure that you have an opportunity to talk with the therapist about your views. Therapists are not all alike, and each will have different beliefs about how to work with people. These views come from various theories on how people learn and how to help people grow.

Do Expect to Talk

Additionally, your therapist may help you identify behaviors that get you into trouble. Remember, your therapist is not psychic. If you do not tell the therapist about things that are problems in your life, don't expect your therapist to somehow guess. Expecting them to guess what you are not disclosing will only set you both up for failure and frustration.

It's important to talk to your therapist about how you react to the discussion of certain topics. If you feel like you want to hurt yourself or cut yourself after you have therapy or every time you have any dialogue about your childhood, tell the therapist. Often you will leave the therapist's office somewhat confused, because you are beginning to look at things in a new way. It's more than likely that your therapist will not know what you are experiencing following the session unless you bring it up. It's also likely that your therapist can help you handle these disturbing feelings or behaviors and tailor your sessions to prevent this from occurring.

It is reasonable for you to have your therapist help you find ways to create safety if you have trouble talking about certain topics. You may want to discuss ways that you can create a safe place in your home and what you can do when you become overwhelmed. There are some ideas about this in chapter 5.

It's also important for you to be clear on what you can expect from your therapist if you are in crisis. Ask if your therapist will make emergency appointments and what the policy is for returning telephone calls so that you can figure out when and how to provide safety for yourself.

Do Expect Support, Insight, and Help with Your Situation

If you are in crisis and get into see a therapist on this basis, you may eventually find that you want to find someone who is more directive, as the first therapist you see may be focused on helping you end the crisis. If you want to better understand yourself and learn how to change habits that do not work, you will be in for a longer process. Therapists cannot simply give you the answers to your questions. Instead, they will help you find these answers within yourself. You are the expert on your life, not the therapist. Although you may not have a perfectly clear understanding of your life and all that has occurred in your past, you will gain more answers and more clarity through the course of therapy.

It's important to remember that your therapist is not your parent, supervisor, or other authority figure. This person is only a guide who can help you to understand yourself better. The therapist's role is to facilitate your learning process about yourself. If you were given the message that you were not worth anything growing up, the therapist will help you recognize the origin of these messages and understand that these messages weren't and aren't true. Your therapist should give you support and help you understand the truth about yourself, and they can help you sort out the misinformation and inaccurate beliefs you have about yourself.

Do Expect to Learn, Grow, and Change

The primary goal of most therapies is to help the client learn and grow. As a client, you should expect this to occur. There are many ways in which your therapist can guide you to learn more about yourself and how you relate to the world. You will develop more self-awareness and understanding of your thoughts, feelings, and behaviors. While learning, growing, and changing are usually positive in the long run, in the short term these things may be difficult. You've established patterns in your life and certain ways of being. Trying to change these patterns takes time and energy. You will probably find that therapy is somewhat draining. Try not to get discouraged or scared by this: change and growth always take effort, and the benefits are an enormous reward for your hard work.

Do Expect to Feel

One thing that therapy will do is to help you learn how to get through the feelings that you have blocked off for years. It's impossible to feel only good feelings, and if you want to start experiencing your feelings, you will likely go through times when you feel worse before feeling better.

Imagine that your fears, pain, and anger were stuffed into a ball. When you could not handle a feeling, it went into this ball, which helps to keep these feelings separate from you. At this point, though, you may only know how to put things into the ball. You may not have yet learned how to let things out. Each year you store more and more feelings in this ball. Even when this ball seems full, you walk around mostly feeling empty. When the ball becomes so full that it is going to explode, you may feel compelled to find ways to reinforce the structure of the ball so nothing escapes. You might excessively work, drink, do drugs, eat, or use other addictions to stop the feelings. Eventually this ball becomes so overstuffed that you have difficulty getting through each day, because you need more and more reinforcement to keep the ball of emotions under control.

Through the work in therapy, you will find ways to release some of the pressure from this ball. At first it will be hard, because these feelings often feel so intense and overwhelming that you may have believed that they would kill you if they ever came out. If you feel this way, letting anything out will be scary. As you work with the therapist over time, it will get easier and easier to release the old stuff. As the pressure in the ball reduces, you can start feeling some of the good things as well as the things that you avoided before, such as anger and fear. Therapy will eventually help you feel better, but try to remember that it takes time and that there are no magical cures or quick fixes.

Do Expect Consistency and Good Boundaries

You should expect your therapist to have clear and consistent boundaries. It is important that your therapist sets boundaries for you. This is not your role as a client. It is important to know that there are certain behaviors that are not part of therapy. It is not okay for a therapist to touch you inappropriately. Some therapists will ask if you want a hug good-bye or if you want them to hold your hand when you are crying. Tell your therapist if at any time you are uncomfortable with any touch they give you. It may be that being hugged upsets you. If so, that is fine, and you can tell the therapist that you don't like to be hugged. If the therapist insists on giving you a hug anyway, saying it is good for you, realize that this is not okay and consider confronting the therapist, notifying the therapist's licensing board, or simply finding another therapist.

What You Should Not Expect from Therapy

Therapy is in no way a normal situation. You spend an hour (which is usually actually fifty minutes) talking to someone you don't really know about the most intimate details of your life. However, sometimes in therapy an event or situation will occur and you will wonder to yourself if what happened was normal. When you're in therapy dealing with issues related to DID, knowing what you should and shouldn't expect can be helpful. The following section will present some things which you should not expect out of therapy or your therapist.

Don't Expect Your Therapist to Always Be Available

Do not expect your therapist to be there every minute of the day for you. There are times that your therapist will go on vacation or not be available for you. Although this may be terrifying, this is necessary so that therapists can take care of themselves. If they don't take care of themselves, they won't be very good at helping you.

Don't Expect Advice or Answers

Don't expect your therapist to tell you what to do or to give you answers to questions about your life. Instead, your therapist will help you find what answers are the best for you and help you to make sense out of your life. Therapists can guide you to make good decisions, but it is still up to you to follow the ideas. Remember, in therapy as well as in your life, you always have choice.

Don't Expect Your Therapist to Treat You as Anything but a Client

You should not expect your therapist to become your friend or lover. Licensed therapists have certain guidelines to follow in order to help keep you safe. Your therapist should never have sex with you or touch you sexually. If your therapist is inviting you to do things outside of your sessions such as going out to dinner, coffee, or the movies, you should end therapy or find another therapist to help you sort out the situation. Therapists should not get into business with you, invite you to be part of their families, or spend holidays with you.

These types of dual relationships are not normal and are not beneficial to you. Even though this extra attention from your therapist may make you feel special or cared for, relationships such as these will be very harmful to you in the long run. There are guidelines set by each profession on the amount of time that should pass before you become friends with your therapist. This is to allow enough time to pass so that this person moves out of a position of power in your life.

Don't Expect to Hear Much about Your Therapist's Personal Life

Therapy is very one sided. When you are in therapy, you are very open about yourself, your life, and your feelings. Your therapist probably knows more about you than anyone else in your life. Although your therapist may be very supportive of you, remember that you are not friends. Therapists should generally not tell you about their problems; however, your therapist may tell you if something unusual has occurred in their life, such as a death, birth, or breakup, if this event is affecting the therapy in some way. For instance, the therapist may be having trouble concentrating because of this issue or may need to reschedule a session. If you begin to feel that you are taking care of your therapist, it is important to discuss this issue with your therapist. If you feel that you cannot do this, find another person to help you do a reality check to see if your relationship with your therapist is good for you.

Retraumatizing

If you have DID, you have probably experienced some trauma in your life. Typically, therapy with sexual abuse survivors involves having the client tell and retell the story of the traumatic experience. However, in treating people with DID, this type of therapy may be destructive. Unless you have safety and communication within your system, you may have difficulty differentiating between the time you were abused and the present day, and you may feel as though you are reexperiencing the trauma over and over while in therapy.

In our opinion, the first step in therapy for someone with DID should be to learn how to communicate with the alters. The alters need to know that life is safe now. They need to learn that the time that they were hurt was long ago. They also need to have ways to feel safe when they get scared.

One way to create safety is to build a safe space into your system. You may imagine that you have a safe room in which adults you trust can support you and help you handle this situation. In this picture, you may have adult alters who promise to keep anything from happening to the child alters. The adults alters in this room could also remind the child alters that the mean people cannot reach them now, and that if one of the mean people tried to get them, the police would be there for protection. Imagining a current calendar in the room, so child alters are able to see and be reminded that many years have passed since the abuse, may be helpful. By creating a room such as this, you can begin to establish a sense of safety for yourself and your alters.

Not all therapists work to establish this sense of safety. This is one reason why some people with DID may be in therapy for years, only to find out that things are not better and are perhaps even worse. Make sure that your therapist does not let you focus on the bad things in the past until you have ways to make yourself safe. You need to have a system of communication set up between your alters so that you can help each one heal from the past, not just relive the experience. It's essential that in therapy you and everyone in your system learn and know with certainty that no one has a right to harm you.

We spent several years working with a therapist who was known for his work with people who had been sexually abused as children. We did not know about DID at the time. We did know that something had happened to us, but did not remember the details. As we started having flashbacks and the bad stuff starting coming up, we would go into therapy and talk about it, draw it, and go home and write about it. We spent most of our time totally dissociated.

We had one inside who managed to keep us going. She would take over when the feelings became too overwhelming. She was the one who got through life; she was really more like a robot: making sure tasks were done, but having no feelings about anything. We would go to therapy three times a week and go over the trauma, and then get in our car and go back to work. Nada (the one who was out) was very good at returning to whatever needed to be done without anyone knowing what we were really living with.

It took several years and some friends scaring us about how bad we were doing to realize that this therapy was more destructive than anything. After a lot of searching, we found someone who was known for working with people who had

DID. She saved our life by teaching us how to learn the difference between the past and present. She also taught us how to have the little ones communicate with us and each other. This allowed us to move through the trauma and learn that life was really fun and worth living. Until we started working with her, we did not understand how to experience life. We knew how to watch time pass, and we spent many hours doing just that—watching time pass.

Recognizing Dissociation

Learning to recognize your own symptoms of dissociation can be quite difficult. While you may be able to realize that you had been dissociating after the fact, identifying dissociation before it starts or as it's happening is challenging.

The first step in recognizing dissociation in therapy is to explore the ways that you can identify when you have been dissociating. For instance, do you suddenly realize that hours have passed and you don't remember anything that took place within that period of time? Do you find that you've engaged in self-destructive or self-injurious activities? Do particular alters come out? Are there other clues that you've dissociated? Once you can identify these clues, you're off to a good start.

Next, take a step back in time and see if you can figure out what was happening right before you dissociated. Were you talking about family issues? Were you discussing some part of the trauma you went through? Did you just feel more removed or as if you were floating? If you're able to identify some of the triggers, you can better predict when you're about to dissociate.

Once you know what you do when you dissociate and why you begin to dissociate, talk with your therapist about these things. Your therapist may be able to help you identify when you are beginning to dissociate and may be able to help you find ways to stay more grounded. You might even discover that your therapist can show you some techniques or strategies that would help prevent you from dissociating during therapy.

Confrontation of Family Members

Whenever you are dealing with topics of abuse and trauma, confrontation of family members is a tough issue. Determining whether or not you should confront your family members is particularly difficult when you have DID. Your family members may or may not be aware of your alters, and raising issues of trauma may also mean coming out about having DID (or vice versa).

Some people believe that family members should never be confronted, as confrontation around matters of abuse often do more damage than no confrontation at all. Most often, when one (or more) of the children in a family develops DID, the families are fairly dysfunctional and often abusive. There is no easy way to confront family or open the dialogue about childhood abuse. One of the dynamics that exists in many families is that you do not talk about feelings, abuse, or anything else of significance. Although you may be making great progress in stabilizing and expressing your emotions, when you face others who have not progressed so well, you are likely to feel frustrated, angry, and perhaps even fragmented. For instance, when you were growing up, you may have been coaxed into doubting your own experiences. Those who abused you may simply deny that any abuse occurred and may make you feel as if you're incorrectly remembering an event, which can be crazy-making. If you confront your family and are told that you must have created these memories, that nothing like what you are describing ever happened, you may feel confused and it may be difficult for you to remain secure in your conclusions about what happened. The dynamic of denial allows abuse to happen in the first place, and it also allows families to ignore the problems. Denial is a powerful tool, which when used in dysfunctional family situations can make the functional members of the family feel confused, angry, or insane.

If you decide to confront your family members about the original trauma, you may wish to examine several factors prior to the confrontation. First, you will need to clarify the purpose of the confrontation. Are you trying to confirm that abuse actually took place? Are you seeking an apology or perhaps even some form of revenge or forced remorse? Are you simply trying to convey to your friends and family that you are aware of what occurred? While each of these purposes may be valid, only the last is likely to be gratifying to any extent; again, denial by family members of the abuse is likely to occur. You will want to prepare for this denial and examine how this will affect the purpose of the confrontation. If you are able to fulfill the purpose of the confrontation without any specific response from the family, the success of this confrontation will be more likely. For instance, if you simply say to your family, "I know what you did to me and here's how it's affected me," this will work better than if you ask for confirmation of the abuse which occurred (which isn't likely to be provided).

If you decide that a confrontation is warranted, you will also want to determine when and how to do this. You may feel as if it is too soon for confrontation to occur and may worry about fragmenting or decompensating during or after this confrontation. If this is your belief, wait until you feel more ready. You should also ask yourself why you want to confront your family now. You may learn that not all of your alters are so eager to have this confrontation, and you may want to consider encouraging a "group meeting" regarding this topic.

There is also a safety issue to address. Make sure that you are not putting yourself at risk. If you were abused by someone who was part of a cult that had control over you, you must take precautionary measures to make sure you will not be subjected to programming that will bring you back to the cult. Are you likely to be abused by the people you confront? Do the abusers still have power over you (real power, not perceived)?

You need to make sure that you have a good support system set up to help you through this confrontation. It's also important that you spend some time with each of your alters exploring methods of coping and ways that they can each find support, safety, and comfort.

Activity 8.4: Planning to Confront Family

There are a variety of other questions and issues which you should consider prior to a confrontation. In your journal, try to answer the questions that follow. The answers will help you plan the best way to deal with confronting your family members (if you decide to at all).

1. What results are you hoping to have from the discussion with your family?

2. What will it mean to you if you get no information from them?

3. What will it mean to you if they tell you that you are crazy or claim that your therapist planted "all of these crazy ideas" in your head?

4. What would you do if your family members told you that they never wanted to talk with you again?

5. How would you handle your family blaming you for your accusations? How would you feel and what would you do if they told you that you had hurt their feelings by accusing them of such awful things?

Now, in your journal, make a list of all of the reasons why you would want to confront your family members. Make a second list of all of the reasons why you wouldn't want to confront your family members. Which list is longer? How will these pros and cons affect your decision to confront your family members? Make sure in planning a potential confrontation that you take into consideration all of the items on both lists.

Remember that the folks who hurt you have nothing to gain by you getting healthy. It is in their best interest to keep you quiet and under their control. They have lied to you from the very beginning by saying that no one will believe you, and they may say you are crazy. The folks who hurt you were not emotionally healthy. If they've never gone to therapy, they may not even really get how what they did to you was harmful. It is important for you to realize that, in order for them to admit they hurt you, they have to own up to their own behavior and admit to themselves and others that they are responsible for their actions, which may be impossible for them to do. This does not make your own pain any less real, and you do not have to get their confirmation in order to heal yourself.

Before you consider confronting family members (or any abuser), make sure that you have answered the above questions for yourself. Also review the ways that you can remain safe during the confrontation.

It always made me nuts when my father and other members of my family told me he wasn't an alcoholic. This was only a minor issue compared to the abuse. Each time I would bring up my dad's alcoholism, someone would tell me how wrong I was and that he only drank some. Talk about crazy-making, I knew that I would see him passed out, empty booze glasses and bottles of liquor hidden in the house. Yet it only took a two-minute conversation with another family member to make me question my reality and to start my insides going totally nuts.

I have not confronted my family, but this is my personal choice. I do not want to go through the process of their crazy-making, and so I just decided it was not healing for me to pursue their validation. Besides, since they can't acknowledge an obvious problem like alcoholism, I don't think they're going to suddenly acknowledge the abuse I experienced.

PART III

For Others

CHAPTER 9

For Therapists

Where to Begin

Surely you can remember a time when a new client walked into your office, sat down across from you, and looked at you pleadingly, hoping that you could possibly offer some help. Where did you begin?

Working with people who have multiple personalities is in some ways no different from working with any kind of client. As with any new client, once you get past the formalities of introducing yourselves and going over office policies, it's generally a good idea to begin by finding out what it is that is bringing them into therapy. Within the first few sessions with any client, you should be working on figuring out goals of therapy as well as formulating some sort of treatment plan to help meet these goals.

Depending on the information provided by the client, you may or may not have confirmation that your client has multiple personalities. Obviously, the diagnosis of your client will play a big part in the types of therapeutic strategies you provide, so the sooner you can discern this information, the better. You may even decide that you feel more comfortable referring an individual who has a certain diagnosis, such as DID, to another therapist who is better suited for this type of client. In most cases, however, you're likely to be working with a client for a while before you determine that a diagnosis of DID is appropriate. Awareness and recognition of the symptoms and behaviors of DID, as well as of dissociation itself, will help you begin your work with the client.

You may not routinely ask questions that would give you information that may lead you to conclude that your client is dissociative. If you find that clients have been abused or have gaps in the knowledge of their past, you may decide it is helpful to do a dissociative survey (such as the one presented in chapter 2 of this book or a more standardized scale, such as the Dissociative Experiences Survey).

Recognizing Dissociative Behaviors and Symptoms

Dissociation is often difficult to determine. Few clinicians have had training in recognizing the symptoms of dissociation. And, to make things even more troublesome, most people with DID are able to dissociate with few obvious signs. You may think that your client is totally engaged in a conversation with you, only to find out later (from your client's own report) that they had been dissociated, or not really present, during the entire session. People with DID are masters at dissociation (as the name of the diagnosis would suggest) and are able to use this talent so effectively that you will likely have problems determining the extent of their dissociative abilities. You will definitely want to ask some pointed questions regarding dissociation when you assess the applicability of a DID diagnosis.

> *I now realize that many therapists are not aware of how to assess whether a client is dissociative. At one point in time, I was seeing a therapist and I would be "gone" for most of each session. My body was there, it's just that the rest of me wasn't. I thought this was what therapy was—I had never been in therapy before. I just knew that as soon as the mention of family or childhood would come up, I would try to disappear and wait until the session would end. My therapist would sit patiently and wait until I would say something, and then begin talking as if I had not left. At the end of the session, I wanted to hurt myself. I thought this was what therapy was about.*

Diagnostic Issues

If you have already worked with DID clients, you probably already know that diagnosing DID can be very difficult. In fact, people with DID spend an average of six years in therapy before receiving an accurate diagnosis. There are many similarities between DID and other diagnoses, so if you are having (or have had) difficulty diagnosing a client, you are not alone. Most individuals with DID receive diagnoses of schizophrenia, Bipolar Disorder, and Borderline Personality Disorder, as well as various mood disorders, prior to being correctly diagnosed.

There are a variety of reasons why it is difficult to accurately diagnose an individual as having DID. First, you may be seeing several alters in your office, sometimes within the same session. Because of this, it may appear as if your client is rapidly changing moods, problems, and general ways of being. In reality, this is true due to the fact that you are seeing several "individuals," each with their own issues, personalities, and views about psychotherapy. Unless you realize that your client is changing personalities, you may have difficulty ascertaining a diagnosis, and instead only be able to pin down that your client is unable to focus, seems resistant to therapy, has a poor memory, and is inconsistent and unpredictable. But upon obtaining a proper diagnosis, all of these characteristics suddenly make sense: Your client is simply more than one individual, with each personality expressing his or her self.

Another reason why misdiagnosis is so common is that many diagnoses have symptoms which are very similar to those presented with DID. For instance, the alters will each have their own mood state at any given moment. When these alters begin to emerge, it may appear as if the individual sitting in front of you is having wild mood swings. Labile moods are often seen in Bipolar Disorder and Borderline Personality Disorder. You may also notice your client seeming to respond to internal cues, which is one symptom of a psychotic disorder. However, unless you are aware that your client is listening to actual personalities inside them, you might opt for a diagnosis reflecting this seeming psychosis, such as schizophrenia, substance-induced psychosis, certain mood disorders with psychotic features, or an undetermined psychotic disorder.

A third reason why you may have difficulty determining an accurate diagnosis for an individual with DID is that you may actually be diagnosing several of the alters. And while each of these diagnoses may be correct for that respective alter, as the alters change, your diagnosis will also need to change. Without an awareness that your client has DID, you may feel perplexed as to why your client who was depressed the previous week is now sitting in front of you completely problem free.

One challenge that you may face as a therapist is knowing which questions to ask. Individuals who have DID have grown up during their entire lives with the symptoms you are trying to identify, so they may not realize that not everyone has them. They will not come to visit you and say, "Oh, by the way, I have these other people inside me who have conversations, and lately, they have been making it difficult for me to concentrate and focus my attention."

> *By the time we entered therapy, we only knew that something in our life was not working. We didn't have a way to explain what was happening to us to a therapist because we didn't know that what we experienced was any different from any other person. Because we had experienced these symptoms throughout our entire life, we didn't realize that they were unique. I remember how stunned I was when I found out that everyone couldn't become a tree or a bird, or that they didn't hear constant chatter in their head.*

DID can also be a problematic diagnosis to make because it is viewed as rare. Illusory correlation is a social-psychological term that means that humans place what they experience in the world into existing categories within their minds. For example, if you believe that left-handed people are more artistic than right-handed people, and you see a left-handed person sculpting a statue more amazing than Michelangelo's "David," you will use that information to confirm your beliefs. In other words, in your mind you will think to yourself, "Oh, another left-handed artist. I guess they really are more artistic than right-handed people." However, if the same person had been right-handed, you would have most likely ignored the connection between artistic abilities and handedness. Illusory correlation basically means that people see what they believe (which serves to strengthen their beliefs), and they disregard the rest. In terms of DID, clinicians generally do not think of a diagnosis of DID as a possibility because it is rarely diagnosed. Instead, if you are presented with complaints such as dissociation, hearing voices, mood swings, or depression, you are more likely to place these symptoms into a diagnosis which you more frequently use, disregarding information which does not fit that particular diagnosis.

For all of the reasons discussed, as well as factors particular to the individual case, it is extremely difficult to accurately diagnose DID, which is why making the diagnosis generally takes so long.

If You Don't Believe in DID

Many people, clinicians and otherwise, don't believe that DID actually exists. Some of these people feel that the person claiming to have DID is putting on an elaborate act for attention-getting purposes. Some believe that DID is actually facilitated by other clinicians, who persuade their clients to accept false recovered memories, as well as assist the client in splitting personality traits into clearly defined alters. If you are a clinician and you believe that DID is not a true or valid psychiatric disorder, or if you believe that anyone claiming to have DID is simply fabricating symptoms, then you should not be working with this particular population. Referring an individual who presents with symptoms of DID or claims to have DID is your best and most appropriate course of action and serves to protect the welfare of your client.

> *We do not know about other people with the diagnosis of DID, but it was not what we aspired to be when we grew up. If we could make ourselves whatever we wanted, we would choose to be a Nobel Prize winner or at least a successful gambler (maybe we just went to the wrong therapist—we have to look in the ads and find ones who address issues of gambling and Nobel laureates).*

> Karen: *Seriously, though, there are therapists who have diagnosed clients with DID who may not actually meet the clinical criteria for diagnosis. They may encourage their clients to create personalities and may feed ideas and information during the sessions that would reinforce this diagnosis. Unfortunately, the field of therapy has some individuals in it who should not be treating people. These therapists set up their clients and harm their clients by creating and then treating an issue that is not real.*

> *If a client does not have DID and the therapist is treating the client for being DID, the client will not improve and more than likely will deteriorate. It is not possible to treat something that does not exist. Equally harmful to a client is to treat him or her as though the symptoms and*

behaviors they exhibit, which meet the criteria of DID, are a diagnosis other than DID. The client again will not improve, but will continue to have problems functioning in their life.

Karen and the little ones: *For a long time, we wanted to believe that we had made us all up, because it was easier for us to accept that we were so crazy that we made up all of the behaviors. We had read about people who made up their personalities and therapists who created alters, so we knew that was possible. Over time, we realized that even though some bad therapists may have mistreated their clients, that was not true for us. We finally got better when we began to learn how DID works and how to handle the problems that occur with DID.*

It may be particularly harmful to individuals who may have DID if you provide therapy when you do not accept or believe in the diagnosis. People with DID typically have severe problems trusting others. It is important for those with DID to be in an atmosphere where trust is fostered. If you believe your client is fabricating or exaggerating symptoms, you're already damaging the level of trust between you and your client. This, in turn, will further damage your client's already diminished ability to trust. The goal of treatment is not the diagnosis, but helping the person heal. From the therapists we have talked with over the years, we do believe that there may have been a few of those clinicians' clients who made up the symptoms of DID. However, these few should not be allowed to prevent legitimate DID symptoms from being accurately diagnosed. As with any client who is misdiagnosed, treatment can prove to be ineffective and may even result in a decline of the client's level of functioning.

Furthermore, if you neglect to recognize a DID diagnosis because of your personal biases, you may be planning and providing treatment contraindicated by this disorder. For instance, you may be treating your DID clients as if they are simply trauma survivors. In this case, the treatment strategies you would utilize (such as eye movement desensitization and reprocessing [EMDR], or having the client repeatedly share the story of the trauma) may serve to retraumatize or harm your client's well-being.

Regardless of your experience and your ability to work with a variety of clients, if you do not believe in DID and you are considering treating an individual who may have DID, it is in your client's best interest to obtain a referral to another trained therapist who does believe that DID is a valid and treatable disorder. Even if you are accepting of the diagnosis of DID and have had a wide range of experience working with clients who are survivors of sexual or physical abuse, you will still need to seek resources to continue your education. It is unfair to yourself and to your client to believe that all of the things that work with survivors who are not DID will work with clients who are DID. There is very little literature that will provide you with treatment approaches needed to really help your client. It would be important that you attend conferences and seek supervision from someone who is skilled in this area.

Creating Safety for You and Your Client

You would probably agree that for any type of psychotherapy to be effective, it is essential that both the therapist and the client feel safe. Safety allows for more open and honest expression and self-disclosure.

In order for therapists to provide adequate therapy, they must feel safe. Otherwise, they cannot focus on their clients' issues enough to be of help to the client. Recently, Tracy was working with a man in his mid-thirties on issues related to anxiety and depression. This man was communicative, insightful, and enjoyable to work with. After working with him for several months, she found out that he had murdered two people four years prior to seeing her. Once she knew of this fact, her work with him suffered greatly. During their sessions together her focus was on her own safety. Would she be able to make it to the door before him if he decided to attack her? Would someone hear her if she needed to scream for help? Needless to say, she was unable to concentrate on therapeutic issues because the concern for her own safety was so great.

After working with this man in an ineffective manner for several weeks, Tracy began to establish a sense of safety for herself, which allowed her to help him more proficiently. Tracy built safety for herself by physically changing her environment and moving her chair closer to the door than her client's chair. This way, if something was to happen, she would be able to get out of her office and shout for help. Also, Tracy made sure that she scheduled sessions for this client at times when other therapists were sure to be near by. Again, this provided her with a greater sense of security. Tracy also began to explore the situation around the murder. The man had been heavily using methamphetamine at the time and became paranoid and violent during a drug deal, which resulted in the murder of two drug dealers. Immediately following this incident, her client stopped using drugs and has been clean and sober since then. Once she learned more of the details, she began to feel more comfortable and was much more effective at providing therapy.

Although none of the clients you work with may be murderers, some of the alters you work with may have histories of violence toward themselves or others, and if you fear for your own safety, chances are you will not be providing good therapy. It is necessary that you discover a way that you can feel safe while you are working with those who may scare you.

Similarly, your clients need to feel safe within the session. Safety issues for your DID clients stem from a number of sources. First, there are the issues of safety and trust that occur within your office. Your DID clients may not trust you and may even feel as if you are out to hurt them. You need to find a manner of rapport with your clients so that you can discuss these issues and make your office into a safe and comfortable place. Also, your DID clients may feel unsafe with themselves. They may be worried that one of their alters will wants to hurt them in some manner. Self-inflicted violence and other self-destructive behaviors are fairly common among those with DID. Because of this, you will need to find a way to work with the alters who are presenting the potential danger, as well as with the alters who act as protectors, and find some way to instill safety. Lastly, your clients will probably believe that people from the past present a significant danger (and sometimes they might). Usually individuals with DID are threatened or coerced into believing that telling others about the trauma or abuse will result in violence, or possibly even death. In most cases, when you are working with adult survivors of this type of trauma who haven't been subjected to this type of abuse for a significant amount of time, these threats will be unfounded. However, for those clients of yours who are in continued contact with their abusers, you will want to assess for the veracity of these threats. Remember, part of building safety is never placing your client in danger.

There are several ways in which to create safety. First, you will need to make your office a safe place for your DID client. This may involve removing triggering items from your bookshelf, arranging your chairs in a different way, or even adjusting the lights or temperature of the office. You should discuss with your client if any of these or other changes need to be made in order to make the office a place of safety. Additionally, you may want to suggest to your clients that they bring in objects which make them feel more secure. For example, one woman Tracy worked with would bring in a teddy bear for her child alter, which would often appear during the sessions. This helped her to feel more comfortable and safe.

You may also want to schedule appointments with your DID clients at particular times of the day when they feel less scared. For example, it may be very frightening for your DID clients to leave their homes after sunset, and it may be helpful to schedule these clients only in the morning or early afternoon.

Your clients will also feel more secure if they know your availability. You should be direct and consistent with your DID clients about how and when you will be available. It is important that you set boundaries that work with your life, because the work can be intense. You may not have total availability for your clients after office hours. If this is the case, let your clients know when they can expect to hear from you and help them define other backup support.

The most important thing that you need to remember when working with your DID clients and trying to establish safety is to be honest. Your DID clients are very intuitive and perceptive and will usually know when you are being dishonest. Lying to your clients is a sure way to damage any sense of trust or safety you have established with them.

Talking with the Alters

It may take a while before you are able to communicate directly with the alters. Remember, people who have been traumatized often have great difficulty trusting others. As for your client, they may feel they are taking a big risk by allowing an alter to communicate with you. Be patient. Once DID clients feel as if they can trust you and that you won't have a negative reaction to the alters, the other personalities will start to emerge.

Depending on your client and the situation at hand, alters may or may not spontaneously appear. At times you may need to ask to speak with a certain personality. It is best if you do this directly and simply ask to speak with that alter or ask if that alter can come out. Sometimes the answer will be "no," that you cannot talk with a particular alter, and you should accept this (although you can try to inquire as to why).

You will probably be able to identify a change in personalities prior to anything being said. Most alters have their own style of being. Each may have his or her own mannerisms, posture, and way of sitting. Some alters may have even more dramatic differences, such as a desire to curl up in a ball on the floor, or even physical changes such as walking with a limp or needing eyeglasses. Once words have been spoken, you'll usually be able to tell for sure if a switch has taken place. Each alter has his or her own way of speaking and own voice. Some of the alters may sound very childlike, both in tone and language used, while others may sound more mature. As you get to know each alter, you'll also begin to be able to more easily identify who is out.

Learning how to communicate with each alter is very important. Some alters are children and may have a very limited vocabulary. Some may be so young that they are not able to speak, but instead communicate with nonverbal language. You may find that some are more candid than others and some may be more shy. You are, in essence, meeting an entire family. And, just like in any family therapy situation, your job is to develop a sense of each family member and work on communicating effectively with everyone there. Communicating effectively often involves creating a different way of relating to each family member. Thus, when you are learning how to talk with the alters, keep in mind that there will be great variety in the way you communicate with each of them.

Boundaries

In performing psychotherapy with any client, boundaries are essential. Clients need to understand and adhere to the limitations of the therapeutic treatment in order for therapy to be effective. When you are working with clients who have Dissociative Identity Disorder, issues of boundaries and limitations are sure to be present.

Because many of those with DID were physically, sexually, or emotionally abused as children, their ideas of boundaries may be a bit skewed. Through the abuse, these individuals developed a warped set of boundaries. For instance, most people learn that their bodies are not to be touched inappropriately or by people they don't know or trust. Many individuals who have been sexually or physically abused are taught that they don't have control over and can't have limitations for their own bodies—that any boundaries can be broken or ignored. This lack of appropriate boundaries may spill over into other areas of their lives, including therapy.

Boundaries may also be difficult for those clients with DID because in many cases you will be the only person who knows about the DID. You may be your client's only source of support or release for issues related to DID. In fact, some of the alters may have no contact with other individuals besides you. Thus, the demands for your attention and assistance may raise boundary issues.

Setting up boundaries with your DID clients may be a bit different than with your typical clients. First, because there is not always co-consciousness between alters, you will want to put statements regarding your availability and unavailability in writing and have your client agree to place this list in a spot where all of the alters can access it. This list of your accessibility will not be useful unless it is able to be viewed by the alters who need it at that particular moment. Also, you should verbally discuss these boundaries with your client and give clear examples of your limitations. You may need to do this with each alter. For instance, if you do not return telephone calls on weekends, inform your client of this verbally and in writing, and offer some options to your client. If you charge for time spent on the telephone, notify your client of this.

Specific areas in which you may want to delineate your boundaries with clients include:

- Fees: How much do you charge for a session? How much do you charge for phone consultation (if you do this)? Do you charge clients if they miss a session (and is there a specific amount of time required to cancel a session without financial penalty)?

- Availability: When are you generally available for sessions? Do you ever see clients on weekends or holidays? How often do you take vacations (and how long is each vacation)? How can you be reached outside of the scheduled session? Do you carry a pager? How often do you check messages? How do you respond to emergencies or crisis calls? What other options do your clients have if they are unable to reach you?

- Boundaries within the session: How long is each session? Are there any circumstances in which you would extend the length of a session? Are you willing to schedule longer sessions (this may be helpful if it takes certain alters a substantial amount of time before they feel comfortable enough to appear in your office)? Are there certain behaviors which you will not allow (e.g., being verbally or physically violent)? Are there certain behaviors in which you will not partake (e.g., you will not touch or hug clients under any circumstances)?

Most problems related to boundaries can be averted if you are clear, direct, and consistent about your own rules and limitations. Although being consistent may be difficult, it is essential in work with DID clients. Through the abuse they likely suffered and through the trauma they have endured, they completely understand inconsistency and surprise. It is your responsibility as a therapist, and as someone who truly wants to help for them, to teach your clients that they must adhere to and expect limitations and rules related to therapy. In doing so, you are teaching them about personal responsibility and you are keeping yourself from feeling overwhelmed or burdened by your clients.

You will play a greatly important role in the lives of your clients with DID. While you are not expected nor required to meet all of the needs of your clients, you should be direct and consistent with your clients in terms of what you are able to provide to them by way of availability, services, support, and ethics.

Adverse Treatment Strategies

An overwhelming majority of the time, DID is at least partially caused by some form of overwhelming trauma. The type of trauma, the duration of the trauma, and how the trauma is experienced emotionally and physically will be particular to each individual with DID. It will be important to assess, as well as you are able to, the nature of the trauma or abuse which occurred.

Although most clinicians receive extensive training and experience in dealing with issues of abuse and trauma, few are trained to work with DID clients. There are some significant differences between treating issues of trauma within the general population and with individuals with DID. If you choose to treat your DID clients as if they were simply survivors of abuse or trauma, you may be creating the potential to harm your clients.

Traditional treatment of trauma involves having the client tell and retell (many times) the story of the trauma. In many cases, this is an entirely effective approach in working with trauma survivors, as it helps the traumatic event lose its power and helps the client regain a sense of empowerment. However, with clients who have DID, this approach may backfire. Having the DID client relate stories of abuse, without taking specific precautions, will often lead to direct retraumatization, allowing some of the alters (particularly the very young ones) to feel as if they are currently being traumatized. Some alters have difficulty discerning the present from the past. These alters may feel as if events from the past are occurring at the present time. Flash-backs like this are more likely to occur when something triggers them, such as the recall of memories surrounding traumatic events. Thus, when you ask your clients to repeatedly recall and relate abu-sive events, you are creating a situation in which some of the alters will feel as if they are reexperiencing the original abuse. This reexpe-riencing of the abuse can be as terrifying and traumatic as the original abuse which occurred.

It is extremely important to find ways to help the client with DID create safety for the host and the young alters prior to having the client work on the trauma. The young alters do not know that life has changed. Often, the little ones do not know that there are other ones that can help them feel safe. The little ones that experienced the hurt often go back inside after the trauma is over. The host personalities safety was maintained by keeping the little ones with the hurt iso-lated, so that the host personality would not be aware of anything bad. Until the little ones learn that there is a difference between the past abuse and the present safety, they may react to discussions of the abuse as if they are currently in danger.

It can also take a while for the little ones to realize that there are adults that do not hurt little ones. In their world, adults are bad and there to hurt the child. Part of establishing a sense of safety in the lit-tle ones is teaching them that it was bad adults that hurt them, and that there are good adults in the world. If you begin to have the client focus on the trauma before they realize how to communicate among their alters, you will likely find that your client may have a harder time coping day to day.

> *When I began experiencing flashbacks, my first therapist spent a great deal of time having each one of the little ones describe what they were experiencing. He was someone who was known for his skill in working with people with a history of sexual abuse and came very highly recommended. When I began therapy with him, I kept having these weird feelings, thoughts, and pictures that would invade my waking time. These were often abuse pictures which had many bloody images. I did not understand the pictures and rarely discussed them with anyone because I believed that I would be diagnosed as psychotic.*
>
> *Since I was studying to be a clinician, I knew that these symptoms were part of being identified as psychotic. People who study any type of diagnosis often go through the process*

of diagnosing themselves. I never did tell anyone about the discussions that went on in my head, which had been going on since I was five or six.

The gross pictures were more troublesome because they would stay with me during the day, no matter what I was doing. When I would visit my therapist, he would sit down with each of the little ones who were seeing the pictures and have them explain them in more detail. What occurred as a result of this is that I spent the better part of the next two years living with trauma on a daily basis. I did not know how to change the pictures or stop them, so I would visit him frequently when things were really bad—two or three times a week—and try and find a way to relieve the pressure. I know now that this process did not help me at all, because each time the little ones would share their hurt, I would end up reliving the abuse and then have to cut off all feelings so I could return to work.

I have since found that many therapists understand how to work with sexual abuse and resulting Post-Traumatic Stress Disorder, but many do not understand that there is a difference in treating those of us living with DID. When I began to discuss the issues of dissociation with some of my colleagues who were experienced therapists, they did not even know how to begin to ask questions. If the therapist was an abuse survivor, then often they had a better understanding of the coping skills people develop to survive abuse. If you don't know that there is a question to ask, it is difficult to get the information you need.

Recovered Memories

Refuters of recovered memories suggest that some individuals, alone, or with the help of others (such as therapists), create memories of events which never occurred. There is no doubt that people are able to create and distort memories. And there is also no doubt that even when people are remembering an event which actually took place, their memories are laden with inaccuracies. However, while many people may not be able to remember the name of their first grade teachers, they usually do remember that she existed and whether she was pretty or young. Thus, while memory is very subjective and often inaccurate, it is difficult to totally misremember an important figure or event within your life.

We can understand that some people remember events differently from exactly how they occurred, but even so, it seems unlikely that many people could or would "make up" memories that were that unbelievable.

Individuals with DID may be accused of creating and presenting false recovered memories for several reasons. First, the often violent and horrific nature of the memories are difficult for others to believe. So, while most people are able to believe that someone had been molested by a relative, they might not believe that an individual was gang raped or witness to ritualistic torture (or murder), because this type of trauma is so far out of their realm of ordinary experience.

As an analogy, imagine that you're talking to someone you don't know, and he tells you that he has won five dollars playing the lottery. You would probably believe him without a problem. Now imagine the same person telling you that they won five million dollars in the lottery. You might doubt him initially until you saw evidence of his good fortune. Until he was able to produce evidence (the winning ticket, a new car, etc.), you might feel uncertain about the whole story.

Some clinicians won't accept the memories of their DID clients until they are able to see concrete evidence. The difficulty with this is that there is usually no such evidence to present. If any physical damage occurred during the course of the trauma, by the time the individual with DID comes to see you it is likely that many years have passed and any vestige of this damage is gone. Scars or internal damage may have occurred, but are unlikely to be seen or presented during the course of psychotherapy (and may even be unknown to the DID individual). The only evidence of the trauma that you are likely to confront is the presence of DID itself. DID develops as a mechanism for coping with severe trauma that generally occurs over an extended period of time. If your client has DID, you can be fairly certain that this individual has been through some sort of intense trauma.

Another reason why the recovered memories of people with DID may be refuted has to do with how these memories are presented within the therapeutic context. Because of the variety of alters who carry memories of the trauma, the presentation and explanation of the memories is likely to be diverse, and perhaps even contradictory. For example, one alter may inform you that there was no abuse or trauma, while another alter may tell you that he or she has survived severe ritualistic abuse. A third alter may be able to draw pictures of some of the abuse, but may not be able to discuss the abuse.

A different alter may have no verbal memory of the abuse, but may remember the abuse through body memories (see chapter 3 for more information on the topic of body memories). The memories presented to you by your DID client may be scattered, contradictory, and difficult to understand. For these reasons, you may be tempted to view the memories as being invalid. However, when you are hearing these stories and judging their accuracy or validity, try to view them a bit differently. Imagine that you are hearing about an event which occurred from several members of a family. Each family member will have a different take on what actually happened. Some family members may not remember the event, while others may relate the event in a nonchalant manner. Some may even contradict the others. Regardless of how each family presents the memory of the event, you are likely to believe in the existence of the event. Try to use the same strategy when dealing with a DID client. Although there are likely to be inconsistencies in the presentation of the memory, the memory as well as the event which spawned the memory are generally real.

Hypnosis

Individuals with DID are highly susceptible to hypnotism, which makes sense given that dissociation and the ability to be hypnotized are related. However, simply because an individual is able to be hypnotized does not mean that this is indicated psychotherapeutically.

Hypnosis with DID individuals should be used cautiously. Using hypnotism to elicit the presence of an alter and thereby confirm a diagnosis of DID may be indicated, but you can generally gain the same information without the use of hypnosis by simply speaking with an alter. While hypnosis may be useful in recovering memories which cannot be accessed through more traditional forms of psychotherapy, given enough patience, these memories would most likely be discovered later in the therapeutic process.

The use of hypnosis with DID individuals is generally contraindicated for several reasons. First, one of the goals of working with DID clients is to help them be able to control the communication between and the presentation of alters. Hypnosis places the client in a state in which this type of control is diminished. This loss of control is likely to make the client feel very anxious and fragmented. Second, use of hypnosis to recover repressed memories can also cause fragmentation and extreme anxiety for your client. Many of the alters are not able to face the memories of the trauma they endured. Child alters, in particular, may have great difficulty when presented with these often violent and traumatic memories. Hypnosis does not allow for selective screenings of memories. That is, when hypnotized, the individual with DID is not able to choose who may or may not have access to these memories. Because of this, hypnotism may cause some of the alters to feel as if they were reliving the remembered events and may result in actually retraumatizing the client. So, although hypnotism may be beneficial in some circumstances, it is generally not recommended.

> *One time we convinced our therapist to try using hypnosis. We had heard about it forever and had heard that you could use it to get through some blocks that you have in understanding the past. Well, one time was enough for us. Our therapist hypnotized one of us and that one decided to "clean house." We were doing an exercise to see if we could remove some of the troubling pictures that we kept seeing. The therapist had us imagine going into the library, taking out the book that held those pictures, and getting rid of it. Maybe it would have been okay if we had stopped at just one book, but the one who was hypnotized decided it was time to get rid of a lot of books, so she got carried away ... well, let's just say we were so spacey for the next week that we couldn't ever figure out what was going on or function well.*

Medication

Some individuals with DID may require medication for certain psychiatric difficulties, most likely depression or anxiety. When your client's psychiatric symptoms are so severe that they are creating difficulty in daily functioning, medication should be considered.

There are several factors to keep in mind, however, when addressing the issue of medication with your DID clients. Assessing the severity of the psychiatric problem should be a first step. Is your client functioning without medication? If so, medications probably aren't necessary. Is your client suffering great distress, such as severe depression or anxiety, which interfere with daily living? If so, medication may be a possibility.

Secondly, you should assess the complaints and symptoms of each alter. While one alter may be very depressed and even suicidal, another may feel just fine. It is likely that with DID clients, more than one medication may be beneficial, depending on the symptoms of various alters. Make sure to adequately follow the progress of your clients with DID. Often, you will need to spend a good deal of time assessing and reassessing the correctness of dosage and type of medication. When you are checking with your clients, let each alter describe his or her experience of the effectiveness of the medication.

Even if you are unable to prescribe medication, it's important for you to know how your clients are affected by the medications they are taking. Sometimes your clients will tell you much more information about how they are affected by these medications than they will tell the person who prescribed them. It may be that the individual who prescribes the medication doesn't even know about your client's multiple personalities. You will probably want to speak with the prescribing doctor and work as a team in order to provide the best possible therapy for your client.

Third, it will be important for you to understand the potential side effects of each medication and how these side effects may influence DID behavior. For example, some medications have sedating effects, which cause those who use the medications to feel "spaced out" and tired. These medications may increase dissociation, and the additional dissociation is likely to have a severe impact on individuals with DID. While taking these medications, they may find themselves having less control over which alters appear or when alters appear. This change in control over dissociation may be more problematic than the original symptoms for which the medication was prescribed.

Additionally, the physical consequences of some medication (such as liver and heart disease) can interfere with the psychotherapeutic progress. Most medications are designed to alleviate symptoms. In the case of DID, each alter may present with a different symptom, thus making any one medication unlikely to be effective. Also, many psychiatric medications will have side effects such as sleepiness, restlessness, and insomnia which may prevent the individual with DID from being able to accurately interpret or explore the underlying issues.

Imagine that you go to a medical doctor with a complaint of back pain. Your doctor prescribes you a certain medication which numbs your back and eases your pain. However, since taking the medication you find yourself unable to concentrate, sleepy, and a bit nauseated. When your doctor asks how you are feeling, you report these symptoms, but don't mention your original complaint—your back. You may still be having great difficulty with your back (the problems may even have worsened), but your attention has been diverted due to the prescribed medication. Thus, you never really get treatment for the cause of the original symptom. This is how medication can affect people with DID.

Finally, it will be important for you to work closely with the person who is prescribing the medication (if it isn't you). Make sure that the prescribing doctor is aware that your client has DID and how this would affect the usefulness of the medications. If the psychiatrist or medical doctor does not believe in DID, you should get your client a referral to someone who does. It will greatly benefit your client if you work as a team, communicating and conferring about the most appropriate course of treatment for your client.

> *You may want to help your client come up with ways to make sure that they do remember to take medicine. It can be hard, even for people who track time well and don't lose things, to remember to take medicine on a regular basis. It becomes even harder with someone who has DID. Some strategies include pill boxes and leaving all the pills in one place that your clients go by during the day, so that over the course of the day they remember to take the medications.*

Hospitalization

Hospitalization of DID clients should be done with the utmost of care and only in extreme situations. While hospitalization is usually effective in reducing suicidal ideation and gives an individual a safe place to be, it also steals from the client a sense of control and independence. Control is extremely important to everyone. People feel better when they are in control of themselves and their environment. They even stay healthier physically when they feel in control of their lives. When people don't or can't have control of themselves or their environment, they react. Some react to a lack of control by being aggressive and rebellious, some by being docile and passive, and some in other ways. These reactions are generally based in fear.

Individuals who have been abused or otherwise traumatized have experienced lack of control as being dangerous. In fact, it was when others (or other forces) were in control that the trauma occurred. For instance, when Jane was three years old, she was repeatedly sexually abused by her uncle. At age three, realistically, Jane had little control over her life, and certainly not enough control to oppose a grown man. Jane, however, was able to control her thoughts, her mind, and how she experienced herself in her body.

She was able to develop alters who were present during the abuse while she protected herself by dissociating from the violent events around her. This was the beginning of Jane's having DID. Like Jane, many with DID have histories of severe and repeated abuse or trauma. When you are working with survivors of abuse, particularly abuse of the severity and intensity found in the histories of most DID individuals, the issue of control is enormous.

The hospitalization of an individual with DID is a bit more complicated than with clients with other disorders. Therefore, with DID clients, the issue of control is primary. When you choose to hospitalize someone with DID, you are taking away his or her power and control. You also run the risk that the hospital staff may not believe in DID, and then your client is put in a no-win situation. There are some facilities that are better about treating this issue than others. If you're unable to help your client maintain support and safety from people in the home, hospitalization may be the best answer during an extreme crisis. But, if you do determine that hospitalization is the best option, make sure to talk with your client about this decision.

Ethical Issues

Many people who have DID engage in self-destructive or self-injurious behaviors (see chapter 3). At certain points within the therapeutic process, this potential for self-harm may become intensified to such an extent that issues related to confidentiality and ethics become relevant. Whenever the welfare of clients is at stake, ethical issues must be addressed. While each licensing agency has its own set of ethical standards, practices, rules, and laws, most postulate that clinicians are bound to act in ways that support the welfare of their clients.

While each case of DID will be unique, it is important to accurately assess the potential for severe self-harm or self-injury. Whenever you are confronted with issues of self-harm, it may be useful for you to consider the following questions in determining whether to take action and, if so, what action to take:

- What is the ethical issue?

- What are the laws, rules, or codes governing this issue? (Your answers to this question will depend on the type of license you have and the state in which you work.)

- Are you mandated by law to take any action, such as in cases of suspected child abuse?

- What are your options?

- What are the benefits and risks of each option?

- What information do you need to make this decision?

- How is this decision likely to affect your clinical work with this client?

- How will you go about implementing this decision?

- How do you think the client will respond to this decision?

Working with DID individuals is likely to raise ethical issues. For instance, one woman Tracy worked with who had DID arrived for her first session with Tracy with a very interesting and difficult treatment goal: She wanted to feel good enough so that she had enough strength and energy to kill herself. Another woman with DID who Tracy treated tried several times to commit suicide by overdosing on sleeping pills. Each time she would take a handful of these pills, one of her alters who didn't want to die (and who also happened to be bulimic) would vomit the pills and successfully thwart the attempt. As you can probably get a sense from these two examples, the problems presented in therapy by those with DID are not so ordinary and may require you to obtain more information and, as always, to use your best judgment. By staying aware of the issues which are particular to DID, you are taking an important step in ensuring the welfare of your clients.

Resistance

Individuals with DID are a unique population to work with in therapy. In essence, you are performing therapy with several (if not more) individuals at one time. Because of this, you will find differences in opinion with regard to the prescribed course of treatment. For instance, while one alter may be really enthusiastic about telling her story of abuse, another alter may forbid this from happening because of previous threats from the original abuser. In your office, you may experience this disagreement between alters as resistance.

Resistance refers to a client's lack of adherence to a prescribed treatment. The client may simply refuse to participate in the suggested treatment activity or may act inconsistently, thus damaging the treatment. For example, at some point in your life, you have probably had an infection and been prescribed antibiotics. Usually antibiotics are prescribed for seven to ten days. If you took the medication for a few days, started to feel better, and then quit taking the antibiotics before the prescribed amount of time, you could be considered resistant to the treatment. Resistance for individuals with DID may appear in a variety of forms, including the refusal of an alter to appear for therapy, the denial of issues which had previously been discussed and accepted in therapy, or a more direct refusal to participate in suggested treatment activities.

Resistance generally stems from fear or from plans for treatment which are viewed as inappropriate by the client. Regardless of diagnosis, most people who enter therapy will find change to be scary and difficult. Most psychotherapy asks that clients alter their patterns of thought and behavior. Because these changes occur on such a fundamental and deep level, they are often met with fear, anxiety, and apprehension. Some of your clients are likely to reject your prescribed treatment simply because they are scared of changing what is familiar to them. Identifying, exploring, and working through this fear is the best way to conquer resistance.

Your DID clients have developed an intricate and effective system of coping with the world. Asking them to change these ways of being is likely to produce a great deal of anxiety and resistance.

Your clients may also be resistant to therapy that does not suit their needs. Your DID clients may not be willing to integrate their alters, even if you feel that this is the best course of action. By suggesting that your clients act in accordance with your wishes and disregarding their own desires, you are creating a situation in which psychotherapy has the potential to be ineffective and possibly harmful.

Additionally, if you are concentrating on integration of the alters, you are essentially asking each alter to give up his or her own life for the well-being of the host personality. Integration is likely to evoke such fundamental fears, including the fear of death, that it will often result in high levels of resistance.

Imagine if you were asked to give up your own life in order to make your family stronger. You would probably not succumb to this plan very easily. This is one reason why we advocate for first establishing a sense of safety and coconsciousness and helping the client develop a coping plan for their current life (which includes all of the alters). It is only after addressing these issues, and only if it is the desire of the client to integrate, that we approve of pursuing the treatment goal of integration.

Each time you work with an individual who has DID, you're sailing in uncharted territory, and you need to approach each of these clients as unique individuals, developing appropriate treatment plans for each of them. When the DID clients you are working with show signs of resistance, it may be a signal for you that the treatment you are providing may not be appropriate for them at that point in time.

In determining the cause and the solution for resistance, it's best if you speak about the resistance you perceive directly with the client. Pointing out to clients that they are not acting in accordance with the treatment plan is a good starting place. From this point, you will be able to determine if the client is being resistant due to fear, disagreement with the prescribed treatment, or because they don't understand what the treatment actually entails. You may be able to resolve resistance through simple clarification of treatment goals.

Group Therapy

The idea of group therapy with a bunch of individuals with DID seems like the beginning of a bad joke. Couldn't you just have group therapy with one DID person? In actuality, however, using groups as a form of therapy for DID individuals does have its uses.

It is true that you can have a group with one person with DID, but it is much more fun with at least two of us. Then all of our alters can all have someone new to talk with!

Group therapy can be effective with DID individuals in several manners. First, because many individuals with DID feel so alone and so isolated, using a group to help build a sense of support and community is very therapeutic. As you know, and as your DID clients will tell you, there is such a sense of shame and secrecy about having DID that many of those with DID tell very few others and keep this secret to themselves. This secrecy and shame supports the idea that DID is only a negative trait. In fact, many aspects of DID are positive (see chapter 6), and the therapeutic benefits are immeasurable for your clients to be able to truly express who they are and get to be fully themselves with a group of people. Group therapy allows DID individuals to connect with others like them and feel support and a sense of belonging.

Group therapy is also helpful in that it allows your clients to present alters which may have to remain hidden in other situations. For example, in a safe, support-group setting, child alters may come out to play or appear for other reasons.

You may also find that group therapy with DID people assists you in understanding the true dynamics of DID, as well as the underlying issues or problems which aren't apparent in your one-on-one work. For instance, within the group you will be able to view specific alters interacting with other individuals. You will see how these alters function in social settings and how they interact with the others.

While there is a potential for great benefit from group therapy, there are also some possible negative consequences. First, some of the issues which may be discussed in group therapy, such as trauma or abuse, may serve as triggers for other members of the group. So, while it may be healing for one member to tell the memory of his or her ritual abuse, these stories may increase the anxiety of other people within the group and may even cause further fragmentation, decompensation, or dissociation.

Also, as in any group-therapy experience, issues of confidentiality are likely to arise. Although group members agree to keep information in the group confidential, the likelihood of complete confidentiality is low. Exposing someone as having DID could have devastating consequences. An individual with DID who is functioning well at work may be viewed more suspiciously or even be asked to leave the job once a diagnosis of DID becomes public.

Integration

Integration refers to the fusion of alters into one consolidated identity. Most therapists have this as the ultimate treatment goal for their clients with DID. While this may be a common long-term goal, it is a goal which should be approached with great caution. Determining treatment goals is something which you should do in conjunction with your clients. Discussing and defining the goals of psychotherapy is an essential component of any successful therapy.

Many individuals with DID may choose to delay integration or refuse to accept the goal of integration altogether. To the individual with DID, integrating, or becoming one, means losing or killing the alters, who are part of that individual's being. For this reason, talking about integration prematurely will severely damage your rapport and work with your client. If your DID clients (or their alters) feel threatened in anyway they will not be amenable to therapy. If you decide that you are going to speak with your client about integration, wait until your client has been in therapy with you for a long period of time and you have an excellent rapport with each other. Generally, only at that point can integration be viewed as a treatment goal, rather than as a threat.

As a therapist, it is natural to have long-term goals for your clients. When working with clients who have DID, you may have the ultimate therapeutic goal of integration. However, there are several issues to consider prior to raising the topic of integration with your client. First, regardless of your long-term goals, you will still need to help your client to function on a daily basis. With your help, your clients can learn strategies to increase coconsciousness and cooperation between alters. Your clients will also be able to improve how they regulate moods and behaviors. These issues, as well as other topics which enhance your client's daily functioning, should (at least initially) be your primary concern and the focus of therapy. Secondly, if and when you decide to speak with your client about the issue of integration, make sure that you are not placing your own needs before those of the client. Although you may wish to see your client integrated, your client may not (and may be functioning very well with multiple personalities). Your client's opinion, insight, and judgment counts at least as much as your own, and you should respect your client's thoughtful choices about the therapeutic process.

Supervision and Ongoing Education

It is important to find supervision from someone who has experience in this area. There is probably a network of professionals in your area who work with survivors of childhood abuse. Someone in this network should be able to give you a referral to a resource or a person who has some previous work in the area of DID. Screen your supervisor as you would screen for a therapist. Ask how many clients they have treated, what the average case was like, and what their beliefs are about treating clients with DID.

While ongoing education in all areas of psychology are extremely important, it is especially critical in the area of DID. Not much was known about DID until fairly recently, and now, with more and more information emerging, the necessity to keep current is vital. Take time to keep up on recent books or journals that have been published. Go to workshops or conferences which deal with issues of DID, dissociation, and trauma. Learn from those around you who work with clients who have multiple personalities. Basically, do whatever you need to do to continue to educate yourself on this topic. Not only will your clients benefit from this education, you will, too.

CHAPTER 10

For Partners

What Happens Now?

So you've found out that your partner has DID. You're probably asking yourself many questions, perhaps including, "What happens now?" Your initial reactions to learning that your partner has DID are likely to be influenced by the manner in which you found out about it. It's one thing to have your partner tell you he or she has multiple personalities, and it's another to walk in on your partner and find him or her sitting on the bedroom floor, speaking in a child like voice, having a tea party with stuffed animals. It may be that you have known about your partner's "moods," "forgetfulness," or "inconsistencies" for quite a while, and you simply haven't been able to put a name to it. Or it may be that these symptoms have more recently appeared and you are just learning of the underlying cause. Regardless, you are likely to have a variety of reactions when you find out that your partner has DID.

As the partner of a woman with DID states, "Sara and I knew each other for many years before we began to date. We would arrange to meet each other for lunch or coffee every so often. About half the time she wouldn't show up. I attributed her forgetfulness to a busy schedule, too many responsibilities, and general flakiness. When she finally told me about the DID, it all made sense."

What You May Feel

Your feelings upon learning that your partner has DID are likely to be intense and they may disturb you. It's highly improbable that you will greet this revelation with enthusiasm and joy (although you will hopefully grow to feel this way). In this society, DID is considered a mental illness, and with that label comes many negative perceptions and related stigma. Thus, it is important to examine your feelings about DID and having a partner with multiple personalities.

You may also wonder what it is about you that made you pick a partner with DID. You may have heard before that people generally end up in a relationship with someone who is somehow like their parents. Well, your parents probably were not DID. However, some of the DID-related qualities your partner has may be similar to qualities your parents had (e.g., changeable, unpredictable, forgetful, driven, dynamic, etc.).

Although you may not have known about the DID prior to seriously committing to your partner, you have probably always noticed the changes in your partner. If you have recently moved in together, you probably see even more changes in your partner than you did when you lived separately. As in any relationship, the more time you spend with each other, the more you'll notice and learn about one another. You did fall in love with at least part of your partner, there's just more to your partner than you planned. Understanding the diagnosis of DID may help you to make much more sense of your partner. After all, the behaviors are not new, it's just that now you have a framework to begin to understand his or her behavior.

Shock and Denial

As you get to further know your partner, you may find out that he or she was abused as a child. As the two of you develop a more open, trusting relationship, you will see the impact of this violation play out in your interactions. Today, many people have a fair amount of understanding about child sexual abuse and trauma, and they have a sense of how it impacts these children when they are adults. Sexual abuse places a difficult strain on any relationship, because the person you love has been violated; it is even more difficult for your relationship when this abuse was sexual, as it impacts your sexual relationship with your partner. Victims of childhood sexual abuse often have to spend time relearning how to be sexual in a healthy way.

Understanding the impact of sexual abuse, however, often will not prepare you for the results of severe childhood trauma and violation, which are generally precursors to DID. Take, for example, Jim and Rose, who had been together for two years. Jim knew that Rose had been abused as a child. The issue had come up in Rose's therapy, and they had spent time talking about how to help Rose heal in order to create a better relationship for them. As Rose became more aware of everything that was happening in her life, she began to wonder if there were events that she had experienced that she couldn't remember. She was having flashbacks, but many of these were feelings that would come seemingly from nowhere. She was also having constant nightmares.

Jim, a therapist who worked with adults who had been abused as children, knew about the impact the abuse had on their lives. He grappled with the issue at work, and then came home to see his wife going through similar trauma. At one point, Jim told Rose that he could handle anything but her having DID. A few days later, one of Rose's alters came out to ask Jim to help keep Rose's family away from her. Rose and Jim just let the incident go and acted as if it never occurred. Rose was exhibiting symptoms that suggested she could have had DID, but neither one of them could handle the issue. It wasn't until many months later that they actually began to acknowledge that DID was what Rose was living with.

Because DID is such a secretive disorder, you may be shocked to learn that a loved one has multiple personalities. You may not have made particular note of many of the signs of DID, such as your partner's forgetfulness, moodiness, or general inconsistency. You probably gave no thought to the frequently misplaced car keys, the lost checkbooks, or the complete changes in wardrobe. DID lends itself to secrecy quite well, in that the alters often stay hidden and can be concealed with relative ease. Also, people are often eager to ignore or deny many of the telltale signs of DID, because the truth initially seems impossible or overwhelming. Thus, when you finally did find out about your partner's other personalities, you may have been shocked.

Related to this feeling of shock is the behavior of denial. Families often overlook the alcoholic or the person with depression, because it is too much for them to deal with at the time. Well, DID is another issue that easily succumbs to denial. It's easy to convince yourself that ignoring something will actually make it disappear. When you learn that your partner has multiple identities, you may be very tempted to deny this fact and pretend that it does not exist. Acknowledging DID would mean not only accepting the presence of the alters and all that comes with them, but also accepting that your partner has had to endure and survive tremendous amounts of trauma in order to develop this style of being. As difficult as it may be to face, it is important that you do your best to accept the reality of your partner having DID.

To deny the existence of the alters will only communicate that you are not interested, not able to help, or do not believe your partner. If your partner is just beginning to understand his or her diagnosis, you will reinforce the issue that he or she is struggling with: that their reality is not real, that they are simply "crazy." Therefore, it is extremely important that, as you are confronted with your partner's multiple personalities, you do your best not to deny the reality of the situation and its implications. Although this may be difficult, responding to the DID, rather than denying its existence, is necessary in order to support and help your partner. This will also allow yourself to learn more about your partner and enjoy the many wonderful aspects of being with someone who has DID.

Confusion

Confusion is a normal reaction when you first find out about your partner having DID. Many people do not understand what having multiple personalities actually means (and now that the name has been changed from MPD to DID, it may seem even more confusing). Some people confuse multiple personalities with schizophrenia, a psychotic disorder believed to be caused at least in part by imbalances of chemicals found in the brain. Schizophrenics can hallucinate, lose touch with reality, become very paranoid, or even enter into and remain in catatonic states (states in which there is no physical movement for long periods of time). DID, on the other hand, is a dissociative disorder which is typically a reaction to a severe traumatic experience. Individuals with DID do not lose touch with reality or hallucinate in the same manner as those with psychotic disorders.

What you do know about DID may mostly stem from stories like *Three Faces of Eve*, *Sybil*, or *When Rabbit Howls*. If you are familiar with these stories, then you may rightly be confused when you see the person in your life acting "normal" (whatever that means) or not exhibiting any bizarre or unusual behaviors. You may also be confused if you had never met any of the alters. Sometimes the alters will decide that they should remain hidden from you. This is usually done as a means of self-protection for your partner. Your partner may feel afraid of your reactions to the alters and may protect herself or himself and the alters by keeping them away from you. Just like anyone, your partner's other personalities do not want to be rejected, ignored, or disbelieved. So even though your partner may have had awareness of the other personalities, they may not have been introduced to you.

Valerie, whose partner has DID, states, "I can remember one time, before I knew about the DID, when I was talking with my partner and she made some comment in a very funny voice. At the time, I wasn't sure if I had imagined it or not. I never mentioned it, because I didn't know what to make of it. Once I found out about the DID, the voice made sense to me, but I was really confused as to who I had been talking to all those years. I mean, was Barbara really Barbara, or was she someone else, and did she remember who I was, or did that change with each of her personalities. I was really confused."

Anger

Anger is another fairly common response to discovering your partner has multiple personalities. Anger in this situation typically stems from one of two sources. First, anger may be a response to feeling as if you have been deceived. You probably did not know that your partner had DID when you first got together. You may be angry due to the lack of disclosure of this information in the earlier stages of the relationship. Although your feelings of anger may be both valid and real (after all, all feelings are real), they will probably not do much to help your relationship with your partner. In sharing with you about the other personalities, your partner has taken a great risk. Your partner is facing possible rejection, abandonment, condemnation, embarrassment, and even potential psychiatric hospitalization. Voicing your anger to your partner will only serve to reinforce these fears.

Anger may also stem from your feelings toward the individual or group of people who perpetrated the trauma or abuse. You may be irate toward those who hurt your partner. Once again, although these feelings are intense, it would probably be best to keep them from your partner. Many people with DID have great difficulty dealing with the emotion of anger, both their own and that of others. By sharing your anger with your partner, you may be harming more than helping.

Sadness

The feeling of sadness is not likely to be an initial reaction to learning that your partner has DID, but rather a feeling that may emerge after you develop a better understanding of the causes of DID. Knowing that your partner has been subjected to severe trauma of some sort is likely to make you feel sad or sympathetic toward your partner. It is difficult to acknowledge the immense psychological and physical pain your partner has been through, causing your partner to create a coping mechanism as elaborate as DID, without responding emotionally. Understanding the extent of your partner's suffering is often a mixed blessing. On the one hand, it allows you to be of more help to that individual. However, it may also penetrate you deeply, causing you to feel intense sadness and psychological pain.

Warren's partner, Janice, has multiple personalities. He states, "It's easy to play with the alters and forget the reason behind their existence. Sometimes when I think of what happened to my partner, I get really sad. On one hand, I'm so glad that all of the others [the alters] are around; I really love them. But, when I think of why they're around ... it's just hard to think that someone could have hurt someone you love so much."

Shame and Embarrassment

Imagine calling your parents and telling them that you've just met the most wonderful person, a person who someday may become your life partner. You tell your parents about this individual's great sense of humor, creativity, insight, intelligence, and tremendous achievements. Most likely, your parents would be thrilled. Then, you add one more characteristic—this person has DID. If your parents are like most of society, this thrill would quickly turn to disappointment, and you could potentially feel ashamed or embarrassed by your partner's alters.

Shame and embarrassment are commonly felt emotions when learning that your partner has DID. You may be hesitant to tell those close to you about this condition. These feelings may prevent you from sharing this information with your friends and family or building a network of individuals who can support you through this discovery. Shame and embarrassment may also make you less open to talking with your partner about DID, which in turn helps to perpetuate the negative ideas associated with DID. If you don't talk about DID with your partner, you won't be able to learn more about what these personalities mean in your own life, and you're likely to continue believing that DID has only negative implications. In other words, shame and embarrassment can keep you from seeing the good aspects of your partner's multiple personalities.

Teresa describes the beginning of her relationship with Michelle: "When I initially began dating my partner, I called my parents and told them all of these wonderful things about her. Since she had been part of my life for a long time before we dated, they were really happy. In the same conversation, I said something like, 'I know that you may not approve of our dating because she has MPD, but I don't really care. I like her very much and we're going to date anyway.' Since then, they have been incredibly supportive of our relationship."

ACTIVITY 10.1: YOUR FEELINGS ABOUT YOUR PARTNER'S DID

This activity is designed to help you assess your feelings about your partner's multiple personalities. In this activity, you will be asked to rate the intensity of your emotions, both when you first learned of your partner's DID and right now. Through examining the extent of change in these emotions, you may be able to understand your own progression through this experience. You will likely find that the more exposure you have to the alters, the better you'll feel, and the feelings you had initially will weaken over time. Once you realize that your emotional reactions will change and lessen, you'll be better able to enjoy you partner and your relationship.

Use the following rating scale to assist you in determining how strongly you experience each of the listed feelings. Blank spaces have been left for you to add feelings which you feel are significant but are not listed.

0	1	2	3	4
not at all		moderately		very strongly

Emotion	Initial Strength	Present Strength
(example) *guilt*	4	2
guilt		
anger		
frustration		
sadness		
fear		
helplessness		
shock		
confusion		
denial		

Once you have finished with making this list and rating your emotions, take a few minutes and look at how and if the strength of your emotions has changed. You will likely find that your emotional reactions now are not as intense as they were at first.

What You May Think

It's no secret that thoughts and feelings influence one another. Julie Andrews' character in *The Sound of Music* aptly taught the Von Trapp children to imagine their favorite things as a way to change their emotions. Just like the characters in the story, your thoughts can affect your feelings and vice versa. When you are thinking negative thoughts, your emotions are also likely to be negative. By simply changing your thoughts and beliefs, you can change your emotions. Of course, changing your thoughts is much easier than it sounds. However, the first step in changing anything is to identify and describe what is occurring.

Your thoughts and beliefs about DID are most likely fairly negative. Society has given DID a bad rap, viewing people with DID as crazy, dangerous, or even dishonest. Some people believe that DID does not exist, and many of these people think that people with DID are either lying or have been persuaded by their therapists to think that they have multiple personalities. Unless you have received some education on DID or have had previous experience with DID, your thoughts may resemble these. As you learn more about your partner and about DID, your feelings about DID will likely change.

There are some common beliefs that partners of people with DID frequently have upon being told of the disorder:

- I should have known.
- I can fix this.
- You're nuts.
- This changes our whole relationship.
- You're not who I thought you were.
- I don't know who you are.

As you take inventory of your own thoughts and beliefs, it will be important for you to assess their accuracy. It is important to be aware of your thoughts so that you can prevent them from creating negative emotional responses; reacting harshly toward your partner can damage your relationship irreparably.

ACTIVITY 10.2: YOUR THOUGHTS ABOUT YOUR PARTNER'S DID

This activity will help you see the ways in which your thoughts influence your feelings. On the left side of this chart, list each of the thoughts you have regarding your partner's DID. On the right side, identify the emotion which is most closely linked with this thought. An example has been provided.

Thought	Feeling
I don't know who you are.	*confusion*

Once you have completed this list, take some time and think about how your thoughts and feelings influence your behaviors. In a journal or on a piece of paper, write about how your thoughts and feelings in regard to DID affect your behaviors. Do you refuse to discuss DID with others because you feel too uncomfortable? Do your thoughts lead to feelings of anger, which make you act irritated with the person who has multiple personalities?

Understanding how your thoughts and feelings combine to influence your behaviors will be important when you are trying to help your partner cope with their having DID.

What to Do and What Not to Do

You may be reading this and thinking to yourself, "Okay, I know that my partner has multiple personalities, but what should I do?" If you're asking yourself this, you have already begun to help. By wondering how to help your partner and your relationship, you are indicating that you have an investment in your relationship and a commitment to your partner. Being with someone who has DID isn't always easy or fun, but often times it can be extremely wonderful and gratifying. All relationships require attention and work in order to prosper, and relationships with those with DID are no exception. However, there are some specific things that you can do (and some that you probably shouldn't do) in order to help your partner, yourself, and your relationship thrive in the presence of DID.

Do Talk about DID

Many individuals with DID are highly vigilant and perceptive. If they believe that you are uncomfortable talking about DID, they will probably do the best they can to not make you confront the topic. They may simply not talk about what it is like to have DID, or they may even prevent you from meeting or being with certain alters. However, the alters exist whether you talk about them or not. As you know, ignoring something does not make it disappear. The same is true with DID: it will not go away because you pretend it doesn't exist.

It is extremely important that you speak to your partner about DID. Talking about DID will allow you to improve the quality of communication with your partner. Also, in talking about DID, you will likely be able to clear up your misconceptions about the disorder and gain critical information as to the ways in which DID will affect or has affected your relationship. By addressing the issues of DID, you are removing the secrecy which surrounds this diagnosis and are thereby reducing the shame attached to this disorder. You are encouraging connection between you and your partner and are helping to create change just by the mere fact that you are willing to discuss DID.

You may not know what to say to your partner. You may not even know how to address your partner: Do you call your partner by his or her name, by the name of an alter, or by some other name altogether? Even by simply acknowledging to your partner that you don't know what to say or that you are confused about names or alters, you are beginning to open the channels of communication.

Activity 10.3: Talking about DID

This activity will give you some ideas as to how to approach talking about DID. The following lists some questions and topics you might want to cover when discussing DID with your partner.

- How many alters do you have?
- What are their names and ages?
- Whom have I met?
- Whom am I speaking with now?
- How can I tell whom I am speaking with?
- How did you learn that you have multiple personalities?
- What is it like for you to talk with me about having multiple personalities?
- How often do you switch personalities?
- How open are you about having DID?
- What do each of the alters enjoy?
- What do each of the alters look like?
- How does having DID affect your life?
- What can I do to help?

Only through an open dialogue can these issues be discussed. It is necessary to talk about DID so that your relationship will be able to thrive, rather than waste away in misconceptions and silence.

Do Be Honest

As previously mentioned, individuals who have DID tend to be quite vigilant and perceptive. Awareness of others and of their environment was a tool used to ensure their survival in a childhood filled with trauma. Because of this vigilance, people who have multiple personalities are very good at discerning truth from lies. Chances are, if you lie to your partner, they will pick up on it.

Although it is sometimes difficult to be honest, it is always for the best when your partner has DID. Most people with multiple personalities were raised in environments filled with lies, deception, and duplicity. They learned that others cannot be trusted and that trust will generally lead to some type of emotional or physical trauma. While it is not your sole responsibility to try to repair this damaged trust, it is your duty as a partner to not damage it any further. By being dishonest with your partner, you are not only damaging the brittle trust which exists, you are giving your partner the covert message that he or she is not strong enough to handle the truth. People with DID are survivors, and honesty, no matter how difficult, will always be more helpful than harmful.

Honesty works best if delivered with a sense of loving and caring. In contrast, information delivered in an angry or hostile way, no matter how honest, can damage your relationship. Statements which carry the message, "I'm being honest with you because I care about you, and I think this information will help you," will be beneficial to your partner and help strengthen your relationship.

Honor Your Feelings

If you are not sure about remaining in a committed relationship with your partner because of the DID or because the two of you have other difficulties, stay true to yourself. It is not fair to you or to your partner to stay solely because you feel bad for what your partner has already experienced or because you believe that your partner will die without you. You have to be honest with yourself about what you need and want in the relationship. If you feel that you are not able to have your needs met in the relationship, it may be better if you leave. It can be potentially more damaging for the person with DID if you leave later in the relationship, after he or she has begun to trust you (though even then, you must be true to your own feelings and needs).

Watching and living with someone healing from child abuse is not easy. Understand that as long as your partner is in treatment with a good therapist he or she is going to get healthier. It is a long uphill battle that has many difficult times and many fun times. There may be times that your partner is unable to do many of the things you used to do together because he or she is having flashbacks, experiencing severe depression, or having to keep all of the alters from taking over. As your partner learns how to communicate with each alter in the system, this process becomes easier.

If you have concerns about any part of your relationship, it is important to be clear with yourself and your partner early on in your discussions about DID. If you are not honest with yourself, you will end up becoming very angry at your partner and resenting the relationship because you do not have what you want. Your partner has survived much worse things than being left. It is not your role to be a parent, savior, or rescuer.

If you sign on for working through the issues that arise as your partner heals, it is your role to be a committed, supportive partner. Remember, the little ones and older ones who come out are all your partners, too. Each one has been created to help the person you love survive. Even the ones who are angry and mean kept your partner alive. As you build your relationship with your partner, remember that he or she is the total of all of the wonderful, fun, angry, hurt, playful, and prankster parts that you see. It is important to keep this in mind, or you may miss out on the best parts of having a relationship with someone who has DID.

Do Be Supportive

Each person has different needs when they are feeling down, upset, or simply in need. You are not expected to read minds and know how to best support your partner. However, by talking with your partner about how you can be supportive, they can assist you in knowing what you can do to help in these situations.

Your partner's alters may differ in what they need to feel supported. For instance, one alter may think that being brought a cup of hot chocolate in bed is the absolute greatest, while another may prefer to snuggle on the couch. Talking with your partner and each of the alters will help to clarify the ways in which you can be supportive. You may find that, depending on which alter is most in need, your methods of offering support will change.

Do Get to Know Each Alter

Throughout life, people meet many individuals who play major roles in their lives: new bosses, new in-laws, new friends, and so on. If you're like most people, you probably feel a bit frightened about meeting someone who will be in your life to such a degree. Just like in these situations, it will most likely be a bit scary the first time you meet an alter. You probably won't know what to expect and may fear the worst. You may also feel awkward, because you'll be asked to interact with your partner in a way you never have. For example, while your partner may be quite articulate and well-spoken, some of the younger alters may not enunciate very clearly or you may not understand the language of a three year old very well, and you may feel strange about asking this alter to repeat something or even to be talking to a child at all. Although it may be difficult initially, do the best that you can to meet and speak with each of the alters. What you will likely find is an immense amount of creativity, knowledge, sensitivity, and individuality within each alter—things you definitely should not pass up.

Don't Discourage Alters from Appearing

Choosing to ignore certain alters or to speak only with the host personality indicates to your partner that you are not really interested in knowing his or her true being. This apparent disinterest will negatively affect your communication, honesty, and overall relationship with your partner. You have to remember, your partner has multiple identities. Being unwilling to interact with all of the identities indicates that you don't really want to know your partner totally, and that you only want to know the parts of your partner that are comfortable or pleasing to you. Avoiding that which is uncomfortable will damage your relationship with your partner.

Don't View Your Partner as "The Sick One"

Although DID is a verifiable mental disorder, resist the temptation to view your partner as the "sick" or "damaged" one in the relationship. Just because a person has multiple personalities does not mean that individual is to blame for all of the ills of the relationship. Having DID simply means having multiple identities, it is not suggestive of the psychological or emotional health of each of the personalities. If your relationship has problems, don't jump to the conclusion that the difficulties are due to DID. Most likely, the problems you face in your relationship are caused by more typical relationship problems such as difficulty communicating or lack of honesty. Make sure that the focus of the problems does not become DID. The other dynamics in the relationship are just as important. It is sometimes easier to focus all of the problems on the person who has more visible and definable issues. However, you also have your own baggage, and you also need to work on yourself and your relationship.

Don't Think You Can Fix Everything

As much as you may wish you could, you can't change or take back the trauma that occurred and caused your partner to develop DID. Similarly, you cannot change the perceptions of others regarding multiple personalities, and you cannot change the difficulties that your partner will face because of DID.

It's also important to remember that DID is not a condition that needs "fixing." Like everyone, your partner will have ups and downs, good days and bad days. Although your partner may have additional difficulties created by having DID, it is not your job to try to eliminate these problems. As a partner, your responsibility is to be supportive, loving, communicative, and kind. While you may strive to understand what your partner is going through, you do not need to change it. If your partner needs more help and support than you can provide, assist your partner in finding a qualified therapist.

Remember that the person you are involved with is a survivor. You are not the parent, and you are not the one in charge. You are a friend, a supporter, and a lover who has a very wonderful partner who was badly hurt as a child. This person has already lived through the worst and survived in a very creative way. It sometimes is hard to remember that when your partner is in the middle of a flashback or has been triggered by something and begins to have body memories. You can help your partner by asking for the adult to come out and by reminding him or her that no one is hurting him or her (if your partner wants you to do this). Your partner is an adult and can leave if a situation bothers him or her. When your partner was a child, there was no place to go and they could not control what happened to them. Now they are adults, and they can call the police or leave a bad situation if they wish. It is not your job in any relationship, let alone a relationship with a partner who has DID, to "fix" everything. Your job is to simply love your partner and give your partner, your relationship, and yourself the very best support and effort you can.

We know that when we are having a bad time, those around us get upset. Since the ones that are really hurt only get to come out at home or at therapy, the one who often sees them is our partner, Tracy. We know she wants to make us feel better. Sometimes we really do try to put away the ones who feel so bad, and we just want to sit and cry because we know how hard it is for her. What is most helpful, though, is for us to just have the time to experience what we are feeling. It passes much quicker when we don't try to ignore the pain from the past or the feelings of being lost.

Do Get Help for Your Own Needs

Sharing your life with someone with multiple personalities can be challenging and even distressing at times. It's easy to overlook your own reactions and concentrate on what is occurring for your partner. It is essential that you find ways to help yourself cope with your own needs and get support for yourself.

Because DID is draped in secrecy, it may be difficult for you to find others with whom you can talk. You may feel ashamed or embarrassed that you are in a relationship with someone who has multiple personalities. However, it may be this very shame and embarrassment that you need help dealing with. Entering into psychotherapy may be a viable option for finding someone you can talk to about your partner, your relationship, and, most importantly, yourself. You may also want to seek out a support group for partners of those with DID or a similar mental illness. It may also be helpful to confide in some friends so that you can build a support network. If you are in a relationship with a person with DID, you are affected by what has happened to your partner. There will be times when it will be difficult and distressing for you to watch their pain being relived in flashbacks, nightmares, and body memories.

It is also hard to find people to talk to who really understand what you experience on a day-to-day basis. Some people will ask why you stay in the relationship. This is a question that you should think about seriously. If you are staying because you feel that your partner could not make it without you, then it may be time to reconsider what a relationship means to you. If you are staying because you are in love with your partner and you can see some of the benefits to DID, you are probably in the right place.

At times, it will be difficult for you to get your needs met because your partner is having extreme difficulties or it is a bad time of year (anniversary of traumatic events). This improves over time, as everyone in your partner's system learns how to separate the past from the present and cope with their DID. As in any relationship, there are times when the balance of support you are giving one another is uneven. However, this shouldn't last forever; it may be helpful to track bad times and good times, so that you have a perspective of how things really are going in your life.

Keep in mind that you are likely to have reactions to your partner's multiple personalities which may be fairly disturbing to you. The better you are able to handle your own reactions and care for your own needs, the more you will be able to help your partner.

Creating Safety

As your partner deals with some of the issues which accompany DID, you may need to help your partner identify ways that he or she can feel safe. Working through issues of past trauma can be extremely difficult and disturbing for your partner and yourself. At times, your partner may be terrified or inconsolable because memories of the trauma are resurfacing. You may find that your partner is changing personalities more often and may even seem to have little control over which alter is present at any given time. During these times, it is important that you attempt to create a safe space for you and your partner.

When you see that your partner is in distress, you can ask if he or she knows what is going on. Ask your partner if there is someone inside who can help make him or her feel more safe. If he or she is really in a crisis, you can ask the alters that come out what would make them feel better. If they tell you that they want to hurt themselves, run away, or die, you can let them know that these are not options.

It is helpful to have your partner develop a crisis plan with his or her therapist. You may want to attend a session to talk about options. There may be times that you do have to take your partner to the hospital, but it is best to have this discussion when you first address both of your concerns about DID. Often, hospitalization is not needed and the crisis that your partner is experiencing will pass. He or she may just need some quiet time, a visit or phone call to the therapist, or some ice cream and some time to sit and watch a movie.

In order to do your part to create safety, you will need to talk with as many of the alters as possible. You may learn that some of your daily activities or possessions are actually contributing to your partner feeling uneasy or unsafe. For example, you may discover that the fillet mignon you have sitting in your refrigerator is causing your partner to have flashbacks to a time when he or she witnessed animal sacrifices. Or it may be that you frighten your partner every time you come home and shout "hello." Without speaking to your partner (and the alters) about creating safety, you will probably be unaware of what simple things you can do to make your environment better for both of you.

ACTIVITY 10.4: CREATING A SAFE ENVIRONMENT

This activity is designed to help you work with your partner to create a sense of safety. In this activity, you will be asked to speak with your partner and each alter and identify current behaviors that contribute to safety, current behaviors that make your partner feel less safe, and future things you can do to encourage a sense of safety. You will want to repeat this activity with each of the alters and record your responses in a journal or something similar. An example is provided below.

Name: Mary

Age: 4

What I do to encourage safety currently:

I give you hugs at night.

I always have ice cream in the freezer.

What I do that makes you feel unsafe, scared, or uneasy:

I slam the door when I come home.

I don't stop tickling you when you first ask.

What I can do to make you feel more safe in the future:

I can always leave a light on in the house.

I can talk with you when you look like you might be zoning out.

I can reassure you that I'm not going to leave you.

You may wish to photocopy the following for each of your partners alters to help you keep track, at least initially, of their different needs.

Name: _____

Age: _____

What I do to encourage safety currently:

What I do that makes you feel unsafe, scared, or uneasy:

What I can do to make you feel more safe in the future:

By the time you complete this activity with each of your partner's alters, you'll have a pretty good understanding of how to help create safety for your partner and yourself. Keep your list(s) handy, because you never know when you might need them.

Negotiating Boundaries

As you begin to get to know each of your partner's personalities, it may become necessary for you to set up some rules and establish some boundaries. Boundaries are helpful, in that they provide clearly defined rules regarding your relationship. For instance, you may wish to decide on specific times or places where the child personalities are allowed to emerge. It probably wouldn't be very helpful if your partner's three-year-old alter decides to join the conversation at a dinner with your boss. Similarly, you may request that only particular alters interact with you at certain times (such as during sexual activity).

Once you have a pretty good idea of the alters who are likely to appear, you will need to spend some time with your partner negotiating and deciding on boundaries. The trick with making boundaries work is that they need to be both clearly defined and consistent. Boundaries do no good if they are unclear to you or your partner or if you know they always change.

Challenges You Will Face

Although being with someone who has DID can be quite fantastic and is always an adventure, there are some challenges. One of the most difficult issues in your relationship may be the task of eliminating the misconceptions you have about DID and reducing the shame or embarrassment you feel about your partner's multiple identities. It will take you some time to get used to the fact that your partner has multiple personalities. Your partner is likely dealing with similar issues. Just remember, DID does not simply go away. If you don't feel like you can handle being in a relationship with someone with DID, figure out why, and if this is something you either can't or won't try to change, then have the courage to be honest with your partner about this issue. It may be that you need to leave this relationship.

Another challenge you may face is understanding and accepting the limitations of your partner. People who have DID have been through a great deal of trauma. Memories of and reactions to this trauma often get triggered. Learning to recognize some of the potential triggers and react supportively when the memories do get triggered is essential. Your partner may not be able to do everything you want. For example, you may have to go to scary or violent movies by yourself, because these things may cause your partner to have flashbacks of the traumatic event. Or you may have to cancel plans with your friends because your partner is having a bad day and is somewhat fragmented (many different alters keep popping out). As mentioned previously, finding support and keeping yourself psychologically fit may also present a challenge.

Communication is essential in a relationship with someone who has multiple personalities, though maintaining open and productive lines of communication may be a challenge. Many relationships are able to thrive despite the absence of good patterns of communication. It is unlikely, however, that a relationship with a partner with DID can endure and prosper without excellent communication skills. Therefore, learning how to talk with each other and share openly and honestly is really important and may be a mountainous task.

Sexuality

Most people who have multiple personalities have been though unthinkable trauma or abuse, often of a sexual nature. As you might guess, sexual abuse generally leaves severe psychological scars. Some of these emotional injuries will affect your sexual relationship with your partner. Sex and sexuality with someone who has DID can be challenging. There may be times when your partner simply does not want to be sexual, and it's important that you respect these wishes. There may be other times when your partner is having difficulty controlling their alters, some of whom may wish to be present during sexual acts even though it's not really appropriate. For instance, both you and your partner may have a difficult time if one of the child alters keeps popping out during your lovemaking. You may also have trouble accepting it if some of the alters have different sexual orientations and even different genders, and this may affect your ability to be sexual with your partner.

Many people with DID have one or two personalities who were created to be sexual. These alters may not understand why you do not want them to be sexual with you and feel that they did something wrong or are bad or will be hurt because of it. If you are sensitive to your partner, you will eventually learn to identify when different alters are coming out. You will also learn to recognize when your partner has left you emotionally and is dissociating during sex—it could be that a touch or a sound triggered a flashback. At these times, stop what you are doing and ask your partner if he or she is okay.

One way of building trust is telling your partner that he or she can say "stop" or "no" at any time, and you will stop. This is the control that your partner never had as a child. It was the adult or perpetrator, not your partner, who was in charge of what was done with your partner's body when he or she was a child. If you have a trusting relationship, you will work at having honest communication; sex is hard to talk about in the best of situations—add to this a history of sexual abuse, and there is a whole new level of intricacy to learning healthy sexual behavior.

Communicating with your partner and talking openly and honestly about sex and lovemaking will help you dispel potential difficulties. Establish ways of touching that are "safe." That is, find ways to touch and love your partner that aren't likely to trigger memories or mood states. Making love with your partner can be extremely pleasurable, even if you don't have intercourse or reach orgasm. You will also want to share with your partner what kind of touching and loving you enjoy (as well as what you don't like). What you will find is that through this open communication about sex and sexuality, you will reach levels of intimacy and passion you have only dreamed about up to this point.

It is important that you both talk about your sexual feelings. Sex is generally a part of the abuse that leads to the development of DID. It is helpful to talk about how both of you are feeling when you begin thinking about touching each other; try to have this discussion before you decide to have sex. This provides time for both of you to explore your wants and needs. It also is the time that your partner can work with the little ones, perhaps putting them in a room or some other safe space where they can stay during adult time.

You will definitely want to discuss what you are feeling and thinking when your partner tells you that he or she does not want to be sexual (and this will happen sometimes). You may be able to devise some things that will help you to connect with each other in ways that are comforting and safe for both of you. If you ignore the issue of sex, it can result in emotional distance between the two of you. If you want to become close, it is important to find ways to talk about how to connect. It is nice and even fun to find ways to be physical without being sexual. Sometimes it helps if you talk about what you want to do, as this allows you both to enjoy the anticipation.

※

Activity 10.5: Learning How to Be Sexual

Prior to being sexual, talk to your partner about how he or she is doing emotionally. It is also helpful to ask to talk to the one who can give you the most information (it may not always be the big one). When you get ready to talk about being sexual, explain to the little ones that this is big people or adult talk, and that the little ones need to go into their rooms or into the play room.

Try to take the time to explore and enjoy this exercise. Find a time when you will not be interrupted by friends dropping in or children coming home and wanting attention.

In this activity, you and your partner will spend time touching each other on various parts of your bodies. As you touch each other, ask what it feels like and notice whether or not your partner has dissociated or zoned out. When you are finished, record your responses. This is one activity that you'll want to repeat many times, so that you can determine what kinds of sexual play work best in your relationship (it's also kind of fun).

Touch	What does it feel like?	Are you still here?
(ex.) legs, gentle	nice, soft, a little scary	yes

As you and your partner learn to communicate about what sexual activities feel good, you will build a strong foundation for your relationship. Part of a healthy relationship is connecting in different ways. It is important to connect emotionally, physically, and sexually. Talking is important for both of you to learn how to build your relationship in a healthy, positive way.

If your partner is having a particularly hard time with flashbacks and body memories, it is probably not a good time to be sexual. Sometimes couples start hugging less, kissing less, or touching less because the person who is abused is afraid that the touching behaviors will lead to sexual activity. It is good to discuss what is going on if your partner does begin to pull away when you go to give him or her a hug. Often, you can build trust between you and your partner by telling him or her that you just want to hug, cuddle, or kiss, but that you aren't expecting them to be sexual. This can bring back the fun for both of you, and it allows your partner to control the touching of his or her body. Talking about when touching is nonsexual and when it is sexual can result in a positive change in your physical interactions with your partner.

Enjoy Your Partner and Have Fun

Bruce has been living with his DID partner for three years. He states, "It's hard for me to imagine life without my partner. She is the most incredible woman, and I love her immensely. She is an inspiration to me in many ways. That she has multiple personalities only makes our relationship more interesting. There is so much about her which is unique, creative, and wonderful. I love playing with and getting to know each of her alters, and I'm continuing to discover more about her each day."

Much of this chapter has focused on the extra work that you and your partner will encounter due to DID. However, along with the work come bonuses. Being with someone who has multiple personalities is a true gift, and if you are still committed to the relationship, you are in for the adventure of your life. Explore the amazing aspects of each of the alters. It seems incredible that so many wonderful characteristics can be included in one body (see chapter 6 for a discussion about many of the good things that go along with having DID). Let yourself play and have fun. Just as your partner gets to have many hobbies, talents, and characteristics, so do you. Allow yourself to join your partner and watch cartoons on Saturday mornings. Have your partner teach you how to paint or sculpt. Give yourself time to spend with your partner talking about daily life or philosophical issues.

Think of your partner as a group of your best friends, and learn to enjoy them together and separately. Your relationship may be a struggle at times, but the fun and excitement that you will find in your partner will be well worth the struggle. You will have many stories that outsiders may not understand, but that your friends in your support circle will definitely enjoy. Basically, enjoy your partner by being open to discovering new and wonderful parts of your partner and yourself, and allow yourself to express and make use of these discoveries. Have fun!

C H A P T E R   1 1

For Family Members

Before you read this chapter, you may want to complete activity 11.1, which is designed to help you to better understand your family. Learning more about the dynamics of your family will allow you to get more out of reading this chapter.

ACTIVITY 11.1: THINKING ABOUT YOUR FAMILY

In order to do this activity, you will need paper and a pen. As you read and answer each of the questions, simply write down what comes to your mind immediately. Do not try to think about the answers or try to determine if they make sense. There are no right or wrong answers, and no one has to see what you have written. These questions are designed to get you thinking about the dynamics that were going on in your home when your family member with DID was a child.

    1. List all of the members in your family and their respective ages when the abuse occurred. Be sure to include yourself.

If there were people outside of your nuclear family who played a major role in your life, you can list them as well.

2. Spend a few minutes thinking about these people. Then, see what you can remember about communication in your family when your family member with DID was growing up. How did your family communicate about issues during that time? Did you talk with each other as issues arose, or did you ignore important things that were happening in your family? Did the parents of your family member with DID get angry and scream? Did they not talk at all? Write down what you remember about communication in your family. You may want to think about your family as a whole or separately, listing how each family member communicated with you and others.

3. Now take a minute to think about how you communicated with your family. Was it safe for children to talk about scary things to the adults in the home? Did the children have anyone close to them either within their family or outside of their family that they could talk with about things that bothered them?

4. Did the parents of your family member with DID or anyone else in the family use alcohol or drugs? Thinking back about the members of your family, do you think they had substance abuse problems? If so, what were they using and how much? Do you think they now have a problem with substance abuse?

5. Reflect on the ways in which anger was demonstrated in the childhood home of your family member with DID. Was there a lot of yelling? Did anyone get hit or hurt during these times? How were the children disciplined?

6. What was the general mood in the home where your family member with DID grew up? Would you describe your family as being happy? Do you think others (friends of yours, etc.) would say that you and/or your family member with DID had a happy home?

7. Sometimes families present different images in different situations. Did the adults in your family act like things were fine in public, though you knew that things were different?

In doing this activity, you may have realized some things about your family that you hadn't thought of before. The better you understand your family dynamics, the more you'll be able to understand how your DID family member's multiple personalities played a role in your family.

Your Potential Reactions to DID

There are many ways that families react to information. If a member of your family is telling you about having DID, you will probably handle this information the same way that your family has always handled unpleasant information. If the tendency is to ignore problems, you may be tempted to do so. If you generally get angry or mistrustful when problems arise, this may be your inclination now. But if you want to continue to have a relationship with your DID family member, you will probably need to confront your family member openly, honestly, and calmly about your feelings.

> *We decided that we were going to tell our cousin about having DID. She was the closest person to us in the family, and we decided that if we were going to tell anyone, she had the best chance of hearing us and maybe even understanding us. We scraped together all of our courage and said, "Let's go for a walk. We want to talk to you about something." We figured if she freaked out it would be okay, because we were outside and she wouldn't want to make a big scene.*
>
> *So we finally told her that one of the issues we had been struggling with was finding out that we had DID. There was a moment of silence, and then she changed the topic. At first we wondered if we really did tell her, and then we all checked in with each other and knew we had. Then we just quit trying to talk about it; after all, what do you say after no response? At the end of our walk, she went home, and that was the end of the subject. We forgot that in our family we never did talk about anything serious, and for that matter, we rarely talked about anything at all.*

Nadia told her sister, Vera, through a letter. The two sisters hadn't spoken in years. The last time they did speak, Nadia had raised questions about their family and the possibility of abuse. Vera had responded by saying, "You're being silly. Nothing like that ever happened in our family." Vera refused to discuss the topic any further, simply ignoring Nadia's continued probing. Nadia left Vera's house feeling frustrated, betrayed, and uncertain of her own sanity. Several years later, after a great deal of hard work in psychotherapy, Nadia wrote Vera a letter explaining about being DID and what her life was really like. Only a few days after mailing the letter, Nadia received a telephone call from Vera. At long last, the dialogue had begun.

Your reactions to learning of a family member's DID are likely to be extreme. You may have many of the reactions which were discussed in the chapter for partners—fear, disbelief, sadness, anger. You may also wonder about your own mental health, especially if you are a peer who suffered the same extreme abuse.

One of the differences between learning of a friend's DID and a family member's multiple personalities is that you, as family, will have quite an extensive history with that DID family member, generally much more so than the history you have with your friends. You may have lived under the same roof for well over a decade. You've probably had similar experiences with your family as your DID family member's. You may or may not have known of the abuse or trauma that your family member endured, and you, yourself, may or may not have been abused. Regardless, you are likely to be surprised, if not shocked, to learn of your family member's DID.

How you react to learning that your family member has multiple personalities is likely to be greatly influenced by your own experiences and personality. You may begin to question your own reality. You may begin to review your past, looking for answers or information to verify the diagnosis of your family member.

If you don't believe or accept that trauma occurred, you will have more difficulty understanding the possible origins of multiple personalities and may not believe in its existence at all. You may also have strong beliefs about issues such as DID and other psychological concerns. You may also begin to question the qualifications and intentions of the therapist who has been providing treatment for your family member.

On the other hand, you may be very aware of the abuse which took place in your home, as well as the symptoms of DID which your family member exhibits. Chances are, if you're reading this book, you are fairly open to the possibility that DID actually exists and that your family member is dealing with this issue. At least you have some amount of curiosity about this strange information, and you may have started thinking about all the media-portrayed characters with DID to see if your family member is similar.

Your reactions to learning that a family member has multiple personalities will also be altered by who that person is within your family. For instance, your reactions may differ quite a bit depending on if it's your mother, father, sibling, or extended family member who has DID. Typically, children are closer to and depend on their parents much more than their siblings or more distant relatives. So, if it is your parent who has DID, it's likely to impact you more severely than if the person with DID is a different member of your family.

The type of relationship you had with your DID family member while you were growing up will also make a difference. If you were very close to the person who has DID, then learning of the diagnosis is likely to affect you more deeply. Similarly, the type of relationship you have now with your DID family member will figure into the extremity of your reaction. The closer you are to that family member, the more impact this news will have on you.

Handling Your Reactions

As you learn of your family member's multiple personalities, you will probably have many strong reactions. Here are a few simple guidelines that may help you better handle your initial reactions to learning of the presence of DID in your family.

- **Your feelings are not wrong.** You are feeling whatever you are feeling. Honor your reactions to the information, both about your family member sharing his or her diagnosis and the information they share about what happened to them. While it may be best to vent your feelings and misgivings, at least while your emotions are volatile, to someone other than your DID family member, it is important that you give yourself the permission and space to do so.

- **It's okay to ask questions.** Questioning is not the same as denying. In fact, asking questions may indicate to your family member that you are interested in what he or she is telling you. You will probably be told some things that may seem incredible to you, and these things may make you wonder about your own experiences and what you are being told. DID is not the easiest phenomenon to understand. Learning more about what went on in your family and for your family member will help clarify some of what you are questioning.

- **Do not tell your family member he or she is crazy or accuse him or her of lying.** Hopefully you will have read this guideline prior to learning of your family member's multiple personalities. Even if you're not sure you believe your family member about having DID, it's important that you don't denounce his or her statements. Think of how you would feel if someone told you that you were crazy or accused you of lying about something you believe. Reacting in a way such as this could create serious negative consequences for your relationship with your family member.

- **Listen to what your family member is telling you.** If it is too overwhelming, ask the person to give you some time and then go back when you are able to talk about what happened. It's taken your family member a long time and a lot of courage to tell you about having DID. It may also take you a while before you're able to discuss this. There's no problem with taking some time to process this information; just be sure to tell your family member that that's what you're doing.

- **Get help for your own reactions.** As mentioned earlier, you will probably have some intense emotional reactions to learning that your family member has multiple personalities. You will need someone to talk with about this. Use your support system—your friends, family, or even a therapist. You'll find that with proper support, this information doesn't need to be so disturbing.

Questions You'll Probably Have

When you learn of your family member's DID, you're likely to have many questions. In addition to the questions presented in the chapter for partners, which have to do with generalities of DID (e.g., How many alters do you have? What are their names, ages, etc.?), you may have questions which are more specific to your family.

Can This Be True?

One of the primary questions you're likely to ask is, "Can this be true?" You may not believe that your family member has multiple personalities, particularly if that person has not shared with you his or her alters. You may know your family member as one individual rather than as an individual with many others existing inside. Because you haven't experienced or noticed the presence of other personalities (this is fairly common), you may not readily accept that your family member has DID. Once you meet the alters, assuming they're willing to show themselves to you, you may be more likely to believe.

You may also have your own personal beliefs about the existence of DID in general. As stated earlier, many professionals are not sold on the fact that DID is real. Some people think that multiple personalities can simply be created by very imaginative and manipulative people with or without the help of their therapists. Some believe that DID is an extension of "false" recovered memories, and that extensive, detailed memories, particularly relating to abuse, can be created or completely misremembered.

When you're trying to determine the legitimacy of DID, think about the great difficulty someone would have to undertake to create and maintain multiple identities, each with his or her own elaborate histories and manners of being. It would be incredibly challenging to perform this task for several minutes, let alone several decades, without "blowing one's cover," so to speak. After simply thinking about the difficulty of this task, you may be more of a believer in the existence of DID.

If you accept that DID is real, you may still be left wondering, "Does my family member really have multiple personalities?" Although you may not want to believe this to be true, chances are, if your family member is telling you that he or she has DID, it's probably the case. You may want to question your family member as to how this determination was made. For instance, it would be important to find out if he or she was diagnosed as having DID by a therapist or if he or she simply read a book and decided that they had DID. Obviously, professional diagnoses are more likely to be accurate than reading a book. So, as part of your accepting your family member's revelation that he or she has DID, you'll definitely want to consider the source of the diagnosis.

Why Is This True?

Once you've accepted that your family member has DID, you may begin to wonder about its origins. As described in the first section of this book, DID is most often born out of severe trauma or abuse (see chapter 2 for more detailed information).

Although most of those diagnosed with DID have undergone some form of severe, long-term trauma, you may have some difficulty believing that this could have happened to someone who was so close to you. It is perfectly plausible that your brother, sister, mother, father, or more distant relative could have been severely abused or traumatized without your knowledge. Just because you didn't know about it doesn't mean that it didn't happen. If you are having a hard time believing that anything like this could happen in your family, you may have difficulty accepting your DID family member's claims of abuse. If you possibly can, at least try to listen to their experiences and reality. If you are not ready to do so, tell them this and ask them to give you more time.

You may find that you have different reactions to learning of your family member's multiple personalities depending on who was the perpetrator. If the perpetrator was a person in your family, then it is highly probable that there was some level of dysfunction in the home. If the abuser was someone in the family you were or are close to, you may have a difficult time even listening to your DID family member tell about what he or she experienced. Add to this issue the difficulty in accepting a diagnosis of DID; you will need to honor your feelings and the time it takes you to process this information.

Am I DID, too?

Another question which you're likely to have pertains to your own mental state. You may be wondering if the presence of multiple personalities in your family member will make you have DID as well. The answer is most definitely "no." Simply because your family member has DID does not mean that you have or will develop DID also. You may or may not have been exposed to some of the same traumatic events to which your family member was exposed. And even if you did experience trauma, you may have utilized different coping devices than your DID family member. For instance, while your family member was dissociating and developing multiple personalities, you may simply have been repressing, or blocking out, this experience.

If the DID family member is a sibling, you may wonder if the same thing happened to you. Not all children experience the same treatment in a family. If you do wonder about your own way of handling your past, you may want to reread chapter 1. This chapter offers a brief initial assessment for DID, which could be helpful to you if you are wondering if you, too, may have this diagnosis. If you begin to get really scared or upset, try to talk with your friends or other people in your support system. You may want to begin going to therapy to receive assistance in coping with this information. Plenty of people who are not mentally ill see therapists; think of therapists as people who can guide you through your own journey of self-discovery and self-acceptance. It is not unusual to be upset that this level of abuse happened to someone in your family. You may also be upset that your family member has the "nerve" to bring up any of the issues connected to your past.

✳

ACTIVITY 11.2: YOUR OWN REACTIONS

Once you learn that your family member has DID, it's important that you take a few minutes to assess your own reactions. Understanding your reactions can help you better determine the impact of this information and the areas which may be distressing for you. Once you know how you're reacting, you can work on any areas which may be creating difficulty for you.

For this activity, you'll need to write down your responses. It would be a good idea if you recorded your answers in a place that you can go back to later. You may be interested in the future to see if and how your reactions have changed. Just like for the last activity, spend a few minutes thinking about and responding to each of the following questions.

1. Who in your family has DID?

2. How did you learn that this person has multiple personalities?

3. What was your initial reaction? How did you feel? What did you think? What, if anything, did you do? What did you say?

4. As your family member with DID was growing up, what was your relationship to this person? Were you close? How did you communicate with each other?

5. How do you think that your family member's multiple personalities affected your relationship when he or she was growing up? What about now?

6. How did this person explain the origin of his or her multiple personalities? Was there abuse or trauma that took place? If so, what happened?

7. If your family member has told you that he or she was abused, was the abuser someone who lived with you? Do you still have a relationship with that person? Were you around during the time the abuse took place? Were you aware that this abuse was occurring? Were you also abused?

8. Why do you think your family member shared this information with you?

9. How do you think you will be affected (or how have you been affected) by your family member's multiple personalities?

10. What have you done or what can you do to help you through this experience? Who can you talk with about this?

Your answers to these questions should help you better understand your own reactions to learning of your family member's DID. As time goes by, you may want to return to this activity and look over your responses to see if anything has changed.

How to Explain DID to Others

Before you begin to decide who to tell about your family member's diagnosis of DID, you should first talk to him or her. Remember that this person decided to trust you with this information. It is not easy for people with DID to open up. The reality for your DID family member is that many people may think she or he is crazy, lying, or just trying to get attention. If you have any of these same questions or concerns, you may want to set up a time to talk with your family member, perhaps with his or her therapist, so that you can have your questions answered and your concerns alleviated.

If your family member with DID does not want to tell the other family members, you need to decide if you can respect that request. It would be best to be honest at this point and tell him or her that, to provide yourself with support, you may need to talk about the issue. If you want to have an ongoing relationship with your DID family member, it is important to keep or build trust. Once you have worked out the details of who to tell, you can begin the next phase of telling family members.

There are several things to consider before you begin to tell others that your family member has multiple personalities. One of the first things to think about is why you want to tell others of this fact. Are you looking for support for yourself? Are you simply sharing gossip? Are you trying to elicit sympathy from others because you're family is "screwed up," and you believe that having someone in your family who has multiple personalities "proves" this? Or are you sharing this information with others to help explain why your family member acts as he or she does? Obviously, the best reason to tell others about DID in your family is so that you can get the support that you need to deal with this issue. The information about someone having DID isn't the same as finding out that he or she just graduated from school or is having children—it probably shouldn't be shared as casual chitchat.

If you do decide to inform others that your family member has DID, there are several things to take into account. Who, where, and when you tell are all primary concerns. Deciding who to tell may be the easiest of these determinations. You should tell people who you believe need to know so that you can be provided with appropriate support, or so that the person with DID can obtain more support or acceptance. The list of people you share this information with may be very short.

You will also need to figure out where to inform others about your family member's multiple personalities. It would be best if you could do this in person, rather than over the telephone. Also, it would be good if you tell others in a place that is quiet, private, and in which you can talk. Telling others about your family member's DID over dinner in a crowded, noisy restaurant will not work very well. You need to have the focus be on the conversation, not on other things going on around you. If you are telling someone who always runs at the slightest hint of conflict, you may decide not to tell them. If you still decide to tell them, you could start by telling them that you have something you'd like to tell them, and that it is important for them to hear you out before they end the discussion. If they cannot agree to stay for the entire discussion, you may want to rethink the decision to tell them about your family member's DID.

Deciding when to tell others about your family member's multiple personalities is another tough one. Usually you will be sharing this information when you need support. Since you are most likely to need support right after you find out about the DID, this is a pretty good time to talk to those close to you. However, there may be additional times when you decide to talk with others about this issue (e.g., if your family member later has more serious problems related to multiple personalities, and you want to discuss this with others). For instance, you may learn that your sister, who has DID, is abusing alcohol. You may need some support to help you through this issue, so you may decide to tell someone close to you about the alcohol problem and the DID.

It will be difficult for you to tell even those closest to you about your family member's DID. Don't expect this to be an easy or simple conversation. Also, don't wait until you feel comfortable to have this conversation. Chances are, by waiting, your fear and anxiety around sharing this issue will only escalate.

How to explain DID to others may also be complicated. Hopefully after reading this book you'll have a better understanding of DID and can offer some insight to those you are talking with. Nevertheless, those who you speak with about your family member's multiple personalities are likely to have many questions, probably many of the same questions you had when you learned of this information. Do the best that you can to explain multiple personalities and how this plays out for your family member with DID. You don't need to have all of the answers.

Handling Family Boundaries

For people with multiple personalities the issue of family can be very difficult, particularly if the trauma or abuse which occurred happened in the presence of family members. The person in your family who has DID may or may not want contact with any or all family members. Contact with family may be extremely difficult for that person if some or all of the family does not believe or acknowledge the existence of multiple personalities or the precipitating factors (abuse within the family). For this reason, it's helpful for you to extend your support and acceptance to the person in your family who has DID, but also to respect his or her desire for distance.

Epilogue

Karen and Tracy

This book was designed to help you or those that you love learn better ways to live with DID, not to change the fact that DID is present in your life. Hopefully you have found some of this information useful. Having DID can, at times, be quite a challenge. It's important that you remember that you have already survived the worst that life can offer and that, in comparison, learning to accept yourself and your life as a person with DID is quite achievable.

Just as living with DID can be trying, loving someone who has DID can also be an adventure. If you have someone in your life who has DID, we hope this book has shown you DID from several perspectives and given you a glimpse of what the person you love who has DID goes through. Hopefully, you have come to view the DID person in your life as someone with amazing skills and talents, who is able to bring something truly unique and wonderful to your life just by being themselves.

Everyone learns to survive in various ways. It takes determination for people with DID to learn how to live life, after being taught as children that they should really be dead. Writing this book has given us the chance to attempt to clarify what living with DID means, including the way in which is it an intricate and successful survival mechanism.

Tracy

Working on this book with Karen was not only incredibly fun and interesting, but it was also educational. Through discussions with Karen, I came to see that my way of viewing DID and the implications of DID were fairly limited. I had no idea how different Karen's world is from my own. I have come to view DID as a wonderful gift that allowed for survival during horrific times. I have come to view those with DID as exceptional individuals, each trying to live in the world in a way that works for them. Hopefully the experience of reading this book was as fulfilling and meaningful for you as was the experience of writing this book for me.

Karen

When I first became aware that I was a person living with DID, I was ashamed. Ashamed because the only thing I knew about DID was from television or movies, which made people with DID seem like freaks. Actually, some of the films did portray some of the experiences of people living with DID fairly accurately.

In retrospect, I realize the same I was experiencing was because of the reactions others have to DID. DID has been a topic of great debate. Does it really exist, or are people just making up these alternate personalities? Over time, I heard therapists, psychiatrists, news reporters, family members, and friends debate the existence of DID.

So, needless to say, when I first realized that all the ways I behaved and functioned were because of being traumatized as a child and was DID, I went into shock. When later I began to understand and accept that I was one of "those" people who really was DID, I went into hiding. I worked, went to school, and went home. I was afraid that, at any moment, someone I hadn't told would discover that I had DID or someone I had told would call me a liar.

When I went to bookstores to find information about DID, I would buy every book, hoping to find answers on how to live with or how to cure this problem. None of the books helped.

As I have explored this topic with Tracy, I have learned more about how people with DID do things differently. We discussed different questions and approaches to this book. For example, I was reluctant to include any exercise that would have people focus on the trauma they endured. From Tracy's perspective, and the perspective of many other therapists, including these exercises would not be unreasonable in a book such as this. Even as we talked about it, all my inside little ones came out and began crying, trying to explain how hard it is to even think about what happened. Tracy saw the distress this topic brought up in us, and we removed the exercise and recommended only going over past trauma with the help of a trained therapist. The information in chapter 2 covers some of the causes of DID. Tracy did most of the work on this chapter, because I did not want to experience the feelings that continue to be brought up whenever I read about ritual abuse.

Throughout my life, there have always been times of the year that were extremely hard. I now know that these are times that in some way related to what happened during my childhood. As I've worked to recover, heal, and grow, I have been able to make the worst days a little better with each passing year. I now try to plan for the "usually bad" days by finding things to do that are fun and nurturing. Some days it is sitting in a movie theater, other days I will go for a walk on the beach or in the desert.

I realize that it can be hard to understand the terror that was created by severe abuse unless you see the reactions of the people who were victimized. I do know that the feelings of terror have lessened and will continue to do so over time. I also know these feelings will never completely go away.

My therapist, Pam, always said that if I was to end my life because I felt so overwhelmed and controlled by the past, the abusers would win. She was right. My goal now is to really enjoy my life and to live it the best way I can. I believe we all can grow and heal. I also know that it isn't easy and can be extremely scary, and many of us living with DID do the best we can to improve ourselves. I guess in some ways I will always try to prove to myself that life can change and get better.

For others with DID, remember that the things you were told—that you aren't worth living, that you're bad, that no one will believe you if you tell them about the abuse you've endured, that you have to kill yourself or hurt others—are all lies. Although DID is the result of horrible things that were done to you, having DID can be quite fun. You have so many skills and talents, many of which you may just be beginning to realize. As you went through this book, I hope that you began to appreciate yourself. In truth, you can do many things that the singletons around you cannot even begin to do. Think about it—when was the last time you heard your singleton friends say that they went flying with the birds or became as strong as a tree, or that they had their own comedy show in their head?

Karen and Tracy: A Final Thought

Each person has a choice: You can be a victim of the past, or you can use the past to grow into the future in a healthy, strong way. We hope that this book has helped you decide to choose the latter.

References

Alderman, Tracy. 1997. *The Scarred Soul: Understanding and Ending Self-Inflicted Violence.* Oakland, Calif.: New Harbinger Publications.

American Psychiatric Association. 1994. *DSM-IV: Diagnostic and Statistical Manual of Mental Disorders,* Fourth Edition. Washington, D.C.: American Psychiatric Association.

Bass, Ellen, and Laura Davis. 1988. *The Courage to Heal: A Guide for Women Survivors of Child Sexual Abuse.* New York: Harper & Row.

Braun, Bennett, editor. 1986. *Treatment of Multiple Personality Disorder.* Washington, D.C.: American Psychiatric Press.

Chase, Truddi. 1987. *When Rabbit Howls.* New York: Jove Books.

Cline, Jean Darby. 1997. *Silencing the Voices: One Woman's Triumph Over Multiple Personality Disorder.* New York: Berkeley Books.

Cohen, Barry, Esther Giller, and Lynn W. 1991. *Multiple Personality Disorder from the Inside Out.* Baltimore, Md.: Sidran Press.

Davis, Laura. 1991. *Allies in Healing: When the Person You Love Was Sexually Abused as a Child.* New York: HarperCollins.

Gil, Eliana. 1983. *Outgrowing the Pain: A Book for and about Adults Abused as Children.* New York: Dell.

———. 1988. *Treatment of Adult Survivors of Childhood Abuse.* Walnut Creek, Calif.: Launch Press.

Los Angeles County Commission for Women. 1991. (Report of the Ritual Abuse Task Force.) *Ritual Abuse: Definitions, Glossary, the Use of Mind Control.*

Putnam, Frank. 1989. *Diagnosis and Treatment of Multiple Personality Disorder.* New York: Guilford Press.

Ross, Colin. 1997. *Dissociative Identity Disorder: Diagnosis, Clinical Features, and Treatment of Multiple Personality.* New York: John Wiley & Sons.

Ryder, Daniel. 1992. *Breaking the Circle of Satanic Ritual Abuse: Recognizing and Recovering from the Hidden Trauma.* Minneapolis, Minn.: CompCare Publishers.

Spiegel, David, editor. 1993. *Dissociative Disorders: A Clinical Review.* Lutherville, Md.: Sidran Press

Whitfield, Charles. 1995. *Memory and Abuse: Remembering and Healing the Effets of Trauma.* Deerfield Beach, Fla.: Health Communications, Inc.

Yalom, Irvin, and James Spira, editors. 1996. *Treating Dissociative Identity Disorder.* San Francisco: Jossey-Bass Publishers.

Bibliography

Abuse

Adams, Caren, and Jennifer Fay. 1989. *Free of the Shadows: Recovering from Sexual Violence.* Oakland, Calif.: New Harbinger Publications.

Bass, Ellen, and Laura Davis. 1988. *The Courage to Heal: A Guide for Women Survivors of Child Sexual Abuse.* New York: Harper & Row.

Beckylane. 1995. *Where the Rivers Join: A Personal Account of Healing from Ritual Abuse.* San Francisco: Jossey-Bass Publishers.

Davis, Laura. 1991. *Allies in Healing: When the Person You Love Was Sexually Abused as a Child.* New York: HarperCollins.

Enns, Greg, and Jan Black. 1997. *It's Not Okay Anymore: Your Personal Guide to Ending Abuse, Taking Charge, and Loving Yourself.* Oakland, Calif.: New Harbinger Publications.

Gil, Eliana. 1983. *Outgrowing the Pain: A Book for and about Adults Abused as Children.* New York: Dell.

———. 1988. *Treatment of Adult Survivors of Childhood Abuse.* Walnut Creek, Calif.: Launch Press.

Matsakis, Aphrodite. 1996. *I Can't Get Over It: A Handbook for Trauma Survivors.* Oakland, Calif.: New Harbinger Publications.

Richardson, Anna. 1997. *Double Vision: A Travelogue of Recovery from Ritual Abuse.* Trilogy Books.

Rose, Emilie. 1996. *Reaching for the Light: A Guide for Ritual Abuse Survivors and Their Therapists.* Cleveland, Ohio: Pilgrim Press.

Addictions

Fanning, Patrick, and John O'Neill. 1996. *The Addiction Workbook: A Step-by-Step Guide to Quitting Alcohol and Drugs.* Oakland, Calif.: New Harbinger Publications.

Schuckit, Mark Alan. 1995. *Educating Yourself About Alcohol and Drugs: A People's Primer.* New York: Plenum Press.

West, James. 1997. *The Betty Ford Center Book of Answers: Help for Those Struggling with Substance Abuse and for the People Who Love Them.* New York: Pocket Books.

Depression, Anxiety, and Other Moods

Bilodeau, Lorraine. 1992. *The Anger Workbook.* Minneapolis, Minn.: CompCare Publishers.

Bourne, Edmund. 1995. *The Anxiety and Phobia Workbook.* Oakland, Calif.: New Harbinger Publications.

Copeland, Mary Ellen. 1992. *The Depression Workbook: A Guide for Living with Depression.* Oakland, Calif.: New Harbinger Publications.

Ellis, Thomas, and Cory Frank Newman. 1996. *Choosing to Live: How to Defeat Suicide through Cognitive Therapy.* Oakland, Calif.: New Harbinger Publications.

Dissociative Identity Disorder

Chase, Truddi. 1987. *When Rabbit Howls.* New York: Jove Books.

Cline, Jean Darby. 1997. *Silencing the Voices: One Woman's Triumph Over Multiple Personality Disorder.* New York: Berkeley Books.

Cohen, Barry, Esther Giller, and Lynn W. 1991. *Multiple Personality Disorder from the Inside Out.* Baltimore, MD: Sidran Press.

Putnam, Frank. 1989. *Diagnosis and Treatment of Multiple Personality Disorder.* New York: Guilford Press.

Self-Inflicted Violence

Alderman, Tracy. 1997. *The Scarred Soul: Understanding and Ending Self-Inflicted Violence.* Oakland, Calif.: New Harbinger Publications.

Trautmann, Kim, and Robin Conners. 1994. *Understanding Self-Injury: A Workbook for Adults.* Pittsburgh, Pa.: Pittsburgh Action Against Rape.

More New Harbinger
Self-Help Titles

THE SCARRED SOUL

Tracy Alderman explores why the victims of self-inflicted violence hurt themselves and shows readers how to take steps to overcome the psychological traps that lead to self-inflicted pain.

Item SOUL Paperback $13.95

TRUST AFTER TRAUMA

Guides survivors of traumatic events through a process of strengthening existing bonds, building new ones, and ending self-perpetuating cycles of withdrawal and isolation.

Item TAT Paperback, $13.95

THOUGHTS & FEELINGS

The second edition of this classic workbook covers all of the major cognitive-behavioral techniques for taking control of your moods and your life.

Item TF2 Paperback, $18.95

BETTER BOUNDARIES

If you feel like you have trouble saying no to others, at work or at home, this book can help you establish more effective boundaries.

Item BB Paperback, $13.95

CONSUMER'S GUIDE TO PSYCHIATRIC DRUGS

An empowering guide to how the drugs used to treat psychiatric disorders work and what to expect in terms of side-effects, interactions with other drugs, dietary restrictions, and danger signs.

Item CGPD Paperback, $13.95

Call toll-free 1-800-748-6273 to order. Have your Visa or Mastercard number ready. Or send a check for the titles you want to New Harbinger Publications, 5674 Shattuck Avenue, Oakland, CA 94609. Include $3.80 for the first book and 75¢ for each additional book to cover shipping and handling. (California residents please include appropriate sales tax.) Allow four to six weeks for delivery.

Prices subject to change without notice.

Some Other New Harbinger Self-Help Titles

Dr. Carl Robinson's Basic Baby Care, $10.95
Better Boundries: Owning and Treasuring Your Life, $13.95
Goodbye Good Girl, $12.95
Being, Belonging, Doing, $10.95
Thoughts & Feelings, Second Edition, $18.95
Depression: How It Happens, How It's Healed, $14.95
Trust After Trauma, $13.95
The Chemotherapy & Radiation Survival Guide, Second Edition, $13.95
Heart Therapy, $13.95
Surviving Childhood Cancer, $12.95
The Headache & Neck Pain Workbook, $14.95
Perimenopause, $13.95
The Self-Forgiveness Handbook, $12.95
A Woman's Guide to Overcoming Sexual Fear and Pain, $14.95
Mind Over Malignancy, $12.95
Treating Panic Disorder and Agoraphobia, $44.95
Scarred Soul, $13.95
The Angry Heart, $14.95
Don't Take It Personally, $12.95
Becoming a Wise Parent For Your Grown Child, $12.95
Clear Your Past, Change Your Future, $12.95
Preparing for Surgery, $17.95
Coming Out Everyday, $13.95
Ten Things Every Parent Needs to Know, $12.95
The Power of Two, $12.95
It's Not OK Anymore, $13.95
The Daily Relaxer, $12.95
The Body Image Workbook, $17.95
Living with ADD, $17.95
Taking the Anxiety Out of Taking Tests, $12.95
The Taking Charge of Menopause Workbook, $17.95
Living with Angina, $12.95
Five Weeks to Healing Stress: The Wellness Option, $17.95
Choosing to Live: How to Defeat Suicide Through Cognitive Therapy, $12.95
Why Children Misbehave and What to Do About It, $14.95
When Anger Hurts Your Kids, $12.95
The Addiction Workbook, $17.95
The Mother's Survival Guide to Recovery, $12.95
The Chronic Pain Control Workbook, Second Edition, $17.95
Fibromyalgia & Chronic Myofascial Pain Syndrome, $19.95
Flying Without Fear, $12.95
Kid Cooperation: How to Stop Yelling, Nagging & Pleading and Get Kids to Cooperate, $12.95
The Stop Smoking Workbook: Your Guide to Healthy Quitting, $17.95
Conquering Carpal Tunnel Syndrome and Other Repetitive Strain Injuries, $17.95
Wellness at Work: Building Resilience for Job Stress, $17.95
An End to Panic: Breakthrough Techniques for Overcoming Panic Disorder, Second Edition, $18.95
Living Without Procrastination: How to Stop Postponing Your Life, $12.95
Goodbye Mother, Hello Woman: Reweaving the Daughter Mother Relationship, $14.95
Letting Go of Anger: The 10 Most Common Anger Styles and What to Do About Them, $12.95
Messages: The Communication Skills Workbook, Second Edition, $13.95
Coping With Chronic Fatigue Syndrome: Nine Things You Can Do, $13.95
The Anxiety & Phobia Workbook, Second Edition, $18.95
The Relaxation & Stress Reduction Workbook, Fourth Edition, $17.95
Living Without Depression & Manic Depression: A Workbook for Maintaining Mood Stability, $17.95
Coping With Schizophrenia: A Guide For Families, $15.95
Visualization for Change, Second Edition, $13.95
Postpartum Survival Guide, $13.95
Angry All the Time: An Emergency Guide to Anger Control, $12.95
Couple Skills: Making Your Relationship Work, $13.95
Self-Esteem, Second Edition, $13.95
I Can't Get Over It, A Handbook for Trauma Survivors, Second Edition, $15.95
Dying of Embarrassment: Help for Social Anxiety and Social Phobia, $13.95
The Depression Workbook: Living With Depression and Manic Depression, $17.95
Men & Grief: A Guide for Men Surviving the Death of a Loved One, $13.95
When the Bough Breaks: A Helping Guide for Parents of Sexually Abused Children, $11.95
When Once Is Not Enough: Help for Obsessive Compulsives, $13.95
The Three Minute Meditator, Third Edition, $12.95
Beyond Grief: A Guide for Recovering from the Death of a Loved One, $13.95
Hypnosis for Change: A Manual of Proven Techniques, Third Edition, $13.95
When Anger Hurts, $13.95

Call **toll free, 1-800-748-6273,** to order. Have your Visa or Mastercard number ready. Or send a check for the titles you want to New Harbinger Publications, Inc., 5674 Shattuck Ave., Oakland, CA 94609. Include $3.80 for the first book and 75¢ for each additional book, to cover shipping and handling. (California residents please include appropriate sales tax.) Allow two to five weeks for delivery.

Prices subject to change without notice.